Jazz Journey

A Guide for Listening

FIRST EDITION

By John Valerio
University of South Carolina-Columbia

Bassim Hamadeh, CEO and Publisher
Michael Simpson, Vice President of Acquisitions
Jamie Giganti, Managing Editor
Jess Busch, Graphic Design Supervisor
Zina Craft, Acquisitions Editor
Monika Dziamka, Project Editor
Natalie Lakosil, Licensing Manager
Mandy Licata, Interior Designer

First published in the United States of America in 2015 by Cognella, Inc.

Trademark notice: Product or corporate names may be trademarks or registered trademarks, and are used only for identification and explanation without intent to infringe.

Cover image copyright © in the Public Domain.

Printed in the United States of America

ISBN: 978-1-63189-056-7 (pbk)/ 978-1-63189-057-4 (br)

www.cognella.com   800-200-3908

Contents

Introduction   1

Prelude 1: How Music Works   2

Prelude 2: How Jazz Works   22

Part 1: Roots and Early Jazz

Chapter 1: Ragtime   40

Chapter 2: Blues   48

Chapter 3: Early Jazz—New Orleans Style, Dixieland   60

Chapter 4: Louis Armstrong   78

Chapter 5: Bix Beiderbecke—Chicago Style   86

Chapter 6: Stride Piano—Harlem Piano School, Eastern Ragtime   92

Part 2: Swing

Chapter 7: Swing Era—Eastern Swing, Fletcher Henderson
     and Benny Goodman   100

Chapter 8: Count Basie—Southwest Swing, Kansas City Swing   118

Chapter 9: Duke Ellington   132

Chapter 10: Singers from the Swing Era   150

Chapter 11: Transitional Figures   174

Part 3: Modern Jazz

Chapter 12: The Bebop Revolution—Dizzy Gillespie
and Charlie Parker   186

Chapter 13: Bebop Pianists—Bud Powell and Thelonious Monk   202

Chapter 14: Cool Jazz   212

Chapter 15: Hard Bop   234

Chapter 16: Great Piano Trios   254

Chapter 17: Miles Davis in the Fifties   260

Part 4: Freedom, Fusion, and Federation

Chapter 18: Bill Evans Trio   280

Chapter 19: Free Jazz—In and Out of Control,
Ornette Coleman and Charles Mingus   290

Chapter 20: John Coltrane   300

Chapter 21: Miles Davis in the Sixties   312

Chapter 22: Fusion in the Seventies   334

Chapter 23: Keith Jarrett   344

Chapter 24: Jazz from the Eighties   356

Bibliography   364

Introduction

This book is intended for a one-semester History of Jazz or Jazz Appreciation course. The major styles and players of jazz are described chronologically from the forerunners of jazz through the 1970s. While many players are left out, most of the major players who have impacted the evolution of jazz are included. The student will learn that jazz is as diverse and varied as any other kind of music, and that there is a rich, evolving history of this uniquely American art form. While some biographical and sociological information is presented, the emphasis is on the music, itself. The history of jazz is told through its performers and their recorded performances.

Since Jazz is a 20th-century phenomenon, we can study the music directly from recordings, films, and videos. The ebook version contains direct links within the text for easy access to audio and video examples. For the print version, the following webpage has links to all the same examples:

http://johnvaleriomusic.com/JAZZ_JOURNEY/LINKS.html

Ideally, the student should listen to the audio examples and watch the video examples as he or she reads the text. Suggestions for what to listen for and listening guides accompany each audio recording. Descriptions for the video examples are provided as well.

Although there are some written music examples, the student needs no background in music or ability to read music to comprehend this book. It is assumed that the student knows nothing about music, formally, and the instructor will introduce and explain the workings of music, and specifics, as need be, in class.

Please report any nonworking links or problems accessing the web material to jvalerio@mozart.sc.edu.

Prelude 1

How Music Works

Music is a most ephemeral art form: notes come and go, sounds vibrate the air then disappear, songs are sung then cease to exist. If any of this is true, how can music make any sense? Where do songs go after they are sung? The answer may be *blowin' in the wind*, so to speak, but more than likely, they reside in our memory. Songs are not things; they are relationships of sounds that proceed in time. Music unfolds and as it does, it is always present, but the present gets there from the past and proceeds to the future; all of which depend on the memory of the listener. Just as language makes sense only within the context that words relate to each other, music relies on notes and rhythms that lie within a contextual framework. Unlike language, however, music is nonspecific in meaning and refers only to itself. Of course language and music often go together to form songs; so do they work in the same ways? Are there words—nouns and verbs—in music? Not exactly, but there are phrases and sentences and a grammar for most music we listen to. Do we need to become music specialists, musicians, or music theorists to comprehend this grammar and syntax? No; no more than we need to be linguists or grammarians to understand language. Culture takes care of all of this for us. While most of us need training to become musicians, most of us need no training to become listeners and perhaps just a little training to become attentive listeners.

The great jazz pianist Bill Evans spoke of a *universal mind of music* that everyone possesses. For Evans, this universal mind was a better arbiter of musical worth than musicians themselves. Specialists often miss the forest for the trees and musicians often miss the music for the notes. This Prelude attempts to show how music works in the broadest sense in order to facilitate the auditory perception of music to thus engage the listener as an active participant in the music-making process.

GOOD VIBRATIONS

Sounds are mere vibrations yet *good vibrations* can delight and even titillate us, but how? Most sounds we hear are vibrations of the air. Usually there is a vibrating body that imparts its vibrations to the air, which transfers those vibrations to our eardrums, which translates those vibrations to our brains as sensory data we call sound. The vibrating bodies include metal strings in the case of string instruments (violins, basses, etc.), thin wooden reeds in the case of reed instruments (saxophones, clarinets, etc.), a player's lips in the case of brass instruments (trumpets, trombones, etc.), stretched plastic or hide membranes in the case of drums, tempered metal in the case of cymbals, and vocal chords in the case of human voices, etc.

Sound waves produce the contraction and rarefaction of the air as shown in the top image below. The sine curve below that is a mathematical representation of any wave.

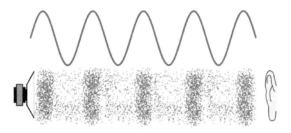

Figure P1.1
Copyright in the Public Domain.

Two aspects of the physics of waves are important for music: the **wavelength** or **frequency**, and the amplitude or height. The faster a wave vibrates, the shorter the wavelength. Thus faster vibrations produce more waves per unit space and have a higher frequency. The **amplitude** of a wave measures its intensity. Amplitude and frequency work independently of each other and do not correlate in any particular way.

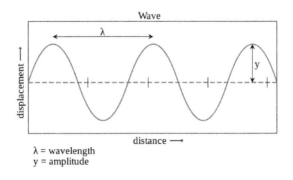

λ = wavelength
y = amplitude

Figure P1.2
Copyright in the Public Domain.

There are two general categories of sound: **noise** and **tone**. Irregular vibrations that have no repeating pattern to them when represented on an oscilloscope are defined as noise. Sounds that generate repeating patterns are tones.

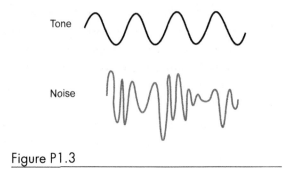

Tone

Noise

Figure P1.3

Both noise and tones are important for music. While tones make melodies and harmonies, rhythms are often played by noisemakers, such as drums and cymbals.

CHARACTERISTICS OF TONE

1. Pitch

Pitch is a product of **frequency** (wavelength). Different frequencies produce different pitches or notes, such as Middle C. Middle C is a pitch that vibrates at the rate of roughly 262 **cycles per second** (cps) or 262 hertz. Anything that vibrates at 262 **hertz** will produce the note we call Middle C. If you could wave your hand back and forth 262 times per second, you would hear Middle C. Not all frequencies are used in music. For western music there is no note for frequencies of 263, 266, or 270 cps. The next highest note is C sharp, which vibrates at roughly 277 cps. Middle C is one of eight Cs on a piano. We call them all C, yet they have very different frequencies. The frequency of the lowest C is roughly 33 hertz and of the highest C is 4186 hertz. There is quite a difference between these frequencies, yet there is something similar between them and among all the Cs. The secret lies with the principle of the **octave**.

The relationship between pitches is measured by intervals: 2nds, 3rds, 4ths, etc. The most curious and special of all the intervals is the octave. It is so special that we use the Latin term *octave* instead of 8th. It is these octaves that have the same letter name and a very definite mathematical relationship. Octaves have a 2:1 ratio between frequencies. The note A above Middle C vibrates at 440 hertz. The A, an octave higher, vibrates at 880 hertz and the A, an octave lower, vibrates at 220 hertz.

A = 220 cps or hertz
A = 440 cps or hertz
A = 880 cps or hertz

Although these As are different frequencies, they are somehow equivalent. They blend so well that when played together it can be difficult to tell there are two different notes present. This is so because the lower A actually contains the upper A. The upper octave is an overtone of the fundamental note. But it does not stop there; there are more overtones and their intervals and vibration ratios have a mathematical pattern.

The ancient Greek philosopher, scientist, and mathematician Pythagoras first discovered the 2:1 relationship. Although different music cultures have different tuning systems, they all recognize the principle of the octave, as the ancient Greeks did before Pythagoras' discovery. Pythagoras was especially interested in whole-number relationships and astounded to discover not only the octave ratio, but other intervallic whole number ratios as well.

The Greeks based their music on a hierarchy of **consonance** and **dissonance**. Notes that blend well together are **consonant**; those that do not are **dissonant**. For the Greeks that hierarchy from most consonant to least consonant was unison, octave, perfect 5th, perfect 4th, major 3rd, and minor 3rd. The ratios are as follows:

Unison	1:1
Octave	2:1
Perfect 5th	3:2
Perfect 4th	4:3
Major 3rd	5:4
Minor 3rd	6:5

The Greeks heard these relationships in this order and when Pythagoras discovered them, he was amazed at the pattern; so much so, he thought of it as proof of the existence of God; there was order in the universe and it was audible to humans.

In Western music, octaves are divided into twelve equal parts. In order to do this, however, compromises are needed for each interval and for various technical reasons this compromise was more or less agreed on by the 18th century. This so-called equal temperament has been with us ever since. Perfect 5ths and 4ths are no longer really perfect and their ratios are no longer exactly 3:2 and 4:3 but octaves are still 2:1.

It is hard to imagine music making any sense without the equivalence of the octave. When a group of men and women sing *Happy Birthday*, they will most likely be singing not in unison but in octaves. Men's voices are usually about an octave lower than women's voices and what sounds like unison singing is really singing in octaves. The notes are different yet the same; therein lies the magic of octaves.

Pitch Range refers to the range of the lowest to highest pitch. It can be used to define the extreme notes of a song or an instrument. The pitch range for human hearing is about 20 cps to 20,000 cps. In music, however, the range is much narrower, from about 27 cps to 4200 cps. All instruments have defined lowest notes but the highest notes on some instruments—wind and string instruments, for example—vary according to the skill of the player. **Register** refers to a region of pitches in general or for specific instruments or voices. For example, the low register for a trumpet is the middle register for a trombone. In nature as well as musical instruments, the smaller the vibrating body is, the faster it vibrates. Thus the small instruments like flutes and violins play relatively high notes, while large instruments like tubas and basses produce the lowest notes. Some music relies on register changes by gradually or suddenly changing among low, middle, and high registers. Much Classical music does this, while much Pop music saturates the pitch range by having all registers present most of the time.

2. Dynamics

Dynamics in music refers to how loud or soft the sounds are. Physicists call it **intensity** and psychologists call it **loudness**. The dynamic level of a sound is determined by the sound wave's amplitude. The wider the amplitude is, the louder the sound becomes. Written music uses Italian terms and symbols to indicate dynamics (see text box). Some music relies on dynamic contrast, while some does not. Much Classical music uses great changes from loud to soft to give the music a sense of drama, while much pop music uses little contrast by starting loud and staying loud; jazz, for the most part, lies somewhere between those extremes.

STANDARD DYNAMIC SIGNS

f = forte = loud *p* = piano = soft *m* = mezzo = moderately
mf = mezzo forte = moderately loud
mp = mezzo piano = moderately soft
ff = fortissimo = very loud *pp* = pianissimo = very soft
crescendo = gradually louder *decrescendo* or *diminuendo* = gradually softer

3. Tone Color (Timbre)

Tone color or timbre refers to the quality of a sound; what makes one voice or instrument sound different from others. A trumpet, a violin, and a piano, for example, can play Middle C but they all sound different from each other because they have different timbres or tone colors. What causes tone color is the most complex aspect of the physics of sound and only a simplified explanation will be given here.

The most contributing factor to tone color is overtones. When a string is plucked, for example, it vibrates not only as a whole but also in half, in thirds, in fourths, etc. The vibrating whole string is called the fundamental pitch and the other partial vibrations are called **overtones**. The overtones or **harmonics** actually relate directly to the Pythagorean ratios described above. The string vibrating in half, vibrates at half the wavelength of the fundamental pitch and thus at twice the frequency, producing a pitch an octave higher. The string vibrating in thirds produces a pitch a fifth higher than the first overtone since their relationship in 3:2. This process continues indefinitely. Thus he plucked string actually produces many pitches simultaneously but we hear only one, the fundamental. This is because the amplitudes of the overtone waves are much lower than the fundamental and serve to color the sound in subtle ways. We perceive the fundamental as the pitch and the overtones as qualifying or coloring the pitch. Depending on the material, shape, and the way the vibrating body is activated, different instruments and voices emphasize different overtones and thus produce different tone colors.

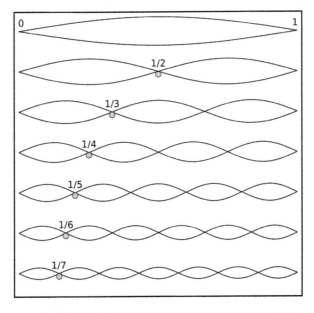

Figure P1.4
Copyright in the Public Domain.

It is hard to imagine music without a variety of tone colors. Traditional orchestras use a variety of instruments in all pitch ranges to maximize tone color and register possibilities. In jazz, big bands of around sixteen players offer the most tone color opportunities and creative arrangers like Duke Ellington took full advantage of all the possibilities by combining instruments in interesting ways. The use of different instruments helps the ear to distinguish multiple parts and layers in the music and makes for more variety and interest. Tone colors are also style specific; for example, orchestras are typical of Classical music, electric instruments are common in Rock, Pop, etc.

PITCH ORGANIZATION

The best way to see how pitch is organized is by looking at a music keyboard.

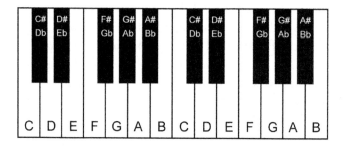

Figure P1.5

Each octave divides into twelve equal parts. Notice there are white keys and black keys and the black keys are grouped into units of twos and threes. The white keys are named from alphabet letters A to G. The black keys are named according to how they relate to the white keys. A few terms need to be introduced to explain this:

HALF STEP is the smallest distance between any two keys
FLAT (b) is a note that is a half step lower than another note
SHARP (#) is a note that is a half step higher than another note.

Notice the black key to the right of C can have two names: C# because it is a half step higher than C but also Db because it is a half step lower than D. There is a theoretical difference between the two but C# and Db sound exactly the same.
WHOLE STEP is the distance of two half steps. For example, the distance between C and D is a whole step since there is key (C#, Db) between them and the distance between E and F is a half step since there is no key between them.

SCALES

Although there are twelve different notes within each octave, most music we hear is based on just seven notes and organized into scales. Scales are an ordering of whole steps and half steps. These seven-note scales, called **diatonic scales**, are the most common in Western music. Each diatonic scale has a distinctive pattern of whole steps and half steps and all use letter names in order. The most common diatonic scale is the **major scale** and is most easily demonstrated by playing all white keys from C to C on a keyboard. This is called a C major scale and the note C is called the tonic. Notice the pattern of whole steps (W) and half steps (H):

W W H W W W H

Knowing this formula, you can construct a major scale beginning on any key. Below are the notes for a C major and G major scales related to the major scale formula. One can sing the familiar do-re-mi, etc., syllables to any major scale.

C   D   E   F   G   A   B   C
W   W   H   W   W   W   H
G   A   B   C   D   E   F#   G

Even though the notes are different the scales sound the same because the relationship among the notes are the same. We say a tune is in the key of C major or G major, etc., if the notes are organized with a major scale beginning on that note. Tunes can be transposed to any key and sound exactly the same. The ability to transpose to any key is one of the advantages of equal temperament (referred to previously).

In addition to the major scale, there is the less often used **minor scale**. This scale has a different sequence of whole steps and half steps. The minor scale is easily demonstrated by playing all the white keys from A to A. Note the pattern is now as follows:

W H W W H W W

The minor scale has a different flavor to it; some say a different color. Although the notes might be the same for both the C major and the A minor scales, the order of the notes makes all the difference. Some equate the major scale with happy music and the minor scale with sad music. While this is not necessarily true, it seems to be that way in the broadest sense. The minor scale has alternate versions that adjust certain notes by half steps but that need not concern us here. There are also other diatonic scales that are usually called modes. These modes will be described in Chapter 17; the time when jazz musicians began to use them.

RHYTHM

Rhythm is the most fundamental element of music. Without rhythm there can be no music. Rhythm relates to the time dimension of music; anything that happens is a rhythmic event. There can be music without pitch—just drums, for example—but there can be no music without rhythm. Rhythm is not just drums, however, although drums are most often associated with rhythm since in general they produce noise without any defined pitches and thus focus on rhythm. *Rhythm* is a word that gets misused and often is confused with the word **beat**.

BEATS

The beat is the fundamental unit of musical time. All musical events are related to the beat. The beat is the ***pulse*** of the music. The beat is something that is felt. When you dance, you dance to the beat. The beat is an important aspect of rhythm but not the only one. The word ***tempo*** refers to the speed of the beat; slow tempos occur when the beats are further apart; fast tempos occur when the beats come at a quicker pace. The beat in music is similar to the second in clock time; it generally is the smallest unit of time and just as in clock time, there are durations longer and shorter than seconds (five seconds, half a second, etc.), there are durations longer and shorter than beats (three beats, half a beat, etc.). The difference between the two is that seconds are always the same duration, but beats are relative to tempo and vary in duration.

METER

As in clock time, there is a hierarchy of time in music. Just as seconds form minutes and minutes form hours, etc., beats usually are grouped in recurring units called **measures** or **bars** and several measures form sections, etc. For most music we know, these measures are grouped into units of 2s, 3s, or 4s. These groupings are referred to as meter; thus the meter can be duple, triple, quadruple, etc. The metric groupings are usually easy to feel and tend to group naturally. The listener can usually feel the **macrobeat**, the first beat of each measure, which is usually stressed. In triple meter, for example, one counts: ONE—two—three, ONE—two—three, etc. **Microbeats** are each beat, including the macrobeat. In written music a time signature placed at the beginning indicates the meter. Below are examples of three different meters. Bar lines or measure lines are the vertical lines that separate each measure or bar.

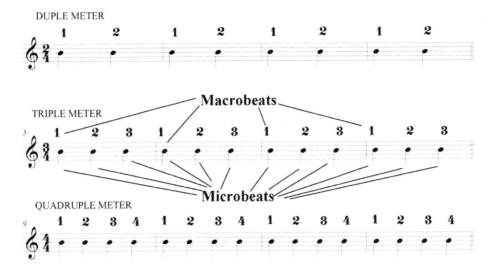

Figure P1.6

Beats and meter organize rhythm in music. Beats do not have to be heard to do so. Beats are **direct** when one or more instruments are playing them and **indirect** when they are not heard. Most jazz and Pop music use direct beats most of the time; Classical music, on the other hand, varies in its use of direct and indirect beats. *Mary Had a Little Lamb* is in duple meter. Notice how the beats organize the rhythm of the melody. Try to tap your hand or foot as you sing the song and notice how the beats naturally fall in groups of twos.

Figure P1.7

Try doing the same to *America* in triple meter.

Figure P1.8

DEVIATIONS FROM THE BEAT

Although beats remain at a constant tempo most of the time, occasionally the tempo can gradually speed up (**accelerando**) or slow down (**deaccelerando** or **ritardando**). Sometimes the beat fluctuates, getting subtly faster and slower according the player's whim. This is called **rubato** and is purely a function of performance, not composition. This ebb and flow of the beat occasionally happens in jazz during introductions but is rare otherwise. Most jazz has a direct obvious beat that remains steady throughout a performance.

<u>MELODY</u>

Melody is a succession of single notes that form a recognizable whole. Whereas most listeners cannot identify individual pitches, most can immediately recognize melodies. Melody is the foreground element of music. When you sing, you sing the melody of a song. Notes of a melody are organized by scales; the examples of *Mary Had a Little Lamb* and *America* shown above are both in the key of C major, which means they are composed from a C major scale. The time and rhythmic aspects of melodies are organized by beat and meter; see the same examples above.

PHRASES AND CADENCES

Melodies work in way similar to speech. In speech, words from phrases, phrases form sentences, and sentences form paragraphs. In music, notes form phrases, phrases form periods, and periods form sections. The relationship among all of these parts in music, however, is different from those in speech. Music relies on three basic relational parameters: **repetition**, **contrast**, and **variation**. A key to appreciating music is to be aware of how these relationships unfold.

At the end of a phrase is a **cadence**. Cadences act like punctuation marks in language and can be divided into two general categories: incomplete cadences and complete cadences. An **incomplete cadence** acts like a comma and implies an incomplete thought that needs continuation. A **complete cadence** acts like a period and completes a musical thought. In speech, a complete thought would form a sentence; in music the term *period* is used as if to indicate the punctuation mark at the end of a sentence.

Music theorists analyze phrases, periods, and sections by using letters of the alphabet. Lowercase letters are used for phrases; uppercase for periods and longer sections. They work as follows:

Repetition	a	a	second phrase is same as first phrase
Contrast	a	b	second phrase is different from first phrase
Variation	a	a¹	second phrase is similar in some ways but different in other ways from the first phrase
Sequence	a	a¹	a common type of variation—second phrase has the same pitch and rhythmic relationships as the first phrase but begins on a different note.

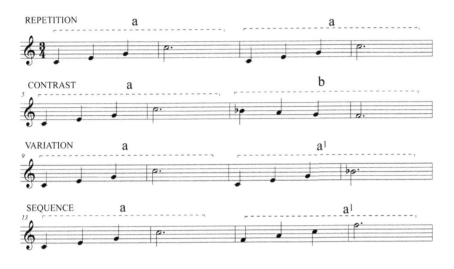

Figure P1.9

Below are examples of song phrases using contrast and variation. Notice in each case the first phrase ends with an incomplete cadence and the second phrase ends with a complete cadence. The cadences are even indicated by the punctuation of the words: comma and period.

Figure P1.10

In the first song, the second phrase is clearly different from the first.

There is a connection, though; the rhythm of the end of both phrases is the same (*gently down the stream* and *life is but a dream*) but this is not enough of a connection to warrant the second phrase a variation since everything else is very different. The second phrase of the second song exhibits a typical kind of variation: it starts the same as the first phrase but changes at the end. This is usually done to have the second phrase end in a complete cadence.

The following song has four phrases.

Figure P1.11

When analyzing longer songs or sections of music, letters and numbers are used in order as needed; for example: a a b b¹ a¹ c a² b² d b³ e.

MOTIVES

A motive is short musical idea that gets used and manipulated during a music composition or performance. They are like seeds that grow into something else. Motives usually have strong identifiable pitch and rhythmic characteristics. Composers use motives in various ways in every kind of music, and as we shall see in later chapters, improvising jazz musicians do as well. The most famous motive is the one Beethoven uses in his Symphony No. 5. The four-note motive is heard at the start of the first movement and is immediately sequenced a step lower.

Figure P1.12

This motive has a well-defined rhythmic character (three short notes followed by a long note) and a well-defined pitch character (three repeated notes followed by a note that is a 3rd lower). Beethoven then develops his motive by make a longer melody from it.

Figure P1.13

Once he planted the seed, Beethoven grows his idea through a process known as **motivic development** in which the motive evolves as it grows and changes. Motives are used in jazz and pop tunes in various ways but do not necessarily develop as Beethoven's does.

Harold Arlen used motives in subtle ways when he composed *Over the Rainbow*. The first period consists of two phrases and the phrases are made from two motives. Motives a and b overlap during the first two measures. The a idea is characterized by an upward leap of an octave followed by a step down. In measures 3 and 4 he uses the same idea but the leap is now a 6th rather than an octave (a¹). In measure 5 he states a¹ again but on different notes and overlaps it again with the b motive. The b motive also is used three times but begins on a different note each time. The back-to-back use of the b motives during measures 6 and 7 is the mark of a great composer who sets up expectations then thwarts them; on the first hearing we expect the a motive in measure 7 since it was used in measure 3.

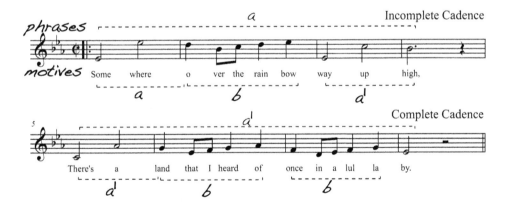

Figure P1.14

Not all music uses motives but many composers make good use of them by getting the most mileage from just a few ideas as Arlen did in *Over the Rainbow*.

HARMONY

Harmony relates to how notes sound together to form **chords** and how these chords relate to each other to form **chord progressions**. While melody is the foreground in music, harmony controls the background and gives focus and direction to the melody. While melody is the horizontal dimension of music, harmony is the vertical dimension. These terms relate to how music is written; melody reads left to right, as the notes are played separately, and harmony (chords) is written up and down, as the notes are played simultaneously.

Harmony, as we know it, is unique to the Western European music tradition. What began as polyphony during the 9th century evolved into full-fledged functional harmony during the 17th century. **Polyphony** is musical texture that uses two or more simultaneous melodies. The science of polyphony governed the separate voices with rules for the resolution of dissonances (intervals that clash) into consonances (intervals that blend well). Although the voices originally were conceived as melodies, the sounding of concurrent notes formed harmonies. During the 17th century, consistent patterns of these harmonies began to guide the melodies and formulaic chord progressions came into use. These chord progressions became the foundation of Western music and remain with us today.

Harmony is the most intellectual element of music. It is what links our music with music from the past. The same chord progressions that Bach and Mozart used during the 18th century are still used today. Bach and Mozart would have no problem identifying chord progressions they might hear on the radio today, although everything else—melody, rhythm, tone color, etc.—would sound very strange to them. Music theory deals mostly with harmony since it is common to most music we hear, both old and new.

TRIADS

Triads are the simplest types of chords. In their basic form they contain three notes arranged in 3rds.. Below is a C major chord. C is the lowest note; the next higher note E is a 3rd higher and is called the 3rd of the chord; the highest note G is a third higher from E and is called the 5th of the chord since it is a 5th higher from the root, C. This triad is called C major because C is the lowest note, the root of the chord, and the 3rd, E is a major 3rd. Intervals are qualified according to their specific intervallic structure; some 3rds are major and some are minor, etc. For example, if the same chord had an Eb instead of an E natural, it would be a C minor chord. We need not worry about these technicalities for the purposes of this discussion.

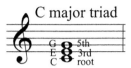

Figure P1.15

Triads can be inverted, which means the positions and order of the notes can be different from the basic form shown above. Any combination of the notes C-E-G in any octaves, with or without duplicate pitch names (doublings), is a C major chord. Inversions are named according to the lowest sounding note of the chord. Below is a C major triad in root position, first, and second inversions, and spread out in a few different possible ways.

Figure P1.16

Chords relate to each other within a key and triads can be built from each note of the scale of that key by building thirds.

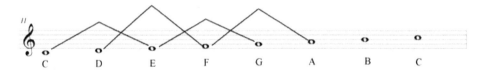

Figure P1.17

Within each key, each chord has a function based on its root's position within the scale of that key. The functions are indicated by Roman numerals based on the position of each chord within the scale; this ordering of chords is referred to as diatonic triads. While the Roman numeral indicates the function of a chord, chord symbols represent the name of each chord. In the examples below, three types of triads are indicated: major, minor, and diminished. A single letter is used to indicate a major triad, for example, (C) = a C major chord; an (m) after a single letter indicates a minor triad, for example, Dm = a D minor triad; the abbreviation (dim) or the symbol (°) indicates a diminished triad, for example, B dim = a B diminished triad.

The example below shows the diatonic triads for the key of C major with their chord symbols and functions.

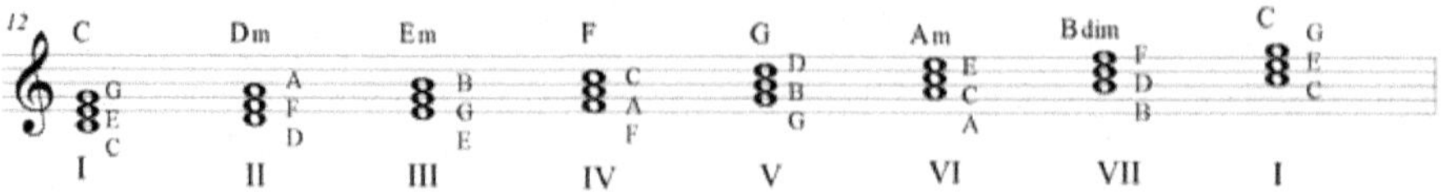

Figure P1.18

Like scales, chord progressions can be transposed to any key and like transposed melodies, the relations will sound the same in any key. Below is a I-IV-V-I progression in the keys of C and G major. They are written in two different ways: first in all root position chords and then with inversions. The inversions smooth out the voice leading (how one note moves to another) by moving each note to the next by the least possible distance.

Root Positions----------------------- With Inversions----------------------

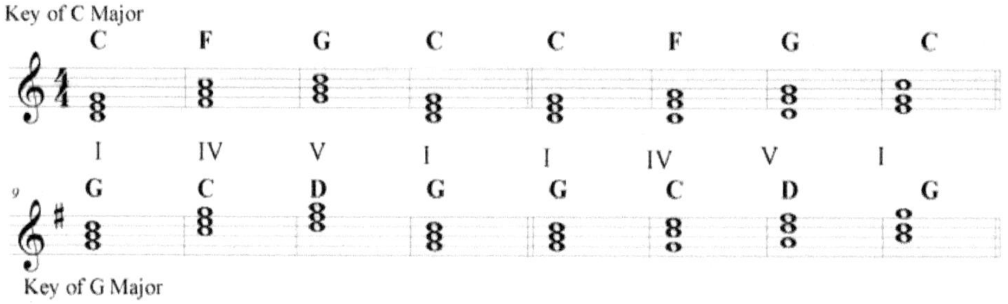

Figure P1.19

Chord progressions cannot be copyrighted and many musical compositions from different styles and eras use the exact same chord progression; in music, only melodies and lyrics are copyrightable. There are literally thousands of Blues tunes that use the exact same chord progressions. Music is often reharmonized with chords different from the original ones inserted or substituted for. Jazz musicians commonly reharmonize the material they play on.

SEVENTH AND EXTENDED CHORDS

Chords, more complex than triads, are formed by adding on more thirds. Seventh chords, which are four-note chords, are fairly common. They are called seventh chords because the interval from the root to the highest note is a 7th; likewise there are ninth, eleventh, and thirteenth chords. There are no chords more complex than thirteenth chords since adding another third would simply double the root. Below are some examples of some of these chords in their simplest position with their chord symbols.

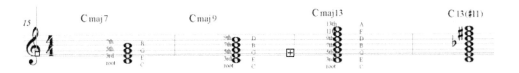

Figure P1.20

Below are some rich complex chords voiced for piano with two hands.

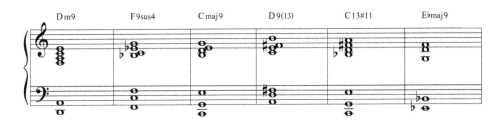

Figure P1.21

As western music evolved over the centuries, the harmony became more and more complex. Not all styles of music, however, make use of complex chords. Much Pop music from the 1950s on still relies primarily on triads. Jazz, on the other hand, evolved a very complex system of harmony that makes use of complex chords and complex chord progressions. Prelude 2 describes how this complex harmony is used in jazz.

Just as beats do not have to be heard to organize rhythm in music, chords do not have to be heard to organize harmony in music. Many melodies can be played unaccompanied but still imply the harmony. Chords can control what an accompaniment plays but might never be heard as a simultaneously sounding unit. Below is *Mary Had a little Lamb* with its implied simple chord accompaniment and then with a more active accompaniment based on the chords without ever sounding a full chord.

Figure P1.22

The elements of music described in the prelude are purposely oversimplified to give the reader only a generally concept of the inner workings of music. Actual music often is much more complex. **Modulation**, for example, is a common feature in much music. Modulation refers to the changing of keys and tunes can change keys several times. A tune can begin in the key of C major and modulate to A minor and then again to F major before coming back to the tonic key of C major. Meter might also change in the middle of a composition, although this is rare in most jazz. Chords can be altered by making notes flat or sharp, etc. Throughout the book more theoretical concepts will be introduced as they apply to the music being studied.

Prelude 2

How Jazz Works

J azz is hard to define but most know it when they hear it. Jazz is an attitude about music more than anything else. The material itself is not nearly as important as what one does with the material. Any music can be turned into jazz simply by performing it as jazz. Jazz, most of all, is a performer's art. The history of jazz is told through its players and singers, not by its composers, and its history is documented through recordings, not written music. The opposite of this is true for Classical music; its history is told through its composers and their written music. But what makes jazz jazz and what makes one a jazz musician? Jazz is characterized by certain sounds and rhythms as well as certain forms and procedures. This prelude will examine what these sounds, rhythms, forms, and procedures are.

JAZZ HARMONY

For the most part, jazz musicians prefer complex chords that are rich and varied. Triads are rarely used and seventh chords are generally the simplest chords used. Sixth chords, which are four-note chords formed by adding a sixth above the root are used as well. Extended chords (ninth, eleventh, and thirteenth chords) are common and alterations to these chords are used often (b9, #11, b5, etc.). These chords are a big part of the sound of jazz and their continual use can make anything sound like jazz, independent of any jazz-like rhythms. *Mary Had a Little Lamb*, for example, can sound very much like jazz by reharmonizing it with some rich complex chords. The example below shows the song with the original chords and a reharmonized version. It is also rewritten in four-four time instead of the original two-four time as shown in Prelude 1. The feeling of the music in four beats rather than two beats per measure is more typical of jazz; the music's rhythmic relationships are exactly the same as in the two-four version.

Figure P2.1

SWING

Most jazz is played with a swing feeling. Swing is a quality that is difficult to define. It is an approach to the beat that is best described as a *playing on the beat* rather than a *playing with the beat*. As will be described later, jazz, in general, is a playing *on* something. Swing also has a going-against-the-grain quality that often puts rhythm at odds with the formal and harmonic structure of the music. Music that swings often has syncopated rhythms. **Syncopation** occurs when notes are stressed on weak beats or in between beats. In tradition Western music the first beat of each measure is naturally stressed. In quadruple meter, beats 1 and 3 are called strong beats, as the third beat gets a subsidiary stress, and beats 2 and 4 are called weak beats. When this norm gets upset with a stress on the second or fourth beats, for example, syncopation occurs. On another level, notes occurring on beats, in general, get more stress than notes in between beats, and if the opposite occurs, syncopations result. Syncopation is not new with jazz, it had been part of the European tradition for centuries, but what was the exception in that music became the norm in jazz. African music influenced this rhythmic practice in jazz and Part I of this book describes why and how this occurred.

Jazz musicians often play swing eighth notes. Normally, eighth notes are equally divided between quarter-note beats. Swing eighth notes, however, are played unevenly; the note occurring on the beat is slightly longer than the note in between the beats. Jazz musicians know when to swing the eighth notes and when not to even though they are written in the same way in written music. Sometimes writers indicate that the eighth note should be swung by the following indication:

Swing!

Figure P2.2

One can still swing without playing swing eighth notes and more modern styles of jazz tend to not use them. Swing is a very complex phenomenon and attempts to define it usually fall short, but as the cliché says: "you'll know it when you hear it."

THE SOUND OF JAZZ

The sound of jazz relies on its characteristic complex harmonies and rhythms. Anything can be turned into jazz if it is played with a jazz attitude using the basic elements of jazz harmony and rhythm. A good example of this is Vince Guaraldi's treatment of **O Christmas Tree** that was used in *A Charlie Brown Christmas*, the animated television special based on the *Peanuts* cartoon strip. Notice in the example below how the chords and rhythm are changed to turn the traditional German carol into jazz. The chords and the chord progression are more complex, and the meter and the rhythms of the melody are changed to make it swing. This is just one example of many different ways this can be done with this tune.

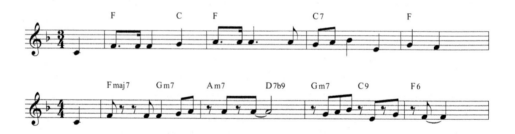

Figure P2.3

THE JAZZ ENSEMBLE

Jazz is played by various sized ensembles, from solo instruments to big bands. Small jazz bands are sometimes called **combos**; combos usually have between two and six players. **Big bands** usually have between twelve and sixteen players. There are ensembles somewhere in between combos and big bands as well, and we will encounter all sizes during our jazz journey.

Most jazz ensembles are divided into two sections: the rhythm section and the section of instruments (or one instrument) that play the main melodies; this can be called the front line, or horn section, or by whatever the instruments are.

RHYTHM SECTION

The **rhythm section** usually has three or four players and each player fulfills a certain role. The overall role of the rhythm section is to supply the pulse (the beat) and the harmony (the chords). A four-piece rhythm section usually has drums, bass, piano, and guitar. Most three-piece rhythm sections have drums and bass with either piano or guitar.

In most jazz performances, the beat is obvious and prominently played by one or more members of the rhythm sections. In general, the roles of each rhythm section instrument within a modern jazz setting are as follows:

DRUMS—provide a steady beat along with various fills and accents
BASS—plays a bass line in one of the following ways:
       - plays a note on every beat (walking bass)
       - plays a note mostly on beats 1 and 3 (2 feel)
       - plays other rhythms appropriate to style
PIANO—plays chords in a random-like manner (comps) or in a rhythm pattern
       appropriate to style
GUITAR—similar to piano

Below is what a three-piece rhythm section of piano bass and drums might play in a medium tempo straight ahead or swing feel while accompanying a lead melody.

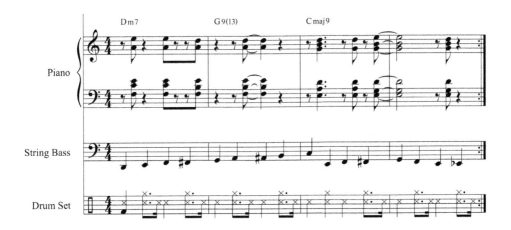

Figure P2.4

MELODY INSTRUMENTS

Wind instruments have played an important role in jazz from its very beginning. Early jazz emerged in part from brass and marching bands. Wind instruments are usually divided into brass and woodwind instruments.

BRASS

Brass instruments produce their sound from the player's lips vibrating against a mouthpiece. All of them have a similar timbre or tone color that varies mostly according to the pitch range of the instrument. The most commonly used brass instruments used in modern jazz are the **trumpet** and **trombone**. The **cornet**, which is virtually the same as a trumpet but has a slightly different shape and sound, was actually used more than the trumpet in early jazz but has become relatively rare since the 1930s. The **flugelhorn**, another brass instrument related to the trumpet, has become fairly common since the 1960s. The trombone plays lower notes than the trumpet and is unique in its use of a slide to lengthen or shorten the instrument's tubing. Other brass instruments, like the trumpet, accomplish this by pressing down valves. The slide makes possible the gradual sliding from one pitch to another, a unique characteristic of the trombone and an effect that is sometimes comical.

The **tuba** was an important instrument in early jazz and was used primarily as a bass instrument in the rhythm section. In more modern jazz styles the tuba is used occasionally as a low brass instrument in a large ensemble. The **French horn** has been used rarely in jazz and usually as a member of a larger brass section.

One of the unique aspects of brass instruments is their ability to be muted. **Mutes** change the sound of a brass instrument and there are many different kinds of mutes that can be used. Some mutes can be manipulated by the player and this gives a vocal-like effect to the sound of the horn. Several recordings referred to in this book demonstrate the use of various mutes.

WOODWINDS

Woodwind instruments produce their sounds in different ways from brass instruments and are not necessarily made from wood.

Reed instruments include saxophones and clarinets. These are single-reed instruments. Their sound is produced when a player blows air through a mouthpiece that vibrates a thin wooden reed. Lengthening or shortening the tube by covering or uncovering holes in the tube produces different pitches.

The **clarinet** was a standard member of the early jazz bands; its use came directly from marching bands. The clarinet has a wide range and typically plays notes both higher and lower than the trumpet or cornet. The **bass clarinet** is pitched one octave lower than the clarinet and its use is relatively rare in jazz.

The **saxophone** refers to a family of instruments that encompass the full range of the pitch spectrum. The most commonly used are the soprano, alto, tenor, and baritone saxophones. Saxophones are played similarly to clarinets and often players *double* on both instruments. Saxophones, more than any other instruments, are identified with jazz. During the 1920s, jazz saxophonists turned what was considered a novelty instrument into one of the most expressive and versatile of all jazz instruments.

Flutes are less common than reeds but have been used with some regularity since the 1960s. Although there are a few exceptions, most jazz flute players are saxophone players who *double* on flute.

Double-reed instruments (oboes and bassoons) are extremely rare in jazz.

STRINGS

Other than the string bass, which is more often plucked than bowed, string instruments are less associated with jazz than wind instruments are. There are and have been some great violin soloists but virtually no viola or cello soloists. Strings are occasionally used in arrangements for singers or instrumental soloists in large ensemble settings.

LEAD SHEETS AND FAKE BOOKS

If jazz musicians read music at all, they usually read from lead sheets. A lead sheet is a written form of music that indicates only a melody and chord symbols without any indication as to how the chords should be played. A collection of lead sheets is called a fake book. Fake books are called that because the musicians must fake their parts; that is, they improvise their appropriate parts from the bare amount of information that is on the lead sheet. For a typical jazz quartet of saxophone, piano, bass, and drums, for example, all four players can read from the same music but each would play something different. The saxophone player most likely would play the written melody or some variation of it. The pianist would play accompanying chords from the chord symbols by voicing them and rhythmically placing them any way he or she wanted. The bass player would invent a bass line derived from the chord symbols and the drummer would play accompanying rhythms, and/or a groove, along with fills and accents, based on the style of the tune, structure, and rhythms of the melody, and whatever everyone else was playing. This process is very different from the Classical music tradition where each player plays a specific part from different sheet music. The jazz process is much freer and more spontaneous and relies on the skill and knowledge of the players to effectively fake their parts.

Below is a lead sheet for **O Christmas Tree** rewritten in quadruple meter, along with an analysis of the phrase structure. Normal lead sheets do not have the phrase analysis. We will use this lead sheet to also explain how improvisation works in jazz.

O CHRISTMAS TREE

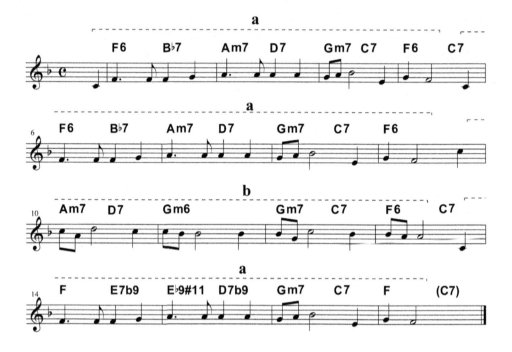

Figure P2.5

This lead sheet version is already different from the original carol, both rhythmically and harmonically, but jazz musicians are always free to change things, including the melody and chords. The form, however, stays intact. The melody here is not written is a swing style as in the previous example; it is up to the player of the melody to manipulate it in such ways that it does swing. Notice that the tune has four phrases in the form of aaba. This song structure is very common and will be described further below.

JAZZ IMPROVISATION

The highlights of most jazz performance come during improvised solos. While improvisation is not unique to jazz, the great jazz soloists have taken the art of improvisation to very high levels. In order to understand how improvisation works in jazz, it is important to know the forms and structures that jazz musicians play on.

O CHRISTMAS TREE

John Valerio Trio

John Valerio—piano
George Hoar—bass
Tim Blackwell—drums

Listen to jazz version of **O Christmas Tree** inspired by Vince Guaraldi. Notice how the music swings and when the piano and bass take improvised solos. Try to hear the head somewhere in your mind while the improvisations go on. Notice how the pianist comps chords for himself with his left hand while the right hand plays the lead melodies. Remember the players are repeating the form of the tune over and over again. This also serves as an introduction to the many listening guides used throughout the book.

Measures	4	4	4	4
Phrases	a	a	b	a
CHORUS 1	piano plays head making it swing———————————————			
	bass plays in a 2 feel—mainly on beats 1 and 3———————			
	drums play swing rhythm with brushes—————————			
CHORUS 2	piano solo———————————————————————			
	plays variations on the head (written melody)———————			
	bass still plays in 2			
CHORUSES 3–7	piano solo continues—————————————————			
	Moves away from head but refers to it occasionally			
	bass plays in 4—on every beat			
CHORUSES 8–9	bass solo——————————————————————			
	piano comps chords in background			
CHORUS 10	piano plays head with variations———————————			
	Bass plays in a 2 feel			
CHORUS 11	piano play head————————————————————			
	Bass continues in a 2 feel			
TAG	repeat of the last a phrase			
	bass uses bow			
	ritardando—music slows down till the end			

Many listeners and even some non-jazz musicians do not understand how jazz improvisation works. The process is actually quite simple. First, the tune is played through as described above, with everyone playing their parts according to their roles in the band. The given tune, itself, is called the **head**. After the head is played, the players start from the beginning of the tune and play through it again but this time one player, let's say the saxophone player, ignores the head (the written melody) and improvises a new melody based on the written melody and/or the chord progression. It all makes sense because the accompanying players still base what they play on the same parameters of the tune as on the head, only this time listening to what the soloists play and fitting in accordingly. This process repeats as players take turns improvising solos and typically ends with a repeat of the head. Each time through the whole form is called a **chorus**; thus the head is the first chorus, and the players proceed from there playing one or more choruses each until the final chorus, which is usually a repeat of the head.

SONG FORMS

There are two kinds of forms for the majority of tunes that jazz musicians play: 12-bar Blues and 32-bar Pop Song Forms (12-bar Blues form will be described in Chapter 2 on Blues). Jazz and Pop music were intertwined for much of the 20th century and continue to be into the 21st century, but while both were roughly contemporaneous for the first half of the 20th century, jazz and Pop, for the most part, have parted ways. The older Pop songs continued to be played after the newer Rock 'n' Roll–related Pop styles emerged during the 1950s, and even though the newer Rock-related music affected much of the sounds and rhythms of some post-fifties jazz, the newer song forms did not.

Most of the Pop material jazz musicians play come from the **Great American Songbook**. These songs were written primarily during the 1920s–1940s and are often referred to as Pop standards or Jazz/Pop standards or simply as standards. These uniquely American Pop songs have served jazz singers and instrumentalists alike as endless sources of interpretation and improvisational fodder. Their typical 32-measure structure, like 90 feet between bases in baseball, seems to be just right. Since both jazz and pop performances rely on chorus repetition, anything shorter, other than Blues, would be too repetitive and anything longer would be hard to remember. Remembering the initial tune leads to a greater appreciation of how the improviser is changing it. Most of the songs of the Great American Songbook consist of four 8-measure periods in one of the following forms:

AABA

ABAB[1]

ABAC

These forms are in order from the most common to the least and it is no coincidence that the order follows from the most repetition to the least. Pop music from all eras is not only a style of music but also a commercial product designed to be bought and sold, and repetition is a key factor in having melodies linger in the memory of listeners who potentially buy records and sheet music of their favorite songs. There are some songs with slight variations added to the basic models, such as: AA^{1}BA, AABA^1, ABA^{1}C. There are also some well-known songs that do not follow one of these models, as well as longer and shorter forms.

The melodies of these songs are flexible and can be interpreted and performed in many different ways; they are not too notey, as are many of the more contemporary songs, and there are plenty of spaces, either long-held notes or rests, that can be filled. The chords and harmonic progressions give a sense of forward motion with subtle key changes that provide just the right amount of tension and release. The newer Pop songs and Pop song formats from the fifties on are more static and redundant with less room for interpretation and variation. These songs are not nearly as flexible since there are usually specifics built into them; bass lines and background parts, for example. The great standards can be performed in myriad styles, tempos, and arrangements.

Familiar Songs in Standard 32-Measure Pop Song Forms

A A B A Form
Over the Rainbow
Blue Moon
Yesterday
Something
Hey Jude
Satin Doll
Body and Soul
Misty
Just You, Just Me
It's Only a Paper Moon

A B A B^1
Fly Me to the Moon
Days of Wine and Roses
Love Is Here to Stay

A B A C
The Shadow of Your Smile
All of Me

Although some of these songs are written in a jazz style, most are not and were never intended as jazz music. Again, jazz is more a manner of performing music rather than a particular kind of music. Many jazz original tunes are based on the chord progressions of these standards and ones that have new chord progressions usually adhere to one of the standard Pop song forms.

IT'S ONLY A PAPER MOON

This is one of the songs from the Great American Songbook. It was written in 1933 with music by Harold Arlen and lyrics by Billy Rose and E.Y. Harburg. It is in an AABA 32-bar form. The melody and lyrics are very catchy and easy to remember. The form with the lyrics is as follows:

A   Say it's only a paper moon
Sailing over a cardboard sea
But it wouldn't be make-believe
If you believe in me

A   Yes it's only a canvas sky
Hanging over a muslin tree
But it wouldn't be make-believe
If you believe in me

B   Without your love
It's a honky-tonk parade
Without your love
It's a melody played
In a penny arcade

A   It's a Barnum and Bailey world
Just as phony as it can be
But it wouldn't be make-believe
If you believe in me

IT'S ONLY A PAPER MOON 1956

After Midnight Sessions
Nat King Cole

Nat Cole—Vocal, Piano
Charlie Harris—Bass
John Collins—Guitar
Lee Young—Drums
Harry "Sweets" Edison—Muted Trumpet

Intro—whole band
  8

	8	8	8	8
	A	A	B	A
Chorus 1	vocal———————————————————————			
Chorus 2	trumpet ———————————| guitar————| trumpet		
Chorus 3	piano ———————————	piano and trumpet———— trade 2s call + response		
Chorus 4	xxxxxxxxxxxxxxxxxxxxxxxxxxxxx	vocal———————————		

Coda (Outro)—whole band- same as Intro
  8

Listen to the 1956 jazz version by Nat "King" Cole. Nat Cole (1919–1965) was an innovative jazz pianist during the 1940s who became a very successful Pop singer and recorded many hit records during the fifties and sixties. This recording of *It's Only a Paper Moon*, made is 1956, is a jazz performance with improvised solos. Try to follow the form as the music proceeds by keeping the original melody (the head) in your head as they improvise.

Part 1

Jazz is a uniquely American phenomenon that began, as far as anyone can tell, in or around the year 1900. This also makes it a product of the 20th century and, as we shall see, could not have evolved at any other time before the 20th century. Jazz, invented by Black Americans, is a unique blending of African and European musical elements. The American imported slave trade ended in 1807 and from that time no Africans were legally brought into America to be sold as slaves. Therefore, by the end of the 19th century, most African Americans were far removed from their ancestors' music and culture. Earlier, slaves were discouraged from and even forbidden to perform much of their native music, so much of what was left by the end of the 19th century was not purely African. Certain characteristics and principles were, however, maintained during that time and as they mixed with the Western, European music of White Americans, a uniquely African American music came into being. It is hard to define what this music was exactly since much of it was improvised, none of it was written down, and what did survive came mostly from White Americans' interpretations of what they heard. These interpretations are almost certainly gross simplifications of the authentic African American music of the time.

A key feature of African music is an emphasis on rhythm, so much so that some African music consists only of drums. By focusing on rhythm, Africans developed a very complex rhythmic concept that was far more complex than any European music. European music, however, evolved a very complex system of harmony but at the expense of rhythm. Jazz essentially combined African rhythms with European harmony to create a uniquely American music. Interestingly, Latin America had a similar situation to that of the United States but the music there evolved in different ways. Aside from the obvious cultural differences of their colonizing countries, the languages spoken in the different countries has a lot to do with how their music evolved. The sounds of a language, its rhythms, its cadences, its vowels and consonants, etc., transfer to the music of those who speak that language. Even within the general tome of what is called Western music coming from Europe, the regional differences of language clearly affect

Roots and Early Jazz

the music of those regions: Italian music is flowing and song-like, German music is precise and metric, French music is blurry and subtle, etc. Jazz, originated by Southern Black Americans, from its earliest days took on the characteristics of Southern Black American speech: its rhythms, its cadences, its sounds, etc. Latin American music, on the other hand, evolved in different ways, as we shall see, because of either the Spanish or Portuguese languages that were spoken there.

White Americans seemed to have always had a fascination with *Negro* music. So much so that White entertainers would put on blackface and sing supposed *Negro* songs. Blackface entertainment was enormously popular during the 19th century and by the mid-century the minstrel show became the dominant form of entertainment throughout the country. Minstrel shows featured men in blackface who mostly derogatorily portrayed caricatures of African Americans. As offensive as this seems to us today, racial and ethnic stereotyping remained a staple of American entertainment well into the 20th century. The minstrel songs that were written in a supposed African American style were in reality closer to folk songs from the British Isles. Many of these songs contained a rhythm known as a *Scottish snap*, which contains a short note on the beat followed quickly by another note before the next beat. Such rhythms seemed exotic to most Americans and almost any exotic rhythm they associated with Black music. *Syncopation* is a word that became associated with Black music; it refers to the stressing of notes or beats within a meter that would not normally be stressed. In traditional Western music, for example, in quadruple meter each measure contains four beats but there is a hierarchy of beats that normally gives stress to the first and then third beats of the measure. If there is a stress on beats two or four, or in between beats, it was heard as syncopation. Harmony and melody usually work in such a way that listeners have come to expect these stresses as a natural part of the music they hear. Syncopation then, upsets this norm and comes as something unexpected to the listener. Syncopation had been a part of Western music for hundreds of years (Beethoven was famous for it) but it was the exception that thwarted listeners' expectations and added variety and interest to the music. West African drumming is often polymetric, meaning there can be several different meters going on simultaneously. Western ears heard such music as very syncopated but syncopation is a Western concept and is foreign to African music. Nevertheless, syncopation became associated with African American music and the simplest form of syncopation like the Scottish snap was heard as being African in nature. Stephen Foster used this rhythm in two of his famous Minstrel songs: *Oh! Susanna* and *Camptown Races*.

Figure I.1: Example of African polymetric drumming with four simultaneous meters. The only common beat is the first beat of each measure.

After the Civil War, Blacks, themselves, began performing in minstrel shows, and even wore blackface and characterized themselves. As ludicrous as this seems, it did give Black Americans a foothold in the entertainment world from which they not only found future employment but also would influence mainstream entertainment and music to the present day. By 1900 the effects of Black American music could be heard in the popular songs of the day and White singers began to "rag the tune," which meant they improvised on it, changing notes and rhythms from the original version. Improvisation was a key feature of African music and since songs, etc., were learned by rote, they changed from singer to singer over the years. This oral tradition music differs from European written music and jazz would bridge the gap between them in the same way it did for rhythm and harmony. Jazz musicians write tunes, yet they improvise on them. The tunes might be published in some concrete version, but jazz musicians constantly change them.

Two new types of music emerged during the 1890s: Ragtime and Blues. Both were inventions of African Americans and both merge elements of African and European music. Ragtime was a strict formal written music, while Blues was an informal non-written improvisational music. In the year 1900, Ragtime and Blues mix together to create jazz. This merger of the formal and the informal, the written and the non-written, the strict and improvisational, gave birth to a music that was uniquely American and unique to the 20th century. Although jazz would have begun when it did, it would not have evolved and developed as it did were it not for the new electronic media of records and radio. As we will see jazz is a complex music that is mostly improvised and unlike folk music it bears repeated listening to be learned. It would be impossible to emulate, let's say, a Louis Armstrong solo, without hearing it many times. With records and radio, that was now possible. No longer did someone need to be where Louis Armstrong was to hear Louis Armstrong play. This was crucial for the development of jazz because unlike Classical music, which is also a complex music, none of what Louis Armstrong played was written down. One could only learn jazz by listening to it and now with records and radio anyone, anywhere, any time, could.

Recording is not new in the 20th century; Thomas Edison invented the phonograph in 1877 and Emile Berliner invented the gramophone in 1887. Edison recorded sound onto cylinders lined with tin foil and Berliner used flat wax discs. The two formats competed until 1910 when the flat disc gramophone won out. Although records predate the 20th century, it was not until 1903 when records made by the world famous Italian opera singer Enrico Caruso became available that the music industry realized the huge money making potential in them. The great Caruso, as he was called, was known throughout Europe and American as the greatest singer of his time but very few people had actually heard him. Records made it possible for anyone to hear this magnificent voice, albeit not with great audio fidelity. As the manufacturing of gramophones increased and became more affordable, the sale of records steadily increased until it became a major industry by the 1920s.

Figure I.2: Edison Phonograph.
Copyright © Norman Bruderhofer (CC BY-SA 3.0) at http://commons.wikimedia.org/wiki/File:EdisonPhonograph.jpg

Figure I.3: Berliner Gramophone.
Copyright © Fotokannan (CC BY-SA 3.0) at http://commons.wikimedia.org/wiki/File:Gramaphone_a.jpg

The first jazz record was made in 1917 and that, in effect, ended the Ragtime Era and began the Jazz Age of the 1920s. Jazz evolves very quickly after that and by the thirties the jazz style of 1917 was already obsolete. We will notice a change in the quality of the recording we hear after 1925. Before 1925 records were made by the acoustical process, which used only acoustical energy with no electricity. The sound waves of singers and instruments were collected by a canonically shaped horn that focused the vibrations onto a metal stylus (needle) that marked indentations onto a revolving wax disc on a turntable. For playback, the process was reversed; the indentations on the rotating disc caused the stylus to vibrate, which then transferred those vibrations to canonical horn that projected sound waves back to the air. In 1925 the started to use the electrical process, which used microphones and speakers to do what the horns had done in the acoustical process. The microphone collected sound vibrations and translated them into electrical signals that caused the stylus to vibrate as before onto a wax disc, but since the microphone collects more of the natural sound, the fidelity was much better. For playback, the stylus now translated the vibrations from the disc into electrical signals that caused a speaker to project the sound waves. This electrical process remained unchanged until the late 1940s when magnetic tape was introduced.

Figure I.4: Acoustical recording session at Edison Studio. Jacques Urlus & Soder's Orchestra, New York, circa 1915.

Copyright in the Public Domain.

Figure I.5: Microphone.
Copyright in the Public Domain.

Part 1 of this book will take us from the forerunners of jazz, Ragtime, and Blues and their merger to form jazz, up through the 1920s. This Early Jazz period includes New Orleans or Dixieland jazz and its later offshoot referred to as Chicago style jazz. Several important musicians are covered, from Joplin to Waller, Bolden to Beiderbecke, with Morton, Oliver, and Armstrong in between.

Chapter One

Ragtime

Ragtime was written solo piano music created by Black Americans in the 1890s and gained widespread popularity by 1900. Though not jazz per se, ragtime was an important forerunner of jazz. Practically all jazz piano styles until the 1940s were based on the ragtime model. In fact, several early jazz piano styles were still referred to as ragtime, and because of this, the term *classic ragtime* will sometimes be used to distinguish the original version from later jazz versions such as Eastern ragtime. Ragtime represents the first formal blending of European and West African musical elements. The form and harmony came from Europe; the rhythmic concept came from West Africa. Ragtime in its original form was strictly a written music, another aspect it shares with the European tradition.

CAKEWALKS

Ragtime evolved primarily from two musical styles: the **cakewalk** and the march. The term *cakewalk* refers to a dance and the music played to accompany it. It featured high, strutting movements that mocked the slave owner's pompous walk and attitude, and was usually accompanied by a kind of syncopated music on a banjo. There were cakewalk contests where couples performed the strutting and the winners would receive a cake as their prize. A characteristic syncopated melodic rhythm developed. It is notated below in two ways: the first in cut time and the second two-four time.

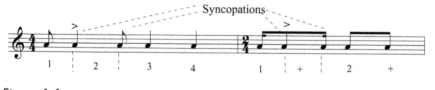

Figure 1.1

This rhythm is typically repeated often during the course of a cakewalk tune. Cakewalks became popular on their own and published piano music using the title *Cakewalk* began to appear in the 1890s. The left-hand accompaniment came straight from the March with its characteristic alternation of bass note and chord, sometimes referred to as oom-pah, oom-pah.

At a Georgia Camp Meeting by Kerry Mills was a very popular cakewalk around the turn of the 20th century. Notice the characteristic cakewalk rhythm or a slight variation on it throughout the first section shown below.

Figure 1.2

RAGTIME SONGS

Cakewalks were simpler forerunners of the much more complex music called Ragtime but once Ragtime became popular, Tin Pan Alley (the name given at the time to the Pop song business) published what they called **Ragtime Songs**. Ragtime songs, however, were really nothing more than cakewalks Sometimes these songs were derogatorily called *coon* songs with stereotyped caricatures of Black Americans on the sheet music covers. ***Hello! My Baby*** by Joe Howard and Ida Emerson is a famous Ragtime Song that is well known today from its use in the famous cartoon, *One Froggy Evening*, in which Michigan J. Frog sings the song several times.

Notice the cakewalk rhythm that is bracketed below.

Figure 1.3

RAGTIME RHYTHM

From the simple syncopated rhythm of cakewalks, Ragtime evolved into a complex solo piano music. Certain aspects of West African rhythmic practice are evident in the rhythmic conception of Ragtime, but Ragtime represents a simplification of that practice. The key aspect present in Ragtime is the concept of rhythmic layers. The multilayered polymetric music heard in West African drumming (see Part I Introduction) is reduced to just two layers in Ragtime and they are clearly separated in the right and left hands of the pianist. The right hand is conceived in eight beats per measure, while the left hand is in four beats per measure. Thus the right hand pulse is twice as fast as the left hand pulse. This two-to-one ratio is much simpler than two to three, etc., relationships found in African drumming. Ragtime reduces the African concept of separate layers going at the same time to two separate layers of rhythmic activity. Although Ragtime was usually written in two-four time, the examples below are written in four-four time to make the relationships clearer.

Figure 1.4

A key difference between the two hands is the left hand almost always plays on every beat but the right hand does not have to play every one of its beats; notes can held for two, three, beats, etc.

The right hand typically groups beats into certain numerical patterns called **additive rhythms**; this also comes from African practice. These patterns are generally in groups of twos and threes, such as: 3+3+2, or 3+3+3, or 3+2+3, etc. These numbers refer to accents with the melodic lines, not to the number of notes played. The example below shows two of the patterns with the first one shown again as held notes.

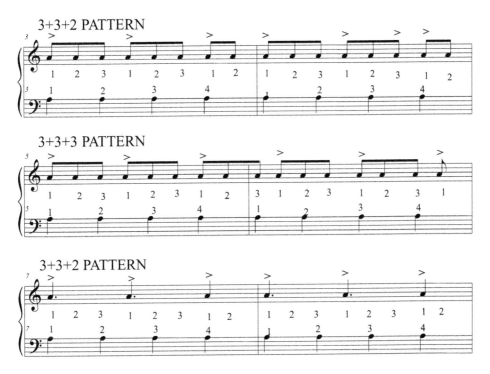

Figure 1.5

In the example above, notice the accents that occur between beats or on weak beats (left hand beats 2 and 4). To Western ears this is syncopation, but the African tradition that this stems from has no concept of syncopation—just simultaneous layers of different rhythmic activity. It is important to make this distinction, although most simply say Ragtime is highly syncopated, because Blues and jazz also work on a layering of rhythmic layers but ones that are different from ragtime.

The left hand usually provides a steady four beats to each measure by playing bass notes and chords. As noted with ***At a Georgia Camp Meeting***, as in the March tradition, it does this by alternating bass notes and chords, for the most part. This is broken up from time to time with several chords or bass notes in a row.

A typical Ragtime left hand may look like this:

Figure 1.6

RAGTIME FORMS

Ragtime pieces generally adhere to March forms consisting of multiple sixteen-measure sections called **strains.** The basic prototype is four repeating strains as follows: AA BB CC DD. The C sections are often referred to as the Trio section, which is a term that goes back to Renaissance dance music when this section was actually played by a trio of instruments. In more modern dance music, marches, and Ragtime, it refers to a contrasting section that is usually in a contrasting key. There are many variations on the formal model. Often, for example, another statement of the A section is placed after the B sections or there may be only three sections or as many as five sections, and an introduction might precede the A section.

SCOTT JOPLIN

Scott Joplin (1868–1917) is the undisputed king of Ragtime. He was born in Texas but famously lived in Sedalia, Missouri, for a while. Joplin was a serious composer who thought of his music in the European tradition. He was adamant about playing his Rags the way he wrote them and hated when someone would play them too fast or improvise on them, as the early jazz players did. In addition to composing Ragtime pieces, he wrote a ballet score and two operas. Joplin is not the only composer of Ragtime but he is the most well known. Coincidentally or not, the so-called *Ragtime Era* ended in 1917, the year he died. But 1917 was also the year that the first jazz record was made and thus the *Jazz Age* began. Although Joplin had a profound influence on jazz, his music was not jazz and he, in fact, hated jazz. Ragtime all but died out during the Jazz Age as it gave way to jazz, itself. Joplin's music, along with that of other ragtime composers, died out for the most part but was resurrected in 1973 when Joplin's music was used for the soundtrack of the movie *The Sting*. The general public became enthralled with the music again and the Ragtime revival that took place continues to the present day.

Figure 1.7: Scott Joplin.
Copyright in the Public Domain.

Figure 1.8: *Maple Leaf Rag* first edition sheet music.
Copyright in the Public Domain.

MAPLE LEAF RAG

Joplin's most famous rag, **Maple Leaf Rag**, was written in 1899. It achieved enormous popularity and made Scott Joplin famous. The form is:

Trio
AA BB A CC DD
Ab-----------Db--Ab

Each strain is 16 measures long.

For the A strain, the left-hand part goes against the standard procedure of alternating bass notes and chords; it does, however, have a bass note or chord on almost every beat. Although Joplin wrote the music in two-four time, we will think of it here as in four-eight time with each eighth note getting one beat. Most of the measures in the other strains adhere to the oom-pah model, for the most part. The example below shows the beginnings of the A and B strains in order to demonstrate how the accents pattern based on additive rhythms in the right-hand eight-beat pulse relate to the four-beat pulse of the left hand. The middle staff shows just the accented notes. Joplin makes the accents clear in these examples by having the accented notes played in octaves. It is the accented notes that occur between the left-hand beats and on the unaccented left-hand beats (beats 2 and 4) that are heard as syncopations but conceptually are the byproduct of two simultaneous metric layers going at their own rates.

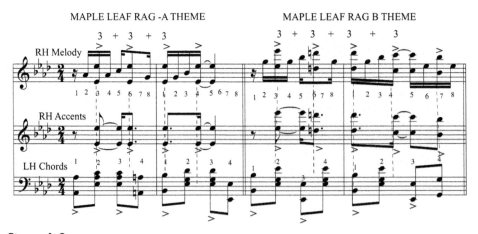

Figure 1.9

MAPLE LEAF RAG 1916

Piano Roll made by Scott Joplin

Although he certainly could have, Scott Joplin made no known recordings. He did, however, make several piano rolls to be played on player pianos. Player pianos, sometimes known as Pianolas, were popular around the turn of the 20th century. They are basically pianos that play themselves by a person pumping air with foot pedals that blows through holes on the piano roll as it scrolls along through a wind-up mechanism. The air then activates certain hammers that strike the appropriate strings. To make a piano roll, someone plays a specially designed piano that makes the holes as a blank piano roll scrolls. This is not exactly the same as making an audio recording since a lot of the subtlety in performance is lost, but it gives at least a decent approximation of a live performance. We are lucky to have this piano roll of Maple Leaf Rag that Joplin made and it gives us good indication of how the composer wanted his Rag played.

What to listen for:

1. The right-hand accents against the steady left-hand pulse
2. The two different layers of rhythmic activity
3. Try clapping the right-hand accents (see listening guide)
4. Try to follow the form
5. Try to notice the key change for the Trio section

Figure 1.10: Chase & Baker player piano, Buffalo, NY, circa 1885.

Chapter Two

Blues

Blues has been a staple of American music for over 100 years. It exists as its own genre, manifested in many different styles, and has had a profound influence on jazz as well as Rock & Roll and related music. The beginnings of Blues are unclear but it seems to have been in place by the 20th century and most probably by the 1890s. Whereas Ragtime demonstrates an African instrumental rhythmic infusion into European music, Blues brings an African vocal practice. African singing generally makes use of an expressive inflection of pitch by bending notes slightly up or down, sliding between notes, and "singing in the cracks," which means singing non-tempered notes that are pitches in between notes, usually a flattened note. The term *singing on the crack* refers to nonexistent pitches that theoretically might exist in the cracks between keys on a piano.

Before Blues there were several important African American genres that influenced the Blues and all make use of African vocal practice. All of this music was not written and thus was handed down by the oral tradition and learned by rote. Improvisation was important and the songs were constantly changing. As songs were performed and listened

Alan Lomax (1915–2002) was a folklorist and ethnomusicologist who collected music from the oral tradition by making field and on-location recordings. He actually continued the work that his parents started in the early 20th century. Since none of this music was written down, his recordings are literally the only record of it. His goal was to capture as much of this traditional music as possible before it would die out completely. He went to various places in the American South, from the Appalachian Mountains to the Mississippi Delta, to record Black American as well as White American Folk and oral traditional music. We can get a glimpse, at least, of what some of this music might have sounded like in the 19th century and about as close as we can get to it. Lomax recorded most of the audio examples in this chapter during the 1930s.

to by others, the others would sing their versions that were heard by others, etc. The types of songs that predate Blues were all performed originally by slaves on plantations in the South. Three important forerunners of the blues are described below.

ROOTS OF THE BLUES

FIELD HOLLERS

Field Hollers were solo songs sung by workers in the field usually performing a non-rhythmic activity, such as picking cotton. A Field Holler is thus an unaccompanied song sung by one person. It usually has a free-floating sense of time without an obvious beat. The technical term is *rubato*, which means a fluctuating beat that may speed up or slow down as the music is performed. Since there are no other performers, the singer of a Filed Holler is free to perform rubato without the need to coordinate with anyone else.

WILD OX MOAN

Wild Ox Moan is a Field Holler sung by Vera Hall and recorded by Alan Lomax. Notice the pitch inflections and rubato performance.

WORK SONGS

Work Songs differ from Field Hollers in several ways. They are performed by a group of workers while performing a rhythmic activity such as chopping wood or rowing a boat. Work Songs served the practical purpose of coordinating the workers' movements for greater efficiency and thus had a very strong sense of beat. An important feature of most Work Songs is a technique named *Call and Response*. Typically there is a leader who sings the call line to which the rest of the group responds. The response can happen in two different ways: 1) the groups repeats the call, more or less, that the leader sang, and 2) the group sings the same response independent of what the call is, which acts as an unchanging refrain (r).

Type 1 Call and Response: a a, b b, c c
Type 2 Call and Response: a r, b r, c r

EIGHTEEN HAMMERS

Eighteen Hammers is a Work Song sung by Johnny Lee Moore and twelve Mississippi penitentiary convicts and recorded by Alan Lomax. Both types of responses are used in this song. In each stanza the group responds to the leader's first line with "ah ah," and then responds to his second line by repeating the call.

a r, b b
c r, d d
e r, f f etc.

In any of this music the repetitions are not necessarily exact and there is always some improvisation and variation. Notice the strong sense of beat and how the song helps to coordinate the breaking of rocks. Again we hear characteristic pitch inflections.

WORK SONG SUNG BY RAILROAD GANDY DANCERS

Watch this video of a work song sung by railroad Gandy Dancers who were men who physically move railroad tracks with picks that acted as levers. Notice how the song helps to coordinate the workers' movements and keep them in sync, which was necessary to move the tracks. This film was taken near Columbia, South Carolina, in 1929.

SPIRITUALS

Slaves brought to America from Africa were forbidden from practicing their traditional religions and eventually adopted their slave owners' Christian religion. In time, the slaves developed their own services and hymns. These hymns, known as Spirituals, were originally improvised and handed down by rote like other African American music, but were eventually formalized and written down by the 20th century. Spirituals are loved and performed around the world and are arranged for many different vocal and instrumental ensembles. They are also performed by solo singers of wide-ranging backgrounds that include jazz, Classical, Rhythm & Blues, and Pop. Many Spirituals deal with Old Testament stories from the Bible; the American slaves identified with the ancient Israelites who were enslaved in Egypt. The lyrics to some of the Spirituals contained hidden messages that might have even helped some slaves to escape.

IS THERE ANYBODY HERE THAT LOVES MY JESUS

This spiritual is performed closer to the way that Spirituals began rather than the formal music they became; it is improvisatory and loosely performed by the congregation. It is sung here by Viola James and congregation and recorded by Alan Lomax. Although not as common as in Work Songs, Call and Response is sometimes used in Spirituals as it is here. Notice that the congregation is not always in sync and some singers wander off from the melody. This is common in a lot of non-professional congregational singing.

THE BLUES

It is not known when the Blues began or where it cam from. It does not seem to have come from Africa but from African Americans in the late 19th century. It evolved as an expressive way of singing about what is known as "feeling blue." "Having the blues" was nothing new in the late 19th century but singing the Blues was. Blues lyrics often deal with some horrible situations and sad feelings, but it is often said that singing the Blues can make you happy; it can serve as a catharsis for the Blues singer and thereby the listener as well. In many Blues lyrics there is a certain acceptance of the unfortunate hand that life has dealt. Blues is almost always sung in the first person, which makes Blues singing a highly expressive art. Most 19th century American Popular songs were written in the third person and thus the singer sang of someone else. Blues songs are often sexual in nature and many lyrics employ sexual innuendoes. This is in stark contrast to 19th century Popular songs that might mention romantic love but never sex. Both the more direct first-person point of view and the sexual realism of Blues will have a huge effect on American Popular songs of the 20th century. In addition, the whole nature of Blues singing with its expressiveness and manipulation and inflection of pitch will come to bear on jazz and Pop singers and instrumentalists as well.

BLUES TEXT FORM

By the 20th century the Blues evolved into a standard poetic form: each stanza contained three lines with the second line repeating the first and a new third line that can act like a punch line. Thus, each stanza is **aab** in form. The repeat of the first line is very important; it builds tension and anticipation of the punch line. The origins of this also unclear and seems to have been invented by Black Americans around the turn of the 20th century. Earlier Blues stanzas are purported to have been in an **aaa** form for each stanza; the singing of each line three times is not nearly as interesting. Below is a stanza from a Robert Johnson Blues song, ***Love in Vain***.

When the train, it left the station, there was two lights on behind,
When the train, it left the station, there was two lights on behind,
Well, the blue light was my baby, and the red light was my mind.
All my love's in vain.

Next is a stanza from A Frank Hutchinson Blues song, *Cannonball Blues*.

Gonna lay my head down on some railroad line-
Gonna lay my head down on some railroad line
Let the cannonball come and pacify my mind

BLUES SCALE

There is a certain scale that evolved in connection to the Blues. This so-called Blues Scale has been often misunderstood and certainly overused. The origins of the scale are unknown and, like Blues, itself, seems to have been invented in America by African Americans. Most consider the Blues scale to be as follows.

Figure 2.1

This is a C Blues scale. Some eliminate the F#/Gb, while others include notes of the major scale. What is commonly misunderstood is the Blues scale is used only for melodies while the harmony comes from the major scale. The African concept of multiple layers is at work here just as it is in the rhythmic conception for Ragtime. There are two different tonal layers. The Blues scale and major scale are lined up below. Notice that the notes don't always coincide. These clashes are usually called blue notes: the concept being that they are nothing more than flattened notes of the major scale that are used for expressive purposes. In actual vocal performances these blue notes are sung to pitches between the major scale note and its flattened neighbor (in the cracks).

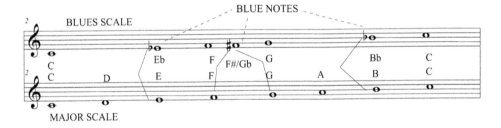

Figure 2.2

If you play or sing just notes from the Blues scale it will sound like Blues. Much like a Pentatonic scale (just the black keys on piano, for example) if you stick to only those notes, nothing will sound bad or like a mistake, hence, the overuse of the scale by beginning improvisers.

12-BAR BLUES OUTLINE

Along with the aab text or lyrics form, Blues settled into a 12-bar (12-measure) form. It is, again, a unique form invented by African Americans and one that is amazingly flexible and resilient; it is still in common use in a variety of musical styles. Each of the three phrases of text occupies four measures of music. These phrases, however, usually last for only two and a half to three bars, which creates gaps that are to be filled instrumentally or vocally. This is a version of **Call and Response** that we first noted in Work Songs. The Call and Response technique is an important one used in Blues and as we shall see also in jazz. Along with the aab text form, there is a basic harmonic progression that goes with it, although not in the same form. The first phrase is accompanied by the I chord for the first four bars. The V chord is played at the beginning of the third phrase. This is the point of most tension in the lyrics, since we anticipate the punch line, and in traditional European harmony, the V chord produces the most tension as well. At the end of the third phrase, the tension is resolved harmonically by going back to the I chord (the Tonic chord). Over the years many variations on the basic harmonic progressive have been used. We will encounter several throughout the book. One common variation is shown below.

BASIC OUTLINE FOR 12 BAR BLUES

```
              1    2    3    4   |5    6    7    8   |9   10   11   12   |
Mel + Lyrics  a————————Fill————— |a————————Fill————— |b————————Fill——————|
              call        response | call      response| call      response |

Harmony            |               | IV    I    | V    I
Key of C          C              | F     C    | G    C

Harm Var      |    IV   I        | IV    I    | V    IV   |
Key of C      C    F    C          F     C    | G    F    C
```

The Blues singer often sings in a free rubato-like rhythm like a Field Holler even though the accompaniment is in strict beats. This free-floating melodic line against the strict background again shows the African concept of separate rhythmic activity but in a way that is different from Ragtime.

COUNTRY BLUES

The original style of Blues is known as Country Blues. It also is called Delta Blues and is the most basic form of Blues. It most probably began in the Mississippi Delta region and spread throughout the South from there. Country Blues is usually sung by a male singer who accompanies himself on the guitar. It is a very personal, direct form of expression and most Country Blues artists write their own songs. Since there is only the one performer, some Country Blues performances adhere to the model loosely; there may be extra or eliminated beats, longer or shorter phrases, etc., but the model, however corrupted, remains intact.

ROBERT JOHNSON

The most famous Country Blues singer, Robert Johnson (1912–1938) was born in Hazlehurst, Mississippi. He acquired legendary status even within his own short lifetime. Little is known about his personal life; he would mysteriously leave and show up in towns throughout the South and his death is a mystery as well. It was rumored he sold his soul to the devil in exchange for his musical talents. He was also into voodoo. He was apparently a womanizer who dazzled the ladies with his singing and songs. Alan Lomax discovered Johnson and brought him to a recording studio in 1936 and between then and 1937, Johnson recorded many takes of many of his songs and many of these are available today. Johnson has become an idol of more modern Blues and Rock players since the Sixties; Eric Clapton and Keith Richards are among the faithful.

HELLHOUND ON MY TRAIL 1937

Hellhound on My Trail is one of Robert Johnson's best-known songs. The lyrics relate to his vagabond lifestyle, the devil, voodoo, and sex. Hellhounds are fictitious supernatural dogs that serve as death omens. "Hot-foot powder" alludes to a voodoo spell and "sweet rider" refers to his lover. Johnson is using a bottleneck in his left hand on his guitar; Country Blues players used it to provide a kind of twangy, almost eerie sound as it slides up and down the fret board. The formal lyrics are shown below followed by what Johnson actually sings.

Formal lyrics:

I got to keep movin', I've got to keep movin', blues fallin' down like hail,
I got to keep movin', I've got to keep movin', blues fallin' down like hail,
And the day keeps on worrin' me, there's a hellhound on my trail.

If today was Christmas Eve, and tomorrow was Christmas Day,
If today was Christmas Eve, and tomorrow was Christmas Day,
All I would need my little sweet rider, just to pass the time away.

You sprinkled hot-foot powder, mmm around my door,
You sprinkled hot-foot powder, mmm around my door,
It keeps me with a rambling mind, rider, every old place I go.

I can tell the wind is rising, the leaves trembling on the trees,
I can tell the wind is rising, the leaves trembling on the trees,
All I need is my little sweet woman, and to keep my company.

Transcription of what Johnson sings:

I got to keep movin', I've got to keep movin', blues fallin' down like hail, blues fallin' down like hail
Umm-mm-mm-mm, blues fallin' down like hail, blues fallin' down like hail
And the day keeps on worrin' me, there's a hellhound on my trail, hellhound on my trail, hellhound on my trail.

If today was Christmas Eve, if today was Christmas Eve, and tomorrow was Christmas Day
If today was Christmas Eve, and tomorrow was Christmas Day (*spoken: Oh wouldn't we have a time baby*)
All I would need my little sweet rider, just to pass the time away, ah-ah to pass the time away

You sprinkled hot-foot powder, mmm around my door, all around my door
You sprinkled hot-foot powder, around your daddy's door, umm-mm-mm
It keeps me with a rambling mind, rider, every old place I go, every old place I go

I can tell the wind is rising, the leaves trembling on the trees, trembling on the trees,
I can tell the wind is rising, the leaves trembling on the trees, umm-mm-mm-mm
All I need is my little sweet woman, and to keep my company, hey-ey-ey-ey, my company

---

MISSISSIPPI FRED MCDOWELL

GOIN' DOWN TO THE RIVER

Mississippi Fred McDowell (1904–1972) is another legendary Country Blues singer. Watch this video and notice all the Blues characteristics. Like Robert Johnson, he uses a bottleneck on his guitar and also takes liberties with the Blues formal model. The first part of the first Blues chorus is cut off from the beginning of this film.

CITY BLUES

By the 1920s Blues made its way to the large cities in the North. In the early 20th century many African Americans migrated north in search of employment, bringing their music with them. By this time jazz was fully developed and jazz and Blues strongly influenced each other. City Blues, also known as Classic Blues, was more sophisticated and polished than Country Blues and used more complex chords and chord progressions. The basic 12-bar structure and outline, however, remained intact. Blues became popular during the 1910s and more formalized with the publication of Blues songs. W.C. Handy, an African American, known as the Father of the Blues, wrote the first published Blues song, *Memphis Blues* and later the most famous published Blues song, *St. Louis Blues*. City Blues were sung mostly by women who were accompanied by piano or a small band. The lyrics often dealt with lost love or the harsh realities of inner-city living at that time. The first City Blues singer of note was Ma Rainey. Other famous City Blues singers are Bessie Smith, Sippie Wallace, Ida Cox, and Alberta Hunter.

BESSIE SMITH

The greatest and most famous City (Classic) Blues singer is Bessie Smith (1894–1937). She possessed a full, powerful voice and became quite popular in the twenties and thir-

ties. She was known as the Empress of the Blues and performed in New York theatres and films. She recorded often and had several hits, including her version of W.C. Handy's *St. Louis Blues* that also featured a young Louis Armstrong on cornet. She also sang it and acted in a short film called *St. Louis Blues*. She is truly one of the great singers of the 20th century and personifies what great Blues singing is about.

Figure 2.3: Bessie Smith.
Copyright in the Public Domain.

LOST YOUR HEAD BLUES

Bessie Smith—Vocal
Joe Smith—Trumpet
Fletcher Henderson—Piano

Lost Your Head Blues is a good example of City Blues; a small band accompanies the singer, the music is jazz influenced and sophisticated, and the lyrics tell of a woman mistreated by her man. Notice the constant Call and Response between Bessie and Joe Smith on the trumpet; he fills in every gap that she leaves. Notice, also, Bessie's Blues inflections and the power of her voice, which is especially noticeable during the last section when she sings:

...Days are lonesome, nights are so long,
Days are lonesome; nights are so long,
I'm a good gal, but I just been treated wrong.

Chapter Three

Early Jazz—New Orleans Style, Dixieland

Jazz seems to begin in New Orleans in the year 1900. Historians may quibble about the exactness of these claims, but this is certainly not far from the mark and it makes for a convenient well-rounded starting time and place. Why New Orleans? Why 1900? What is jazz? A simplified formula is

RAGTIME + BLUES + MARCH MUSIC = JAZZ

But how and why did they all come together when and where they did?

During most of the 19th century, New Orleans was a unique American city that was more European and, even more specifically, French in culture. Gambling and prostitution were legal, and music played an important part in the everyday lives of those living there. Music accompanied many indoor and outdoor activities and social dancing was very popular. Opera thrived there as well as marching bands and dance orchestras. New Orleans had a very diverse population that included many Black Americans, French, Spanish, and Caribbean people. Not only were Blacks more accepted there, but persons of mixed race were as well. New Orleans had a large a large mixed-race population known as Creoles of Color. Whereas in other parts of the country during the 19th century, anyone with mixed Black and White blood was considered to be a "Negro," which gave them an inferior social status, in New Orleans they were considered White.

The bands and orchestras in New Orleans were separated into Black and White bands. The Creoles of Color, who originally were considered White, played with the White bands and were trained in the European tradition of written music, Classical music, etc. The Black musicians were mostly untrained and learned their instruments, tunes, and songs by rote, relying much on improvisation. By 1900 their music tradition included Ragtime, Blues, Spiritual, and Work Songs, as well as some popular songs and marches. During the 1890s new segregation laws (Jim Crow Laws) came into effect in New Orleans and now the Creoles of Color, because they had some Black blood, were considered to be "Negros," which meant they lost their White privileged status. As far as musicians were concerned, this meant the Creoles of Color were now forced to play in the Black bands. This is when and where the merger of styles took place. The European tradition met the African American tradition head on and jazz burst onto the scene. As the Creoles of Color brought their music to the Black musicians, the Black musicians began to improvise on it by *ragging the tune*, which meant they changed the notes and rhythms around to be more like African American music—in other words they *jazzed it up*. It is impossible to know what the earliest jazz sounded like since none of it was written down and jazz was not recorded until 1917. But we can make reasonable assumptions from the earliest records and accounts given by the early New Orleans jazz musicians.

BUDDY BOLDEN

If you could talk to anyone alive back then, they would tell you that Buddy Bolden (1877–1931) was the first jazz musician. It is unknown if he invented jazz on his own but everyone back then seemed to agree he was the best. Bolden was an African American cornet player who was one of the first to *rag the tune*. A cornet is relatively rare today. It looks and sounds very much like a trumpet. He improvised on everything and changed everything he played. He made each performance unique and his own. He is said to have had a unique sound on the cornet, using Blues inflections and feeling. These are all attributes of jazz to this day. He was able to play extremely loudly and those who heard him said he could be heard for miles around. Unfortunately, there are no known recordings of Buddy Bolden.

Figure 3.1: Buddy Bolden's band around 1900–1906
Bolden is in the top row, second from the left.

STORYVILLE

The red-light district in New Orleans around the turn of the 20th century was called Storyville. This is where the brothels were and by city ordinance they were centralized in this one area of the city in 1897. Although jazz did not begin there, Storyville was an importance place for the evolution of jazz. Jazz was considered to be a very sensuous music and seemed to go well with the activities of the neighboring brothels. In fact, the word "jazz" originally referred to having sex. Good jazz musicians found good work there, mainly in clubs, and made good money as well. Coincidentally Storyville was closed down in 1917, the year the first jazz record was made. Many of the original jazz musicians told of fond memories of Storyville.

JELLY ROLL MORTON AND EARLY JAZZ PIANO

Jazz evolved simultaneously as solo piano music and as small band music. Jelly Roll Morton (1885–1941) was involved with both and excelled in them equally. He is considered to be the **first great jazz pianist** as well as **the first great jazz composer and arranger**. He was born Ferdinand Joseph LaMothe and was a Creole of Color. He was quite a character, too, and was known as a real braggart and teller of tall tales. He clamed to be the inventor of jazz; although this is not true, he was there at the beginning and is one of the "founding fathers of Jazz." He had several side occupations that included being a comedian, singer, pool hustler, tailor and pimp. He found work as a teenager playing piano in Storyville.

Jelly Roll was the first noted pianist to fuse elements a Blues with Ragtime and turn it into jazz. All early jazz piano playing was rooted in Ragtime and remained so until the 1940s. Pianists like Jelly Roll started to improvise on Rags and make them *swing*. He loosened the "even subdivisions" effect of Ragtime—turning "straight" eighth notes into "swing" eighth notes by playing them unevenly in a long–short manner and this more relaxed attitude has stayed with jazz ever since.

Swing in a word that is hard to define; it is famously said that if you have to ask what it is, you'll never know. As elusive as a definition of swing is it something that most listeners can feel. If we play a Louis Armstrong record next to a Mozart symphony, almost everyone will notice that Armstrong swings while Mozart does not. Almost all jazz swings, so what is it? Swing is an approach to music, an approach to the beat that goes against the beat while being fully aware of where the beat is. The example of Jelly Roll Morton's ***Maple Leaf Rag*** that follows clearly swings, as do most of the examples in this book.

Swing relies on more than just the underlying rhythmic feel, however. Swing relates to subtle shadings of dynamics and accents, as well as rhythmic placement. It relates to a "going against the grain" quality that applies not only to rhythm, but also to harmony and melody as they relate to pulse, meter, cadence, form, and each other. Whereas classic Ragtime was in two-four time, jazz is in four-four. This is an important difference. Ragtime adheres to a system of strong beats and weak beats—the bass notes (1 and 2) are emphasized, while the after-chords (the "ands") are significantly weaker. In early jazz, the bass notes are played on beats 1 and 3, and after-chords on beats 2 and 4; thus in jazz, the after-chords occur on the beat level, not as after-beats. Essentially, there are no weak beats in jazz. Jazz makes all the beats equal on the melodic and pulse levels, and any beat can be stressed. Often beats 2 and 4, or even the "ands" in between the beats, are stressed. This equalization of all beats gives jazz its basic underpinning for swinging. The harmonic structure generally adheres to the traditional procedure of changing on the "strong" beats, 1 and 3, but rhythmically, jazz goes against this grain.

The following example shows the difference between classic Ragtime and jazz regarding the pulse.

Figure 3.2

MAPLE LEAF RAG 1937

Played by Jelly Roll Morton

The Smithsonian Collection of Classic Jazz (SCCJ) uses this 1937 recording of *Maple Leaf Rag* to demonstrate the difference between Ragtime and Jazz. It's a valid comparison and the differences are clearly audible. Although by 1937, jazz styles evolved beyond the New Orleans style, Jelly Roll remained true to his roots and thus we can hear this as an example of early New Orleans jazz piano playing. As all great jazz musicians do, Jelly Roll transforms the material; he plays *Maple Leaf Rag* without ever playing *Maple Leaf Rag*. Rather, he plays *on Maple Leaf Rag*. He uses it as a framework on which he improvises his own music. In other words, he makes it his, not Scott Joplin's music. In jazz there are countless ways of playing *Maple Leaf Rag* or anything else. It is a performer's art much more than a composer's art.

Jelly Roll Morton not only improvises constantly on Joplin's Rag, but he also changes the form. He uses the second half of the A strain as an introduction and follows it with ABACCDD. Compare this to the original form (see Chapter 1). Other differences are shown below.

Joplin	Morton
Ragtime	Jazz
Written	Improvised
Does not swing	Swings
Relatively stiff	Looser feeling, more relaxed

Morton alternates bass and chords in his left hand, as in Ragtime, but he breaks it up a lot more by playing offbeat rhythms and counter melodies. His whole approach is orchestral; it sounds as if he is playing parts for multiple instruments. He also treats the second D stain as a **Shout Chorus**, which is an arranger's term for the last chorus or section of an arrangement that builds to an exciting conclusion; it is usually loud and very full sounding. Listen to all or some of the Joplin recording before listening to Morton's version.

NEW ORLEANS COMBO MUSIC

Small groups in jazz are often referred to as combos. Along with solo piano music, combos played an important role in the evolution of Early Jazz. This New Orleans style, also known as Dixieland, is the first band style of jazz. It evolved from Ragtime, Blues, and March music. New Orleans combos were essentially made up of instruments used in brass bands. These brass bands played for outdoor concerts, parades, and other activities, including funerals. As noted at the beginning of this chapter, musicians in these bands began ragging the tune of otherwise "straight" music by improvising ragged rhythms.

The typical New Orleans combos were split into two sections: the rhythm section and the Front Line. The Front Line consisted of wind instruments that played the main melodic material. This first style of jazz is a very complex music that requires careful listening on the part of each player. As you will hear, there is a lot going on and remarkably none of the music is written; each player improvises his or her part on the spot. This not haphazardly played, however, and each player has a certain role to play and fits his or her part in accordingly.

RHYTHM SECTION

The function of the rhythm section was to give the beat or pulse and supply the harmony. There was no standard instrumentation; in the early days various bands used various instruments. Some choices were made based on where the music was performed: outdoors or indoors, concert halls, small rooms, etc. Usually rhythm sections varied between two and four players and consisted of any combination of drums, banjo (or guitar), piano, and tuba (or string bass). Although guitar and bass were used in the very early bands sometimes, banjo and tuba were used more often. The roles of these particular instruments were interchangeable, meaning the guitar could perform the banjo's role and the string bass could perform the tuba's role.

An important part of the rhythm section's job was to supply a strong beat and all players except tuba or bass played on every beat.

DRUMS

The drummer's playing is the least known for the earliest bands. Jazz was not recorded until 1917 and the inferior fidelity of the recording technology at that time was not conducive to drums. The "noise" produced by drums was hard to record and tended to clutter the overall sound. Drums, thus, were often left out of a band's record or drummers greatly simplified their parts. But we can surmise that drummers played something on every beat and most likely played similarly to a marching band's drum line, using snare drum, bass drum, and cymbals.

BANJO

The banjo player strummed chords on every beat. Banjo was generally preferred over guitar because it was louder and could be heard more easily over the rest of the band.

PIANO

The pianist, still based in Ragtime, primarily alternated bass notes with chords on every beat as in Ragtime, typically using both hands instead of just the left hand. Sometimes the pianist would use just the left hand for this while adding chords in the right hand.

TUBA

The tuba player (or bassist) played primarily on beats 1 and 3, occasionally filling in beat 2 or 4. The tuba plays mainly on just two beats per measure for two reasons: 1) to produce a sound on a tuba requires a lot of air and to play on all four beats would be very taxing on the player, and 2) the bass part is born from the Ragtime and March traditions, which typically has the bass parts mostly on beats 1 and 3.

The following diagram shows when each rhythm section instrument plays in a typical measure on four beats.

BEATS	1	2	3	4
Drums	*	*	*	*
	combination of drums + cymbals			
Banjo	*	*	*	*
	chord	chord	chord	chord
Piano	*	*	*	*
	bass	chord	bass	chord
Tuba	*		*	
	bass		bass	(bass)

FRONT LINE

The wind instruments that play the melodies were referred to as the Front Line. They most often were cornet or trumpet, clarinet, and trombone. The cornet was used more often than the trumpet up until the late 1920s. An important aspect of the sounds produced in these instruments was the attempt of the players to mimic Blues singers with all the sliding between notes, inflection of pitch, etc. They engaged in a three-way conversation of sorts, by improvising three different melodies simultaneously. The term *Collective Improvisation* is often used to describe this process. Technically they play a three-voice *Polyphony*. Polyphony is a term that relates to a musical texture of two or more simultaneous melodies. Although this seems like it might lead to chaos, the music is organized around the role that each instrument performs.

CORNET

The cornet (or trumpet) player played the main foreground melody while usually embellishing, ornamenting, and making variations on the tune.

CLARINET

The clarinetist played arpeggiated (broken chord) lines based on the chords of the tune. He typically played notes higher and lower as well as faster than the cornet or trumpet.

TROMBONE

The trombonist played mostly chord tones, bass-like figures, or actual bass notes (especially if there were no tuba present). He usually played notes lower and slower than the cornet or trumpet and clarinet.

Each player, then, knew what his or her role was and carefully performed it by improvising around each other. Below is a score transcribed from a New Orleans band recording. Notice how the Front Line instruments produce their independent yet interlocking parts.

Figure 3.3

In the earlier days of New Orleans Jazz, all players played all the time. It is a later development of this style that real solos were used. Sometimes one instrument came more to the foreground than the others to be featured as a quasi-solo. True solos occur when one player improvises alone with rhythm section accompaniment. Breaks, however, were used from the beginning. **Breaks** occur when the whole band stops for a measure or two and one player fills in the gap by improvising a line. Breaks were an important device used in New Orleans style jazz. Breaks were used more then than in more modern jazz.

THE ORIGINAL DIXIELAND JAZZ BAND

It is ironic that the first jazz record was made by a White group called the Original Dixieland Jazz Band (**ODJB**). This was the beginning of many complaints through the years that White musicians stole jazz from Black musicians and profited much more from it despite their inferior performances of it. While this is true in some ways, jazz may not have survived if White musicians had not exposed this music to the general public. Jazz was never exclusively a Black American music and White musicians are fully capable of playing it as well as Black musicians. Certainly Black Americans invented jazz and have contributed the most to this uniquely American art form. The ODJB has been criticized for playing an inferior brand of New Orleans jazz and attaining commercial success at the expense of more authentic Black bands. Their playing has been called stiff and more like Ragtime than jazz. Their performances seemed to have been worked out ahead of time and there was little real improvisation while performing. Critics have long debated the merits of this band, but their historical importance cannot be denied; they were the first to record jazz and essentially put an end to the Ragtime Era and made a beginning to the Jazz Age.

Nick LaRocca (1889–1961), a cornetist from New Orleans and the leader of the ODJB, like Jelly Roll Morton, claimed to have invented jazz. No one much believed him, of course, and this fantastic boast did not help gain him favor with the critics. He is the composer of ***Tiger Rag***, which was one of the most famous and most often played jazz standards ever. The ODJB's recording of ***Livery Stable Blues*** put jazz on the map for Americans and Europeans as well. It eventually sold over a million copies, and may be the first record to do so. People now became aware that money could be made with this music called jazz, and bandleaders, record companies, and entrepreneurs were eager to cash in on it. The year 1917 was when Scott Joplin and Ragtime died and in the ears of most, when jazz was born.

LIVERY STABLE BLUES 1917
Original Dixieland Jass Band

Livery Stable Blues was recorded by the Victor label and was the B side to *Dixie Jass Band One-Step*. Notice the original name of the band used the word *jass* instead of jazz. They later changed it to jazz. *Livery Stable Blues* became a sensation for several reasons. It was novelty music, which means it was meant to be funny. Sound-wise, it came across well for the primitive recoding technology at the time. The distinct peculiar sounds of the horns worked better on records than other types of music; orchestral Classical music, for instance, did not fare well with the reduced fidelity. The musical medium of jazz worked well on the sound medium of records at the time.

 Livery Stable Blues is a 12-Bar Blues form. Jazz musicians from the earliest days in New Orleans turned Blues into an instrumental form as well as a vocal one. Although the basic harmonic outline remained intact, the aab text form was not always adhered to. In this recording, there is a four-measure introduction followed by three different Blues choruses, each one played twice. The three choruses are then played again with the same repeats. The C chorus features a **break** where each wind instrument imitates a different barnyard animal; the clarinet does a rooster, the cornet does a horse, and the trombone does a cow. This was the novelty aspect of the record that amazed and amused the listeners.

Figure 3.4: Original Dixieland Jass Band.

What to listen for:

1. The 3-way polyphony with the cornet, clarinet, and trombone
2. The playing on the beat of the piano and drums
3. The repetition of the three different 12-measure Blues choruses
4. The breaks in the C choruses where they imitate animals
5. Does this music swing to you?

LIVERY STABLE BLUES 1917
Original Dixieland Jass Band

Nick LaRocca—Cornet
Alcide Nunez—Clarinet
Eddie Edwards—Trombone
Henry Ragas—Piano
Tony Spargo—Drums

INTRO
 4

Chorus	1	2	3	4	5	6
Section	A	A	B	B	C	C
	3-way polyphony————————————				break	break
	Full ensemble————————————				—3—	—3—
Measures	12	12	12	12	12	12

Chorus	7	8	9	10	
Section	A	B	C	C	TAG
	3-way polyphony| break		break		
			3	3	
	12	12	12	12	1

Each chorus is 12-measure Blues form
A Tag is extension of the end of a chorus

LIVERY STABLE BLUES
VIVA LAROCCA

Watch this video of the Dutch band Viva, LaRocca recreate note for note the original record of *Livery Stable Blues* by the ODJB

KING OLIVER

Figure 3.5: Joe Oliver.
Copyright in the Public Domain.

Joe Oliver (1881–1938) was known as "King" Oliver for is prowess on the cornet. He was born in New Orleans and became on of the major exponents of Early Jazz. He emulated Blues singers when he played and pioneered the use of mutes on brass instruments. Mutes change the sound of the horns when inserted into the bell (the front opening). Oliver was adept at moving certain mutes back and forth as he played, which gave the horn a vocal-like quality. He and others almost literally talked through their horn when manipulating mutes. After playing in various bands in New Orleans, he moved to Chicago in 1917 when Storyville was closed down. There he formed his Creole Jazz Band and made several famous recordings. By the 1920s Chicago became the major center for New Orleans jazz as many musicians, like Oliver, migrated North for better work and social conditions. Jazz was popular on riverboats going up and down the Mississippi and many jazz musicians found their way to Chicago after a trip up the river. While still in New Orleans, Oliver tutored a young Louis Armstrong and eventually asked the young cornetist to join his band in Chicago as a rarely used second cornet player.

KING OLIVER'S CREOLE JAZZ BAND

While in Chicago, King Oliver formed one of the finest New Orleans–style bands. They recorded several historic and influential sides during the early twenties, including *Mabel's Dream* and *Dippermouth Blues*. Oliver also wrote *West End Blues*, most famously recorded by Louis Armstrong in 1928. This band featured some of the all-time great New Orleans–style players: Johnny Dodds on clarinet, Honore Dutrey on trombone, Lil Hardin on piano, Bill Johnson on banjo, Baby Dodds on drums, and Louis Armstrong on second cornet.

LIL HARDEN

Pianist Lil Harden (1898–1971) is one of the few women to contribute to Early Jazz as an instrumentalist. There were important singers, mostly associated with City Blues during this time, but playing an instrument in a jazz band was considered by most as not a proper thing for a lady to be doing due to the somewhat questionable lifestyles that many jazz musicians led. Hardin was a pianist, composer, and singer from Memphis, Tennessee, who studied music at Fisk University. She became a key member of Oliver's band in 1921. She married Louis Armstrong in 1924 and played with his famous Hot Five and Hot Seven bands that made some the great jazz records of all time (see Chapter 4). After divorcing Armstrong, she went on to lead her own bands as well as singing and playing solo piano.

DIPPERMOUTH BLUES 1923

Dippermouth Blues is one of the great Early Jazz recordings. It is in a 12-bar Blues form and a good example of a New Orleans–style instrumental Blues. It is credited to Joe Oliver but there seems to be some evidence that Louis Armstrong may have written it. "Dippermouth" was one of Louis Armstrong's many nicknames and no matter who wrote it, the tune was named after him. The band performs it basically in the older New Orleans style that has everyone always playing. There are, however, two "solos" played where one player comes to the foreground over the rest of the ensemble. Johnny Dodds plays a two-chorus solo against a stop-time background. **Stop-time** occurs when the rhythm section leaves out one or more beats in a measure. In other words, the normal procedure of playing every beat of every measure is interrupted. Stop-time can occur in various ways as far as which beats can be left out. In this situation the fourth beat of every measure is silent and the other horns join in with the rhythm section playing on the first three beats. A full ensemble chorus follows the clarinet solo before King Oliver plays his very famous three-chorus solo. This is one of first notable recorded jazz solos in history. It served as a model for cornet and trumpet players for many years. It is very simple yet it very effectively builds, getting higher and higher in pitch for each chorus. He manipulates a plunger mute, which gives a wa-wa effect that makes the horn sound very vocal-like. Mutes of all kinds were an important part of the sound of Early Jazz. In later years the tune became known a *Sugerfoot Stomp* and many arrangements had been made for larger bands that almost always include Oliver's recorded solo as part of the arrangement. The young Louis Armstrong plays second cornet and is mostly in the background except during the fifth chorus where he briefly plays lead cornet.

What to listen for:

1. The dense polyphonic texture throughout
2. The steady beats of the rhythm section
3. The stop-time during the clarinet solo
4. King Oliver's plunger mute solo that increases tension as it gets higher in each chorus
5. The vocal break sung by Bill Johnson at the end of the cornet solo

DIPPERMOUTH BLUES 1923
King Oliver's Creole Jazz Band

King Oliver—Cornet
Louis Armstrong—2nd Cornet (unusual)
Johnny Dodds—Clarinet
Honore Dutrey—Trombone
Lil Hardin—Piano
Bill Robinson—Banjo and vocal break
Baby Dodds—Drums

Intro	Ch 1	Ch 2	Ch 3	Ch 4	Ch 5
Full ens	....	....	cl solo	....	Full ens
	coll imp	....	stop time	....	coll imp
4	12	12	12	12	12

Ch 6	Ch 7	Ch 8	Ch 9	Coda
cor solo	....	....	Full ens	....
plunger mute wa-wa	higher	higher vocal break 2	coll imp	....
12	12	12	12	2

JELLY ROLL MORTON AND HIS RED HOT PEPPERS

Besides being the first great jazz pianist, Jelly Roll Morton was the first great jazz composer and arranger and made some of the finest New Orleans–style records ever in 1926 with a band he called His Red Hot Peppers. Morton was less inclined to trust what other musicians might improvise and liked to control his music more than most jazz musicians at the time. He put together a first-rate ensemble that played his own original material exactly as he wanted it. This is not to say the group did not improvise at all, but that not all of it was improvised. There are two hallmarks to Morton's band style: **Variety** of tone colors and textures and the frequent use of **breaks**. All early

Jazz musicians used breaks but Morton used them more than anyone else; in fact he thought that breaks were a crucial component of jazz. He also liked to arrange the music so that no one sound or texture went on for too long. By 1926 the older New Orleans procedure of all instruments always playing gave way to true solos where only one instrument would play with rhythm section accompaniment. Morton not only used solos but also varied who played in the rhythm section as the music went along. He seemed to want to use as many different instrumental combinations as possible.

GRANDPA'S SPELLS

Glancing at the Listening Guide below, one can see Morton's fondness for breaks and variety of tone colors and textures. ***Grandpa's Spells*** amply demonstrates both of these penchants. Also notice the form is in what by 1926 was considered an old-fashioned sectional Ragtime-like form; there are multiple 16-measure strains. Morton was one of the last of the New Orleans musicians still writing in those forms and by the thirties they pretty much died out completely. But as old-fashioned as Jelly Roll was in that regard, *Grandpa's Spells* shows that he was forward looking at the same time. First, he uses guitar instead of banjo and although the guitar was not totally new, it will replace the banjo entirely in the 1930s. Second, he uses string bass instead of tuba or no bass instrument; again, the bass is not totally new but it becomes a standard rhythm section instrument in the thirties, replacing the tuba entirely. Morton also has the bass play all four beats in the measure during the A2 section and the last C section, the ***shout chorus***. This was not the norm at the time but became the norm in the 1930s.

What to listen for:

1. The breaks every 4 measures during the A and A^1 sections
2. The piano and clarinet breaks during the B section
3. The different instrumental combinations throughout
4. The bass playing on all 4 beats and bass solos during the A^2 section
5. The excitement of the last C section Shout Chorus propelled by the bass playing in 4 again.

GRANDPA'S SPELLS 1926
Jelly Roll Morton and his Red Hot Peppers

George Mitchell—Cornet
Omar Simeon—Clarinet
Kid Ory—Trombone

Jelly Roll Morton—Piano
Johnny St. Cyr—Guitar
John Lindsay—Bass
Andrew Hilaire—Drums

INTRO	A—	—	—	—
Full ens	Gtr	Full	Gtr/pno	Full
arranged	break	coll imp	break	coll imp
4	2+2	4	2+2	4

A¹—	—	—	—
Tpt	Full	Tpt	Full
break	coll imp	break	coll imp
2+2	4	2+2	4

B—	—	—	B¹..........	....	....
Full	Pno break	Full	Cl solo	Cl break	Cl solo
					cont
6	2	8	6	2	8

A² —	—	—	—	—	—
Tbn solo	Bs solo	Full	Tbn	Bs solo	Full
4 on bs	....	....	....	....	....
2	2	4	2	2	4

C	C¹	C²—	—	C³	Coda
Tpt solo	Cl solo	Pno solo	Cl solo	Full	Gtr break
mute		no bass		4 on bs	
16	16	8	8	16	2

Chapter Four

Louis Armstrong

Louis Armstrong (1901–1973) is the single greatest figure in Early Jazz and many would say in all of jazz history. He, practically singlehandedly, turned jazz into an art form during the 1920s. He did this through his improvised solos and by doing so, made the solo a crucial and featured part of any jazz performance. He was more advanced than any other player during the twenties and influenced all who came after him.

Louis Armstrong was born in 1901 in New Orleans. He learned to play the cornet in a reformatory after he was arrested for a childish prank when he was 13 years old.

Figure 4.1 Louis Armstrong.
Copyright in the Public Domain.

He was later tutored by King Oliver and played in Kid Ory's band when he was 18. King Oliver summoned Armstrong to join his band in Chicago in 1923. King Oliver also played cornet and it was unusual to have two cornets in a New Orleans–style jazz band, but Oliver insisted that Armstrong play with him. In 1924 Armstrong played with Fletcher Henderson's band in New York and became known as the greatest jazz musician in the world. In 1927 and 1928 Armstrong made his greatest recordings of his early period. They were recorded under the names of Louis Armstrong and His Hot Five or His Hot Seven, and several other band names. In 1928 he switched from cornet to trumpet and almost every other cornet player did the same. In the 1930s he appeared in several films and was known also as a popular singer and entertainer. His popularity and artistic output waned somewhat during the Swing Era of the thirties and early forties when he led various big bands, but he returned to a New Orleans–combo format later in the forties and continued that way under the name of Louis Armstrong and the All-Stars for the rest of his life. From then on he became more and more popular and served as an official Ambassador of Good Will for the United States while touring around the world. During the 1950s, he made several classic albums with singer Ella Fitzgerald, and in 1964 his recording of *Hello, Dolly!* actually knocked the Beatles off the number-one spot on the pop record charts. He always had a broad appeal as a singer and instrumentalist and it is nearly impossible to imagine what jazz would have become without his enormous talent and artistry.

Some of Armstrong's most important contributions to jazz follow.

CONTRIBUTIONS

1. SOUND—it was brilliant and brassy with an aggressive attack. He was able to player higher notes than anyone before him.

2. SWING—he was the first player to consistently swing. While he was not the first jazz musician to swing, he was the first to consistently do so. He used swing eighth notes but also had a unique approach to melodic rhythms.

3. DRAMA—he was able to create drama in his improvised solos through the process of tension and release.

4. IMPROVISATION ON CHORDS—he was the first player to base his improvisations primarily on the chord changes rather than ornamenting and making variations on the given melody, as was more commonly done in early jazz.

5. SINGING—he set the standard for jazz singing and developed the art of scat singing (improvised singing of nonsense syllables).

6. JAZZ AS ART—he turned jazz into an art form through the aforementioned contributions and showed that the relatively new medium of jazz can be as artful as any other music.

ARMSTRONG'S EARLY JAZZ RECORDINGS
STRUTTIN' WITH SOME BARBECUE 1927
Louis Armstrong and his Hot Five

This is one of Armstrong's best-known recordings from the early period. It features his aggressive, soaring, swinging style that is unique among all early jazz players. Notice how the other wind players, who are among the top players of the time, pale in comparison. Armstrong's wife and pianist, Lil Hardin Armstrong, wrote this tune for him. She also was instrumental in getting him to assume leadership of his own band and recordings. This tune is written in a standard 32-measure Pop song form (ABA^{1}C); these forms as well as Pop songs themselves were becoming increasing common in jazz during the late twenties.

What to listen for:

1. The New Orleans–style polyphony and collective improvisation during the Intro, Chorus 1, and Chorus 4
2. The breaks throughout
3. How the off-beat accents (on beats 2 and 4) during the trombone solo turn into off-beat stop time during the cornet solo
4. The command of his instrument that Armstrong has throughout and his perfect awareness of the beat that allows him to float on top of it with a pure sense of swing
5. The 32-measure pop song form—ABA¹C
6. The steady four beats per measure played by the piano and banjo

STRUTTIN' WITH SOME BARBEQUE

Louis Armstrong—Cornet
Johnny Dodds—Clarinet
Kid Ory—Trombone
Lil Harden—Piano
Johnny St. Cyr—Banjo

Intro—Full ensemble, Cornet lead, collective improvisation
  12

	8	8	8	8
	A	B	A¹	C
Chorus 1	Full ensemble, cornet lead, collective improv——bjo br			
				2

Chorus 2 Clarinet solo————br | trombone solo——— br
                          2   off-beat accents————2

Chorus 3 Cornet solo————br | cornet solo continues—tbn + cl br ext
          Stop time on off-beats | Stop-time on off-beats— 2   2

Chorus 4 Full ens, coll imp   br | full ens——| full ens————Coda
                          bjo | | arranged   2
                          2

EARL HINES

Pianist Earl Hines (1903–1983), sometimes known as Earl "Fatha" Hines, replaced Lil Hardin Armstrong in Louis Armstrong's band in 1928. By this time Hines was considered Louis' equal. He made his way to Chicago from Pittsburgh and met Armstrong in 1927. They hit it off immediately both musically and personally. Hines had an aggressive style that matched Armstrong's. Most pianists at this time still followed the Ragtime model of oom-pah, oom-pah in their left hand, but Hines often broke out of that with off-beat, random-like accents and punctuations that temporarily threw off the regular meter. He developed what became known as **trumpet-style** piano, which is a way of simulating a trumpet on a piano. He did two things to accomplish this. First, he played a lot of his right-hand melodies in octaves; the octaves reinforce each other to produce a louder, clearer, more powerful sound like a trumpet and could cut through the rest of the band more easily. Second, he often played the octaves as tremolos to simulate a trumpet's vibrato. Louis Armstrong and most of the New Orleans wind players played with a lot of vibrato, which is a slight wavering of pitch that goes a little above and below the actual desired pitch to give warmth to the tone. Different wind players, string players, and singers play with varying degrees of vibrato. It is impossible to do this on a piano since once the strings are activated, the pianist cannot manipulate them in any way. A tremolo occurs when two notes are rapidly alternated; the *trill* is used when the notes are only a step apart. While a tremolo is quite different from vibrato, the effect is somewhat similar. Hines played the octaves, with or without tremolos, with the assertiveness and brilliance of not just any trumpet player but of Louis Armstrong, himself.

Figure 4.2: Earl Hines.

Copyright in the Public Domain.

WEST END BLUES 1928
Louis Armstrong and His Savoy Ballroom Five

This is Armstrong's most highly acclaimed recording from his early period. The opening trumpet **cadenza** (solo without any accompaniment or definite meter) and last chorus solo are legendary and universally admired. Trumpet players to this day have learned these segments note for note. This historic recording also marks Armstrong's switch from cornet to trumpet. Most cornet players followed Armstrong's lead and the cornet has been relatively rare in jazz ever since. Armstrong demonstrates his complete mastery of the instrument in the famous opening cadenza and final chorus solo. He also scat sings while engaged in call and response with the clarinet during the third chorus. Scat singing, which the singing of nonsense syllables in an instrument-like manner, was erroneously thought to be Armstrong's invention. Although he did not invent scat singing, he was the first to widely popularize it. Earl Hines plays on this recording and shows brief examples of his trumpet-piano style with octaves and tremolos.

The opening trumpet cadenza clearly demonstrates Armstrong's mastery of his instrument and his unabashed sense of swing. He is a master of producing drama through the careful creation and releasing of tension; he does that here by starting with a relatively high note (G), then he slowly descends then ascends with faster notes that come to a hold on a high C. From there he plays a gradually winding serpentine descending line that comes to rest on a low Ab. The real art here comes from the gradual, subtle way he releases the tension he created from the high C. Similarly, in the last chorus, he begins by holding out a high Bb for almost four full measures. This single held note is dynamic and replete with tension from the sheer length of it and vibrancy of its sound. After a repeated figure he gradually winds the line down then up and down again until he suddenly cuts it off unresolved. After a brief piano fill, he finally resolves the tune and all the tension. Armstrong's solos are transcribed below.

What to listen for:

1. The assertiveness and sureness in Armstrong's playing, and the drama produced through Tension and Release during the opening cadenza
2. The Blues inflections that Armstrong plays during the first chorus
3. The Call and Response between the clarinet and Armstrong's scat singing
4. Hines' light touch at the beginning and end of the fourth chorus and the Trumpet-Piano Style with octaves and tremolos in the middle of the solo
5. The great drama and tension in the last chorus produced by the trumpet's long, high note and the gradual release of tension

---

WEST END BLUES

Louis Armstrong—Trumpet
Jimmy Strong—Clarinet
Fred Robinson—Trombone
Earl Hines—Piano
Mancy Cara—Banjo
Zutty Singleton—Drums

		12	12	12	12	12
INTRO:	Tpt solo	CH1	CH2	CH3	CH4	CH5
	Rubato	Tpt	Tbn solo	Cl +vocal	Piano	Tpt
	Cadenza	Head		C + R	tpt style	Long high note then gradual descent

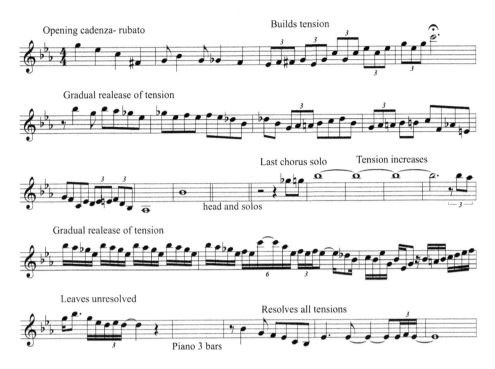

Figure 4.3 Armstrong's opening cadenza and last chorus solo.

BASIN STREET BLUES 1959

Louis Armstrong—Trumpet
Peanuts Hucko—Clarinet
Trummy Young—Trombone
Billy Kyle—Piano
Mort Herman—Bass
Danny Barcelona—Drums

This video shows Louis Armstrong much later in his career and still playing at a high level. This is more modern version of New Orleans style; there is a string bass and the bass plays on all four beats at times, but the group still engages in 3-way polyphonic collective improvisation. Armstrong sings and plays on this old New Orleans favorite. Despite its title, it is not a 12-bar Blues. It is in a verse-chorus form with two verses preceding the 16-measure chorus. All solos are on the chorus section only.

Chapter Five

Bix Beiderbecke—Chicago Style

As Chicago became the major center for New Orleans–style jazz during the 1920s, a group of White musicians inspired by the original Dixieland Jazz Band and also by a newer White band, the New Orleans Rhythm Kings (NORK), developed a different approach to the music that was known as Chicago Style. The Austin High Gang, consisting of some musicians who went to Austin High School in Chicago but also some from other places in the Midwest, were one of the first playing is this newer style. Historians debate what Chicago style actually is, but there seems to be several traits that differentiate it from New Orleans style. Both styles are considered part of Early Jazz in general and Chicago style is an outgrowth of New Orleans style. A few differing characteristics of Chicago style follow.

1. Solos were more prominent in Chicago style. We saw Jelly Roll Morton and Louis Armstrong going this way in their recordings. The Chicago bands still engaged in polyphonic collective improvisation but not as much as the New Orleans bands.
2. Saxophone was commonly used, whereas it was rare in the New Orleans bands.
3. Guitar replaced the banjo almost entirely.
4. The Chicago band played with a less aggressive, more relaxed, laid-back feeling.
5. There were more arranged, pre-planned ensemble parts with the Chicago bands.

Jazz thrived during the Roaring Twenties as bootleg alcohol was being freely served in speakeasies that were run mostly by gangsters. Jazz was becoming very popular and seemed to go along well with the risqué, partying lifestyle of the Flappers and the Gatsbys of the Prohibition era and what F. Scott Fitzgerald labeled the *Jazz Age*.

BIX BEIDERBECKE

Cornetist Leon Bix Beiderbecke (1903–1931) became a real symbol of the *Jazz Age*. He has been romanticized and idolized and his unfortunately short life turned him into a legend. He was born to German immigrants in Davenport, Iowa, and was essentially self-taught on the cornet and piano. He purportedly had some learning disabilities that made reading music difficult and frustrating for him. His parents hoped that sending him to boarding school just outside of Chicago would straighten out some of his learning and behavioral problems, but Bix was spending more time listening to all the jazz Chicago had to offer and was eventually expelled from school. His first prominent playing experience was with the Wolverines; from there he played with the Jean Goldkette orchestras, Frankie Trumbauer, and most famously with the Paul Whiteman orchestra. Whiteman led the top commercial band of the day. They played a variety of music, mostly for dancing, which included the newly popular jazz. While not a jazz band, per se, Whiteman hired a few real jazz musicians to play improvised solos. Bix received maximum exposure with Whiteman who billed himself as the "King of Jazz," a title that had little justification since he was not jazz musician. Whiteman, however, did champion the cause of jazz and introduced it to large segment of the population. He famously premiered George Gershwin's Jazz-inspired composition *Rhapsody in Blue*. Critics have often insinuated that Bix was unhappy and felt stifled playing with such a commercial orchestra but the evidence suggests otherwise; Bix was a featured soloist with the most famous band in the country and making as much as a sideman could make at the time. Bix did, however, have a severe alcohol problem, which led to his death at the age of 28.

Figure 5.1: Leon Bix Beiderbecke.
Copyright in the Public Domain.

Although he was not around for long, he left a lasting influence on jazz. He is considered to be the first great White jazz musician, but more important was his contribution to advancing the harmonic language of jazz. He is also considered to be the first great **cool** jazz music who helped to inspire the Cool school of jazz in the 1950s.

COOL PLAYING

Bix's cool approach was in many ways the opposite of Louis Armstrong's hot style. Whereas Louis used much vibrato and played aggressively and dramatically with many high notes, Bix used little vibrato, played more lyrically, relaxed, and laid-back as well as closer to the middle and low registers of his horn. All of these characteristics are associated with **cool** playing in general, while Armstrong's, like most at the time, are considered **hot**. Bix was one of the few cool players in the mostly hot world of early jazz. Bix and Louis admired each other and Armstrong said that Bix was his favorite cornet player.

ADVANCED HARMONIC PLAYING

Bix was fascinated by some of the newer Classical music of the early 20th century, especially the music of French Impressionist composers Claude Debussy and Maurice Ravel. These composers developed a new harmonic language that explored the use of complex chords and nontraditional chord progressions. Most jazz during the twenties used simple triads along with slightly more complex sixth and seventh chords. The French composers began to use extended chords tones to create ninth, eleventh, and thirteenth chords along with altered notes and exotic scales that were not commonly used in Western Classical music. They also did away with functional harmony, which meant traditional chord progressions and expectations were no longer strictly adhered to. Parallel harmonies like the ones that follow were "forbidden" by the rules of traditional harmony.

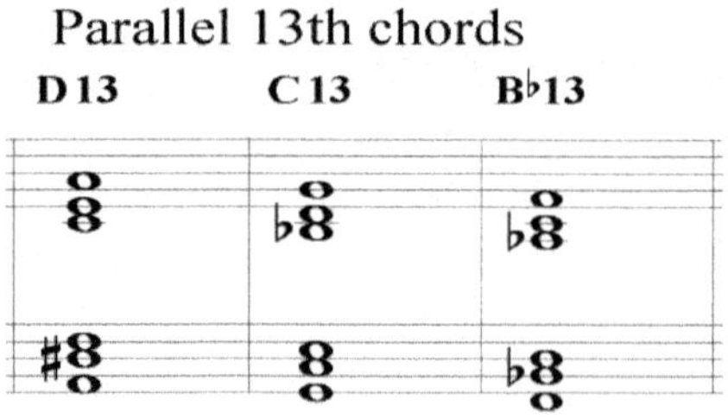

Parallel 13th chords

Figure 5.2

Bix was hearing these sounds in his head and wanted to somehow incorporate them into the jazz he was playing but he was not schooled enough to know exactly how to do it or write it down for others. He did write and record an interesting piano piece called *In a Mist* that combined elements of this harmonic language with ragtime. Since a cornet can play only one note at a time, Bix had to imply these harmonies by emphasizing these extended and altered chord tones in the melodic lines he played. Below is a C major chord followed by possible extensions (upper partials) and alterations.

Figure 5.3

BIX AND TRAM

Saxophonist **Frankie "Tram" Trumbauer** (1901–1956) had an association with Bix Beiderbecke that lasted several years. They played together in Goldkette's and Whiteman's bands and recorded some classic sides under Trumbauer's name. Trumbauer played a C-melody saxophone, which is a rare instrument pitched between an alto and tenor saxophone. Like Bix, he was also a relatively rare **cool** player who had a huge influence on later players. The saxophone was not commonly used as a solo instrument before the twenties and Tram is one of the first notable saxophone soloists in the history of jazz. He set the tone, literally, for future cool players. The great tenor saxophonist of the Swing Era, Lester Young, modeled his sound and style after Trumbauer. He played with same lyrical, relaxed style of Bix Beiderbecke and together they became known as Bix and Tram.

SINGING THE BLUES 1927

Frankie Trumbauer and His Orchestra

Singing the Blues is perhaps Bix Beiderbecke's and Frankie Trumbauer's best known recording. The solos by Bix and Tram were widely imitated by both White and Black musicians. Tram plays the head by himself in a relaxed decorative manner before Bix enters with his famous solo. Bix weaves a delicate but disjunct melody that works off a single idea or motive at the beginning of his solo. He exploits the upper extensions of chords throughout the solo. During the break at the end of the B section Bix plays uncharacteristic rip that slides up to a high note; this is more typical of Louis Armstrong. Like Louis Armstrong's *West End Blues* solo, many cornet and trumpet player learned this solo note for note from the record.

EDDIE LANG

The guitarist on this recording is Eddie Lang (1902–1933). He is considered by some to be the father of jazz guitar. While most guitarists strummed chords on every beat like the earlier banjo players, Lang chose a different approach that was more ornate, decorative, and melodic than most at the time. He often plays countermelodies along with the soloist in a subtle, unobtrusive way.

What to listen for:

1. The more relaxed, laid-back feeling compared to New Orleans style
2. The cool sound and characteristics Bix's and Tram's playing
3. The working off a motive in the beginning of Bix's solo
4. The breaks during the solos
5. The ornate guitar playing of Eddie Lang throughout
6. The polyphonic collective improvisation during the last chorus

SINGING THE BLUES
Bix Beiderbecke with Frankie Trumbauer

Bix Beiderbecke—Cornet
Frankie Trumbauer—C-Melody Sax
Bill Rank—Trombone
Jimmy Dorsey—Clarinet
Paul Mertz—Piano
Eddie Lang—Guitar
Chauncey Morehouse—Drums

Intro
4	8	8	8	8
	A	B	A^1	C

	0:07
Chorus 1	Sax solo-plays head with improv variations————————
	br | br

	1:03
Chorus 2	Cornet solo—improvisation————————————————
	Motive—— br |

	2:00
Chorus 3	Full ensemble | cl solo——— | full ensemble————————
	coll. improv coll. improv
	gt br

Chapter Six

Stride Piano—Harlem Piano School, Eastern Ragtime

As noted earlier, all early jazz piano playing evolved directly from Ragtime. A version of jazz piano evolved in the Northeast became known as **Stride** piano, or sometimes referred to as the **Harlem Piano School** or **Eastern Ragtime**. Most jazz piano players through the twenties thought of the music they played as ragtime when it was really jazz. This shows the close connection between the two. Stride piano's major center was the Harlem section of New York, but other Northeastern cities such as Philadelphia, Boston, and Atlantic City had an active Stride presence as well. The name *Stride* comes from the left-hand action that came from Ragtime of moving (striding) back and forth from bass note to chord (oom-pah, oom-pah). One should not confuse this technique of striding from the distinctive style of jazz piano from the 1920s known as **Stride Piano**.

Stride piano is characterized by it dazzling displays of virtuosity. The impetus for this came from cutting contests that were held at rent parties.

Persons who needed money to pay their rent held rent parties and guests were invited to attend for an admission price that included food, beverages, and entertainment. Cutting contest were competitions for piano players to try to outplay each other. The incentive was cash, and as pianists sought to win these prizes, the music got faster and faster.

Even though some called the music they were playing Ragtime, the music these pianists played was jazz mainly because they improvised and made the music swing. Like Jelly Roll Morton, they fused Blues and Ragtime to create jazz. Below is a list of the key differed between Stride and Ragtime.

1. Stride tempos were much faster. While Ragtime tempos were derived from March tempos, the Ring Shout inspired Stride tempos. The **Ring Shout** was a sort of ritualistic dance derived from an African tradition that slaves did as a form of worship. People would gather in a circle and clap their hands and stomp their feet at very brisk tempos.

2. Stride harmony, chords, and chord progressions were generally more complex with more use of seventh chords and even some ninth chords. Ragtime was mostly triadic.
3. Stride swung, while Ragtime rhythms were stiff (see Chapter 3 on Jelly Roll Morton's piano playing).
4. Stride used Blues devices with blue notes and inflections.
5. Stride used Call and Response patterns either by calling with one hand and responding with the other or by calling and responding in different registers with one hand.
6. Stride players improvised, while Classic Ragtime was totally written.
7. Stride players broke out of the oom-pah more often by playing walking bass lines that consisted of four or more bass notes in a row.

JAMES P. JOHNSON
Father of Stride Piano

Figure 6.1: James P. Johnson.

James P. Johnson (1894–1955) is considered the Father of Stride Piano. Born in New Brunswick, New Jersey, he was a real virtuoso pianist who was classically trained. He was a very eclectic musician who also composed classical pieces, film scores, and Pop songs. His song *Charleston* was the biggest hit of the twenties and is associated with the Charleston dance craze of the time. He made his main living by making piano rolls for player pianos, many of which are still in existence.

CAROLINA SHOUT 1921
James P. Johnson

Carolina Shout is one of several tunes that Johnson wrote using a Ragtime formal model. Like Ragtime, it comprises multiple 16-measure strains. Johnson plays Blues effects by sliding off black keys to neighboring white keys, as well as crushing notes a half step apart at the same time. There are several Call and Response passages. On the repeat of the A section, he plays a characteristic cross-rhythm in his left hand by grouping in threes instead of twos. This is an interesting effect, as the left hand seems to be three-four meter, while the right hand is still in four. The beats are the same for both, so this is not the same as African polyrhythmic or polymetric drumming. An example of this processis

```
     >            >            >
RH   1   2   3   4  |1   2   3   4  |1   2   3   4   |


     >        >        >        >
LH   1   2   3  |1   2   3  |1   2   3  |1   2   3   |
```

Johnson does this by breaking up the 1-2-3-4 oom-pah, oom-pah pattern with a 1-2-3, 1-2-3 oom-oom-pah, oom-oom-pah pattern. Notice the second and third measures below.

Figure 6.2

What to listen for:

1. The clean, precise technique
2. The Blues inflections throughout (crushed notes etc.)
3. The cross-rhythms in the left hand during the A1 section
4. The call and response patterns during the C, and D1 sections
5. The swing feeling throughout

CAROLINA SHOUT 1921
Written and played by
James P. Johnson

	0:15	0:24	0:44	1:03	1:22
Intro	A	A¹	B	C	C
		LH cross-rhy-			Call + Response————
4	16	16	16	16	16

	1:40	1:59	2:17	2:35
	D	E	D	Coda
		Call +Res–		Call + Res–		
	16	16	16	4

FATS WALLER

Figure 6.3: Thomas "Fats" Waller.

Thomas "Fats" Waller (1904–1943), born in New York City, was a multitalented Stride pianist who also composed, played the organ, sang, acted, and made people laugh. Like Louis Armstrong he crossed over into Pop world of entertainment and like Louis Armstrong was no less a great artist for doing so. He wrote many hit songs and several have become standards, including **Ain't Misbehavin'** and **Honeysuckle Rose**. He wrote many comedic songs that include: **All That Meat and No Potatoes** and **Your Feet's Too Big**. He appeared in many films as a singer, piano player, and comedian. He was known as a real *bon vivant*, a party animal who, unfortunately, ate and drank himself to death at the age of 39. He recorded hundreds of solo piano sides during which he was mostly either drunk or hung over, not a hint of which showed from his clean and precise performances.

Waller, like his mentor James P. Johnson, was classically trained and possessed an astounding virtuosic technique. His touch was lighter than Johnson's and he stands midway between the heavier-handed early jazz pianists and the later lighter-touch Swing Era pianists who emerged during the thirties.

HANDFUL OF KEYS 1929

Fats Waller

This aptly named tune is a real tour de force that shows off Waller's musical and technical skills. The form is unusual and serves as a compromise between the old-fashioned Ragtime sectional forms and the newer pop song forms. There is a tune within a tune here with a new tune sandwiched in between another tune.

What to listen for:

1. The clean, precise technique
2. The Blues inflections (crushed notes etc.)
3. The speed and virtuosity
4. The playful variations on the main tune
5. A lighter touch than James P. Johnson's touch

HANDFUL OF KEYS
Written and played by Fats Waller

Intro
| 8 | 8 | 8 | 8 | 8 |

Tune 1
| A | A | B | A |

Chorus 1 0:08
main tune————————————————————————

0:39
Chorus 2
variation on main tune————————————————

1:08
Interlude
4

Tune 2
| A | B | A1 | C |

1:12
new tune—more driving——————————————

Tune 1
| A | A | B | A |

1:42
Chorus 3
new variation on main tunes——————————Break———

2:12
Chorus 4
another variation on main tune————br———br————tag
                                                    2

AIN'T MISBEHAVIN' 1942

In this short film Fats Waller sings, plays the piano, and clowns around with a bevy of young women. This is one of many **Soundies** that he made in the early forties. Soundies were short films of the music stars of the day that were shown in movie theatres before the feature films. This is one of Waller's best-known songs.

Part 2

As the stock market crashed and the Great Depression got under way during the 1930s, jazz was undergoing great changes. The availability of records and radio during the late twenties enabled musicians to quickly absorb the new trends; more musically educated jazz musicians brought a more sophisticated style to jazz, one that relied on written music in addition to improvisation. Commercial dance bands added jazz numbers to their repertoires during the twenties and there were several Black bands that merged New Orleans–style jazz with written arrangements. Historians refer to these bands as Pre-Swing bands since it was these bands that led most directly to the Swing bands of the thirties. Fletcher Henderson and Duke Ellington led important Pre-Swing bands that did just that.

Technology made the playing lighter overall and the use of guitar and string bass more practical. The microphone could amplify the sounds of these softer instruments and their use greatly changed the character of the music. The bass went from playing primarily on beats 1 and 3 to playing on all 4 beats of the measure, and this propelled the music forward in new way that gave the music more drive and evenness. Arrangers figured out how to have multiple instruments play harmonized parts in a way that swung. The simultaneous polyphony of the New Orleans bands gave way to Call and Response exchanges between instrumental sections of the band.

With larger bands of over ten players, written parts were necessary to go along with improvised solos. At first the Pre-Swing bands sounded rather stiff but as we get into the thirties, the players loosened up along with the new momentum provided by the rhythm section. Drummers switched from snare drum to hi-hat cymbals to lighten the sound and texture, and drove the beat forward by playing it on the bass drum. Pianists, still rooted in Ragtime, played with a lighter touch afforded them by the microphone and let the bass carry more of the momentum.

Swing Era

By 1934 the new Swing style was in place and Benny Goodman introduced it to much of the American public on a radio program called *Let's Dance*. Goodman, through the aid of Fletcher Henderson's arrangements, started the national Swing craze that became enormously popular during the Great Depression and World War II. During these hard times, Swing seemed to lighten the woes of most Americans and soon spread around the world. The term *jazz* was often not used anymore and *Swing* became the name of the new style of jazz. Swing was primarily dance music and even during the hard economic times of the thirties, most homes had a radio and people could, at least, roll up the rugs on a Saturday night to dance to the radio. New dances like the Lindy Hop and the Big Apple replaced the twenties' dances like the Charleston and the Black Bottom. The up and down movements of the twenties' dances gave way to the more flowing, forward movements of thirties' dances in order to match the more flowing, forward driving music. Swing was the dominant Pop music of the time and the bandleaders were the major Pop stars.

Some of the great contributors to jazz emerged during the Swing Era, as we shall see in the following pages. Some of the great singers of all time grew up in the Swing Era and continued to perform Swing music for many years after the Swing era ended. After World War II Swing faded in popularity and newer jazz and Pop styles achieved prominence, but Swing was still the thing to those raised on it and remains the popular style of jazz with the general public.

Chapter Seven

Swing Era—Eastern Swing, Fletcher Henderson and Benny Goodman

S wing, the new jazz style, took the country by storm during the 1930s and became the dominant style of pop music as well as jazz from 1934 to 1945. The Swing Era, or Big Band Era, saw the country through much of the Great Depression and all of World War II, and this music served as a relief from the hardships endured during this time frame. **Benny Goodman**, who became known as the *King of Swing*, was the first person to popularize Swing during 1934. Although he did not invent Swing, most Americans first heard this new music on the radio, played by Goodman's band. Radio was a major medium for entertainment during the Great Depression and almost all households had one. Swing has its roots in the dance bands of the 1920s as well as in early jazz itself. As jazz was becoming popular during the twenties, commercial dance bands began incorporating jazz into their repertoire. Often one or two jazz musicians were hired to playing jazz-like improvised solos along with otherwise non-jazz musicians. The bands played written jazz-influenced arrangements with occasional improvised solos to accompany some of the popular dances of the time, including the Charleston and the Black Bottom. Paul Whiteman, a White bandleader, led the most popular band of the period, and was billed as the *King of Jazz*, although he was not a jazz musician himself. He did, however, hire several outstanding jazz players, most notably Bix Beiderbecke and Frankie Trumbauer. Many of the Black dance bands were more authentically jazz bands with more true jazz musicians. It is these bands that led more directly to the Swing bands of the thirties. Historians often refer to the music of these bands as **Pre-Swing** and the evolution from early Jazz to Swing can be traced directly from recordings of these bands. **Fletcher Henderson** led one of the best and most important of these bands and is the one most important to the development of the Eastern Swing Style emerging out of New York.

FLETCHER HENDERSON 1897–1952

Fletcher Henderson born in Cuthbert, Georgia, to middle-class parents and was musically educated by his mother. He received a degree in chemistry and when he could not find work as a chemist in New York, he began working as a musician. He became associated with other Black musicians who also were musically trained and as the leader and pianist of a larger jazz ensemble, was instrumental in evolving the early jazz style into the Swing style of the thirties. Although more of a commercial dance band when formed in 1923, they gravitated more toward jazz when Louis Armstrong played with band in 1924. The musical sophistication of Henderson's band and a few others during this time led to the polished large ensemble playing that was to become a standard in the Big Band Era. Henderson, however, was not so adept at the business side of running a band and often had to disband his ensemble. His music became more known when Benny Goodman purchased several of his arrangements in 1934 and later hired him to arrange new material for his band.

PRE-SWING MUSIC

Fletcher Henderson's contribution to Swing cannot be overstated. He led a premier Pre-Swing band that evolved into the prototype swing band. He hired outstanding musicians and arrangers, and eventually became a great arranger himself. **Don Redman** (1900–1964) arranged for Henderson's early band from 1923 to 1927. He successfully combined elements of New Orleans Jazz within the context of written arrangements. He began to play the brass and reed sections (saxes and clarinets) off each other in a call and response manner that would become a hallmark of the Swing style. He often arranged improvised-like melodies in 3-part harmony with trios of instruments. Clarinet trios were especially popular. After Redman left, Henderson, himself, began to arrange for his band and along with Benny Carter, an alto saxophonist/arranger, forged the new Eastern Swing style that dominated the era. Pre-Swing sounds rather stiff compared to Swing and retained the two-beat feel of New Orleans jazz and twenties dance music. Tuba and banjo were still used in the earlier days before giving way to string bass and guitar. The gradual loosening up of the rhythmic feel and modernization of the arrangements can be heard by comparing Henderson's Pre-Swing band's recordings that follow.

COPENHAGEN **1924**
THE STAMPEDE **1927**
SOMEBODY LOVES ME **1930**

CHARACTERISTICS OF THE SWING STYLE

Swing differed in several ways from earlier jazz styles. It was smoother, yet more driving at the same time. An essential rhythmic characteristic of the Swing style was the evenness of beats. The Swing ideal was for the rhythm section to keep the pulse by playing the beats perfectly evenly with no single beat getting an accent or stress. This differs from the New Orleans–style division of the pulse into units of twos. This evenness of beat was made possible by a few key changes. First a four-piece rhythm section became standardized. It retained the piano and drums from the older style but permanently replaced the banjo and tuba with a guitar and string bass. The more gradual fade of each note on the bass rather than the abrupt cutoffs on the tuba created a dovetailing effect of one note leading to the next. Also, bass players now played notes on every beat instead of primarily beats one and three. Likewise, strumming chords on the guitar made for a more gradual fade and dovetailing of one chord into the next, as opposed to the banjo's more brittle attack and decay. Also, the guitar players strummed each chord with a down stroke, making each strum the same. This differed from the banjo players who alternated down and up strokes, giving every other chord a slightly different sound. Drummers evened out the pulse, by switching from march-like rhythms on the snare drum to a consistent ride rhythm played on the hi-hat. Swing was usually played by Big Bands. Big Bands usually consisted of two main sections composed of between 13 and 16 players.

RHYTHM SECTION	HORN SECTION
Guitar	Trumpets (3 or 4)
Piano	Trombones (2 or 3)
Bass	Reeds (3–5 saxes or clarinets)
Drums	

THE RHYTHM SECTION

As before the rhythm section had two main functions: give the pulse or beat, and supply the harmony (chords). Each instrument performed a certain role.

DRUMS

Most of the time the drummer plays the bass drum on every beat while he opens and closes the hi-hat with his other foot; it is open on beats 1 and 3 and closed on beats 2 and 4 (O and C). With his stick he plays a ride rhythm on the hi-hat while it opens and closes. The drummer at other times plays various other drums and cymbals for fills and accents.

GUITAR

The guitarist strums chords on every beat.

PIANO

Still rooted in Ragtime, the pianist mostly alternates bass notes and chords, often using tenths instead of single notes and octaves for bass notes and plays more walking bass lines than the Stride pianists, using tenths instead of single notes or octaves.

BASS

The bassist typically plays **walking bass** with a note on every beat.

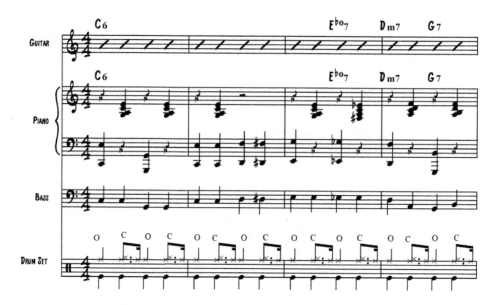

Figure 7.1

ARRANGEMENTS

With the greater number of musicians in the Big Bands, arrangers became crucial to organizing the music. Reliance on each player improvising his part by performing a designated role was no longer feasible as it was in earlier jazz. Arrangers helped to define the sound of each individual band and most bands had several arrangers. The arrangements often pitted the three individual units of the horn section against each other or by dividing them into brass (trumpets and trombones) against reeds (saxophones and clarinets). The reed players mostly played various sized saxophones, typically two altos, two tenors, and one baritone in a five-person reed section, with one or more of the players doubling on clarinet. Melodies were often tossed from section to section and Call and Response between sections was a commonly used technique. Arrangers sought to maintain interest through variety and contrast. Riffs became a major arranging device and perhaps a bit overused. Riffs are repetitive catchy rhythmic figures. The key word is *repetitive*. The word is often misused; if it doesn't repeat, it is not a riff. They were used in a lot of ways and were often played against each other. A common technique was called pyramiding, which happened when different riffs would pile up on each other, often creating exciting climactic endings. Although much of the music was now written, there was still plenty of room for improvisation and improvised solos were featured parts of any arrangement. The most common arranging devices are listed as follows:

1. **FULL ENSEMBLE**
   All sections play together
       a. Unison or octaves
       b. Harmonized melody

2. **MELODY AND ACCOMPANIMENT**
   One or two sections play melody
   One or both of the other sections play simple accompaniment with usually sustained chords in the background

3. **CALL AND RESPONSE**
   One section calls, another responds
   Often quick back and forth

4. **RIFFS**
   Catchy repeated rhythmic figures
   One, two, or three riffs can be played at the same time
   Pyramiding—occurs when riffs are piled on top of one another

5. **IMPROVISED SOLOS**
   Usually one instrument accompanied by rhythm section alone or with 2, 3, or 4 above

WRAPPIN' IT UP 1934
Fletcher Henderson and His Orchestra
EASTERN SWING STYLE

The dominant style of Big Band swing is known as Eastern Swing. Through the influence of several of his band's arrangers, most notably Don Redman and Benny Carter, Henderson perfected this style through his own arrangements for his band in the early 1930s. His arrangement for *Wrappin' It Up* serves as a prototype for all Eastern Swing arrangements. All of the aforementioned arranging devices are used.

Figure 7.2: Fletcher Hendersen and His Orchestra.
Copyright in the Public Domain.

What to listen for:

1. The Call and Response used during the Intro, and the first and fourth choruses
2. The sustained chordal background behind the alto sax solo during the second chorus
3. The quasi-riff played behind the trumpet solo during the third chorus—the riff changes slightly as it repeats
4. The full ensemble passages during the first and fourth choruses
5. The evenness and drive of the rhythm section

WRAPPIN' IT UP
Fletcher Henderson and His Orchestra

Fletcher Henderson—Arranger
Hilton Jefferson—Alto Sax Solo
Red Allen—Trumpet Solo

	————————————12——————————————|
Intro	Call and Response: Brass-Call, Saxes Respond

	8	8	8	8
	A	B	A^1	C
Ch 1	sax melody- brass quick res————|Full Ensemble Melody————| ext			1

Ch 2	Alto sax solo-chord accompaniment————————————————|

Ch 3	Tpt solo————| Full ensemble	Tpt solo——————————| ext
	-sax riff acc call + response sax riff acc 1

Ch 4	Tpt -call	cl solo	sax melody	full ensemble|
	Cl trio res

BENNY GOODMAN

Benny Goodman (1909–1986) was born in Chicago to poor Russian Jewish parents. He began playing clarinet when he was 10 years old and was playing professionally at 14. By the late 1920s he was a successful studio musician in New York. Goodman formed his own band in 1934 and with the help of John Hammond (see insert) was hired as the "hot band" on a NBC national radio show called *Let's Dance* that featured three different style bands on Saturday nights. Goodman bought several Fletcher Henderson arrangements and in many ways his band was a "White" version of Henderson's band. In 1935 Goodman took the band on a cross-country tour that ended at the Palomar Ballroom in Los Angeles. This engagement has become legendary and is often cited as the beginning of the Swing Era. The band performed with limited success on its tour and was about to give up until it met with a rousing reception there. Since his radio time slot was 12:30 AM on the east coast, the band was not that well known in the east, but on the west coast, the show was broadcast in a primetime slot at 9:30 PM. The knowledge of the band's music in California surprised Goodman and the news of his huge success there spread the word that Swing had arrived on the national music scene and Goodman was the *King of Swing*.

Goodman made history again in 1938 when his band performed at Carnegie Hall in New York. At the urging of his manager, Wynn Nathanson, Goodman reluctantly accepted a booking at the hallowed New York concert hall. The concert was a huge success and made jazz a legitimate music in the ears of many who previously thought jazz was a low-class, inferior music to the classics. Goodman also broke down the color barrier in jazz when he hired Teddy Wilson on piano and later Lionel Hampton on the vibraphone (see Benny Goodman Trio and Quartet below). Goodman is widely considered to be the best of the Swing Era clarinetists. He continued playing jazz with various sized groups off and on as well as classical music after the Swing Era for the rest of his life.

Figure 7.3: Benny Goodman.

The World Is Waiting for the Sunrise
Segment
Benny Goodman—Clarinet

JOHN HAMMOND

John Hammond (1910–1987) was wealthy and an heir to the Vanderbilt fortune and used his wealth and influence to champion the cause of jazz, Black American music in general, Folk, and even Rock music. He discovered talent and helped many artists to attain lucrative careers. His discoveries include Benny Goodman, Count Basie, Billie Holiday, Teddy Wilson, and later Aretha Franklin, Bob Dylan, and Bruce Springsteen. During the Swing Era he also was interested in educating the public to the Black American roots of Swing. During his famous Carnegie Hall concert, Benny Goodman gave a brief history of jazz and its origins through musical demonstration. Later in 1938, Hammond sponsored a series of two concerts at Carnegie Hall titled **From Spirituals to Swing**, where he also tried to show the progression from earlier Black American forms such as Blues and Spiritual to the present-day enormously popular Swing music. The legendary Country Blues artist Robert Johnson was hired to appear at one of the concerts but died mysteriously before the performance.

1938 CARNEGIE HALL CONCERT

In January of 1938 Benny Goodman took Swing and thus jazz out of the dance halls and onto the concert stage. Although Goodman thought the idea was risky, through the urging of his manager and John Hammond, he took the chance and succeeded in establishing jazz as a legitimate art form. The event was a major milestone in the history of jazz and was an artistic and commercial success. Although the concert was recorded, it was not made available until 1950. Goodman enlisted the help of some famous musicians who were not part of his band, including Lester Young, Johnny Hodges, Count Basie, Freddie Green, Cootie Williams, Harry Carney, and Walter Page.

GENE KRUPA

Figure 7.4: Gene Krupa.
Copyright in the Public Domain.

Gene Krupa (1909–1973) is the first great drum soloist. Earlier jazz drummers played mostly in the background, keeping the pulse as part of the rhythm section. Krupa made the drum solo a standard feature of any jazz performance and fans loved to watch his animated style of playing. After playing in various Chicago bands, he joined Benny Goodman's band in 1934 and left to form his own successful band in 1938. After the Swing Era ended he led various small combos as well as participated in several "drum battles" with Buddy Rich.

Segment from "George White's Scandals" 1944

Figure 7.5: Benny Goodman performing at a dance hall.
Copyright in the Public Domain.

Figure 7.6: Benny Goodman and His Orchestra at Carnegie Hall, 1938.
Copyright in the Public Domain.

SING, SING, SING 1938
Benny Goodman and His Orchestra
Carnegie Hall Concert

Sing, Sing, Sing is perhaps Goodman's best known tune and one of the most enduring of the Swing Era. It is often heard and recognized to this day. *Sing, Sing, Sing* was written and recorded by New Orleans trumpeter Louis Prima in 1936, but Goodman made it famous. The arrangement is credited to Jimmy Mundy but much of what is played by the time of the Carnegie Hall concert evolved as a *head arrangement* with new parts added by the players during rehearsals and performances. ***Christopher Columbus***, a Fletcher Henderson tune, is even inserted into the arrangement. The whole performance at the Carnegie Hall performance is over twelve minutes and features several extended solos. Gene Krupa, however, dominates the performance with his aggressive drumming and infectious tom-tom rhythms. His drum interludes offset various sections of the arrangement.

What to listen for:

1. Gene Krupa's tom-tom intro
2. The call and response between reeds and brass during the first chorus
3. The drum interludes throughout the arrangement
4. The new tune ***Christopher Columbus*** taking over for ***Sing, Sing, Sing***
5. The riffs and pyramiding during the first chorus of ***Christopher Columbus***
6. The changing riffs and pyramiding until the end of Part 1
7. The inspired solos and new riffs during Part 2

SING, SING, SING 1937

Watch this clip from the 1937 movie, *Hollywood Hotel*. In this scene the Goodman band is rehearsing *Sing, Sing, Sing*. Harry James plays the trumpet solo and Gene Krupa is prominently featured.

SING, SING, SING

INTRO

8	10
Drums	| Tbn + sax vamp (Riff) — Tpt melody

SING, SING, SING

Chorus 1	A	A	B	A
0:19	8	8	8	8
	Reeds-Brass ———————————————————————— |			
	Call + Response			

INTERLUDE 0:54

	4
Full Band	

Chorus 2	A		A		X
0:59	6	2	4	4	8
	Cl solo	|Full Ens	|cl solo	|Full Ens	|Drums
	Sax acc		sax acc		

CHRISTOPHER COLUMBUS

Chorus 1	A	A	A	X
1:26	8	8	8	8
			|Reeds Riff——————— |Drums	
		|Tpt Riff———————		
	Tbn Riff———————			

Chorus 2	A	A	X
2:00	8	8	8
	Tpt Riff————————————— |Drums		
	Tbn and sax background		

Chorus 3	A	A	A1	A1	X
2:25	Sax Riff———————————— |sax background——— |Drums 24				
	Tpt Riff———————————— | Tpt Riff———————				
	Tbn Riff———————————— | tbn background———				

Chorus 4	A2	A2
3:26	Clarinet Riff———————————— |	
	Sax Riff———————————— |	
	Brass Riff———————————— |	

PART 2

Continues with solos and riffs

BENNY GOODMAN TRIO AND QUARTET

In 1935 Goodman, through the urging of John Hammond, hired Black pianist Teddy Wilson and formed the Benny Goodman Trio. Although Black and White musicians had previously performed together on records and informal jam sessions, most thought it risky for Blacks and Whites to be part of the same public performing ensemble. The inclusion of Wilson along with drummer Gene Krupa proved to be a popular as well an artistic success. The trio recorded together and often performed during the intermissions of the full band's performances. Wilson did not play with the full band and was featured as a key member of the trio. The trio gave Goodman and Wilson a chance to stretch out and play in a purer jazz format, unfettered by the need to accompany dancers. The addition of Hampton on vibes added a new more aggressive dimension to the music. It was very unusual during the Swing Era to have a rhythm section without a bass player, but Wilson's remarkable use of walking tenths in left hand made a bass part dispensable.

TEDDY WILSON AND SWING PIANO

Teddy Wilson (1912–1986) is the epitome of the Swing pianist. His playing is synonymous with Swing piano and he is the greatest of the pure Swing players. (Although Art Tatum is technically a Swing pianist, he is really in a class by himself and will be discussed in Chapter 11.) Swing Piano evolved from Stride piano during the thirties and was lighter and more fluid than Stride. The Ragtime roots are still present and the left hand typically keeps the pulse by alternating bass note and chord or often playing walking bass lines in tenths. The use of tenths softens the sounds of the bass notes compared to the traditional single notes or octaves. Wilson was partly influenced by Earl Hines and sometimes employed his trumpet-piano technique of octaves and tremolos. Wilson, however, developed a smoother, more legato style that employed fast right-hand runs and fluid left-hand walking tenths. His left hand was able to walk tenths at incredibly fast tempos and the top notes of the tenths often serve as a middle voice contrapuntal line to his right-hand melody—sometimes even omitting the bass note. Wilson's restrained, elegant style influenced many other Swing Era pianists. He led several bands of his own and famously recorded with many great artists, including Billie Holiday and Lester Young.

Figure 7.7: Teddy Wilson.
Copyright in the Public Domain.

Nice Work If You Can Get It Segment

LIONEL HAMPTON

Lionel Hampton (1908–2002) so impressed Benny Goodman that he augmented his trio to a quartet. Hampton played the vibraphone (vibes) in a percussive yet melodic Swing style. Vibes were relatively new during the Swing Era and Hampton helped to establish the instrument as a mainstay in the jazz world. He led his own successful band in the 1940s that was influential in the new Jump Blues Style.

Figure 7.8: Lionel Hampton.
Copyright in the Public Domain.

BODY AND SOUL 1935
Benny Goodman Trio

Body and Soul, written in 1930, is probably the most often played and sung ballad in jazz history. There are many great recordings of this great Pop standard, including those of Coleman Hawkins (see Chapter 11), Billie Holiday, Ella Fitzgerald, and Keith Jarrett. This Goodman Trio record was a hit in 1935.

This song was always considered a challenge for improvisers because of its distant key changes in the bridge. The song is in a typical AABA form and was written by Johnny Green with lyrics by Edward Heyman, Robert Sour, and Frank Eyton.

What to listen for:

1. The overall sound of this unusual trio of instruments
2. Gene Krupa's use of wire brushes
3. The overall relaxed feeling of the music
4. Benny Goodman's sure tone and articulation
5. Teddy Wilson's precise left-hand and florid right-hand runs
6. The alternation of Goodman and Wilson solos

BODY AND SOUL
BENNY GOODMAN TRIO 1935

Benny Goodman—Clarinet
Teddy Wilson—Piano
Gene Krupa—Drums

	A	A	B	A
Chorus 1	Clarinet———|	Piano———|	Clarinet—|
Chorus 2	Piano———|	Clarinet——|	Piano——|
Chorus 3	XXXXXXXXXXX|	Clarinet——————|	
	Left out———			

I'VE GOT A HEARTFUL OF MUSIC 1937

Benny Goodman—Clarinet
Lionel Hampton—Vibraphones
Teddy Wilson—Piano
Gene Krupa—Drums

Watch this clip from the 1937 movie, Hollywood Hotel. In this scene the Goodman Quartet playing *I Got a Heartful of Music* at an incredibly fast tempo.

Chapter Eight

Count Basie—Southwest Swing, Kansas City Swing

Early Swing bands operating out of the Southwest were sometimes referred to as Territory Bands because they traveled within a small local region. Dallas, Oklahoma City, and Kansas City were the major centers. The Southwest Swing bands differed from the Eastern Swing bands in several ways. Whereas the Eastern bands emphasized their arrangements, the Southwest bands emphasized swing itself, the groove, and the feel of the music. Most of the early arrangements were not written down and not authored by any one person. These bands relied on **head arrangements**, which are arrangements made up on the spot by various band members during actual performances or rehearsals. Three factors made this process workable: 1) The riff was the major arranging devise used, 2) Most of the tunes were 12-bar blues forms, and 3) Improvisation was emphasized. Typically what happens is the rhythm section starts improvising on a blues progression and one of the sax players makes up a riff for a melody. The other sax players hear the riff and join in. A trumpet player might add a new riff to go against the sax riff and the other trumpet players join in, and so on. The riffs would be remembered the next night and new ones would be added, until after a few performances, a full-fledged tune would be composed and arranged and eventually named. The arrangements tended to be more spacious and less cluttered than the Eastern arrangements, allowing the rhythm sections to emphasize the groove and create an infectious dance music. Benny Moten led a pre-swing band in Kansas City that became the forerunner of the great Swing band led by Count Basie. His 1932 recording of *Moten Swing* serves as a prototype of a Kansas City Swing performance and one of the earliest records in the Swing style.

COUNT BASIE

William Basie (1904–1984) was given the name Count to compete with Duke Ellington, King Oliver, and Earl Hines. He was born in Red Bank, New Jersey, and grew up a fan of the stride pianists. He was tutored by Fats Waller and ended up in Kansas City where he played with Benny Moten's band. When Moten died in 1935, Basie formed a new band made up of many of the same players. He soon became known as Count Basie and led one of the greatest big bands in jazz history. John Hammond discovered Basie's band when he heard them on the radio and arranged for them to come to New York. The band was not well received at first, but with some member additions and changes, the band soon gained a national reputation as one of the swingingest bands of the Swing Era. Basie's band is one of the few to survive the end of the Swing Era and to perform almost continuously until Basie's death. In fact, the Count Basie Band has outlived Count Basie. His band was always known for its great rhythm sections that producing a relaxed yet clearly defined groove. Many great soloists have come through the Basie band, including Lester Young, Herschel Evans, Clark Terry, Buck Clayton, Harry "Sweets" Edison, Snooky Young, Thad Jones, Frank Wess, and Frank Foster. Several great singers also performed with the band, including Billie Holiday, Jimmy Rushing, and Joe Williams. Although the band went from head arrangements in the 1930s to more written arrangements by some great arrangers, the band maintained its unique sound and feel throughout its long existence.

Figure 8.1: Count Basie.
Copyright in the Public Domain.

THE COUNT BASIE RHYTHM SECTION

The Count Basie late 1930s rhythm section is considered by most to be the FIRST GREAT RHYTHM SECTION in jazz history. No rhythm section of the entire Swing Era swung more than this one. The Swing rhythm section ideal was the evenness of beats. The difficulty lies in the perfect synchronization of the all four instruments. Basie's four players played as one and the results were like a well-oiled rhythm machine. They played with a lighter feel than most Eastern rhythm sections, which resulted in a buoyant but solid groove.

FREDDIE GREEN (1911–1937) Guitar

Freddie Green is synonymous with Swing rhythm guitar playing. Modern musicians often tell guitarists to "play like Freddie Green" when wanting to hear chords on every beat. Green outlasted Basie in the Basie band and his steady, even quarter-note groove was crucial for defining the famous Basie Swing feel.

WALTER PAGE (1900–1957) Bass

Walter Page originally led a Southwest Swing band named the Blue Devils. He later joined Benny Moten's band, then Basie's. He played with a full sound and emphatic tone and could be heard better than most bass players at the time. He was one of the pioneers of the quarter-note walking bass line that during the Swing Era replaced the two-beat bass parts of earlier jazz. His lines had a sense of forward motion and were more linear (stepwise) than most in the thirties. His more melodic, linear playing influenced the next generation of Bebop players.

JO JONES (1911–1985) Drums

Jo Jones is often referred to as "Papa" Jo Jones to distinguish him from "Philly" Joe Jones, another great drummer. He was one of the most important innovators of the Swing Era. His playing differed from earlier drummers in several ways. He kept time lightly on the bass drum or not at all and maintained the beat more with the hi-hat cymbals, by opening and closing them on every other beat with his foot while playing a ride rhythm on the top cymbal with a stick. He also pioneered the use of brushes. His playing was much lighter and more subtle than Gene Krupa's playing and led the way to the freer, more layered playing of the Bebop drummers.

BASIE THE PIANIST

Figure 8.2: Count Basie.
Copyright in the Public Domain.

Count Basie is a major innovator on the piano who not only developed an original identifiable style but also changed the piano's function in the rhythm section. He is the first notable pianist to shed jazz piano's Ragtime roots. He let go of the piano's pulse-/time-keeping role by not playing bass notes or chords on every beat. Instead, he comped chords. **Comping** is the technique of playing accompaniment chords in a random-like unpredictable manner. The typical Swing pianist kept the pulse by alternating bass notes with chords, as was done in Ragtime or walking bass lines in tenths. Although Basie did this at times, he also began to comp chords freely, feeling that keeping the pulse was redundant as long as the other three members of the rhythm section were performing that role extremely well. By doing this, Basie allowed his rhythm section to sound lighter, and by freely playing chords when he felt they were needed, he added an extra layer of rhythm to the music. Comping became the norm in the next jazz style of the 1940s, Bebop, and continues to this day. The word *comp* is thought to come from the word *accompany* or *complement*, which are exactly what it does.

Basie also developed a unique way of playing jazz piano; one that relied on understatement and few but well-placed notes. While most Swing pianists played extremely fast runs with a continuously beating left hand, Basie was content to play sparse high register notes with little or no left accompaniment. These light, high register, delicate "splinks" and "splanks" became associated and immediately identifiable with Count Basie. Freddie Green is purported to have said: "the Count don't do much, but he does it better than anyone else." Basie served as the foil to his band and his soft sparse interjections and solos contrasted greatly to the full dynamic force of the whole band. He is famous for his "Count Basie endings" that features a few short notes on the piano before a final chord played by the full band.

Figure 8.3

ONE O'CLOCK JUMP
1938

One O'Clock Jump was Basie's theme song and was a major hit during the Swing Era. It is a good example of a head arrangement that spawned various manifestations over the years and is representative of the Kansas City Swing style that stressed Blues, improvised solos, and riffs. It is a 12-bar blues form and features a series of different solos accompanied by different riffs. The solos are by Basie on piano, Herschel Evans on tenor sax, Dicky Wells on trombone, Lester Young on tenor sax, and Buck Clayton on trumpet.

The last three choruses feature an example of pyramiding with three different riffs going on. The trumpets and trombones main their riffs, while the saxophones change theirs each chorus. The riffs that the saxophones play during chorus 9, Riff 8, is usually regarded as the "head" of *One O'Clock Jump* and has remained a constant of this ever changing, evolving head arrangement.

What to listen for:

1. The tightness, evenness, and swing of the rhythm section
2. Basie's light, sparse, high register playing during his solos
3. The riffs going on behind the horn solos
4. The pyramiding during the last three choruses
5. How the pyramiding builds to a climax at the end.

ONE O'CLOCK JUMP 1938

INTRO Piano Boogie-Woogie Style
  8

Chorus 1   Piano Solo, typical Basie sparse style
   12   Listen to tightness and groove of rhythm section

Chorus 2   Piano Solo continues

Chorus 3   Tenor Sax solo (Hershel Evans)
                Riff 1—Muted Trumpets

Chorus 4   Trombone Solo (Dicky Wells)
                Riff 2—Saxes

Chorus 5   Tenor Sax Solo (Lester Young)
                Riff 3—Muted Trumpets

Chorus 6   Trumpet solo (Buck Clayton)
                Riff 4—Saxes

Chorus 7   Piano Solo—Basie—light, high, sparse
                Rhy Sec comes to foreground—Freddie Green-guitar

Chorus 8   3 Simultaneous Riffs
                Riff 5—Trumpets, Riff 6—Trombones, Riff 7—Saxes

Chorus 9   3 Simultaneous Riffs
                R5-Trumpets cont, R6-Trombones cont,
                Riff 8–Saxes new

Chorus 10   3 Simultaneous Riffs
                R5—Trumpets cont, R6—Trombones cont,
                Riff 9—Saxes new

LESTER YOUNG

Lester Young (1919–1959) is the most important saxophonist of the Swing Era, and considered by many to be the greatest soloist of the period. He was born in Mississippi and raised in New Orleans and Minneapolis. He moved to Kansas City in 1933 and became famous playing with the Count Basie band. Billie Holiday, his close friend, gave him the nickname "Prez" ("Pres"), which was short for President of the Tenor Saxophone. Young differed from most players in the thirties in two ways. First, he was a cool player who played with a laid-back feeling and a light tone with little vibrato, and second, he was a horizontal player who thought more melodically than harmonically. In these regards he is usually contrasted to Coleman Hawkins, the dominant pre-Prez tenor saxophonist, who was a hot, vertical player. Whereas Hawkins constructed melodic lines based primarily on outlining chords, Young often seemingly ignored chords for the sake of melodic continuity. Ironically, by doing this he often implied extended harmonies. For Hawkins, chords are like hills that must be traversed by going up and down them. For Young, the chords are more like obstacles that he weaves his way around. His playing was based often on the scale of the prevailing key. Most Swing tenor sax players modeled themselves after Hawkins but Young's influence can be heard on the next generation, the Bebop players. Young was influenced by Frankie Trumbauer, the C-melody *cool* saxophonist who played with Bix Beiderbecke. He even emulated Trumbauer's sound on his tenor.

Figure 8.4: Lester Young.

LESTER LEAPS IN 1939
Count Basie and His Kansas City Seven

In 1939 Count Basie did some recordings with smaller group he referred to as his Kansas City Seven. It featured the same great rhythm section and one member from each horn section: Buck Clayton, trumpet; Dicky Wells, trombone; and Lester Young, tenor sax. The tune served as a feature for Young along with Basie. Lester Young's initial solo inspired a generation of sax players, including Charlie Parker. It ranks up there with Louis Armstrong's West End Blues solos as one that was learned and memorized by other players. The beginning of the third chorus sounds a little disjunct because apparently Count Basie jumped into his solo too early. The players, however, smoothed over this and Young continued his solo uninterrupted. The tune is based on two simple riffs, "Riff A" played during the first chorus and "Riff B" played during the last two choruses. Young and Basie trade fours and alternate solos with each other and the band during choruses 4, 5, and 6.

What to listen for:

1. The two riffs played at the beginning and end of the tune
2. Lester Young's light tone, laid-back phrasing, and horizontal melodic approach
3. Count Basie's light, high register, sparse playing
4. The tightness, evenness, and groove of the rhythm section
5. The Call and Response effect of trading 'fours'

LESTER LEAPS IN 1939
Count Basie and His Kansas City 7

INTRO Piano
       4

	8		8		8		8	
	A		A		B		A	
Ch 1	Riff a	Riff a |	|Riff a	Riff a	|Piano		|Riff a	Riff a
	4	4	4	4	|		4	4
Ch 2	Sax solo————————————————————————————————
Ch 3	Sax and Piano		|Sax——————————		——————— |		——————— |	
	Stop Time———————————————————			————————— |			|Stop Time—
Ch 4	Piano	Sax	|Piano	Sax	Piano	Sax	|Piano	Sax
	4	4	4	4	4	4	4	4
Ch 5	Riff b	Sax	|Riff b	Piano	|Piano		|Riff b	Sax
	4	4	4	4	8		4	4
Ch 6	Riff b	Piano	|Riff b	Piano	|Piano		|Riff b	Ending
	4	4	4	4	8		4	4

Figure 8.5: Count Basie Band with vocalist Ethel Waters from
Stage Door Canteen, 1943.

POST SWING ERA BASIE BANDS

The Count Basie Band continued on after most Swing bands folded. The style changed somewhat but the band maintained its unique identity. The rhythm section was still anchored by Freddie Green and Basie remained himself amid changing styles in the jazz world.

The band acquired a more modern sound by using contemporary arrangements by some younger arrangers. The arranger/composer Neal Hefti helped to develop a newer Basie sound and style. Frank Foster, one of Basie's saxophone players, also contributed many new tunes and arrangements for the band. Dynamic contrasts became a hallmark of the Basie band and the new arrangers fully exploited them.

CORNER POCKET 1962
(UNTIL I MET YOU)

Watch this video of one of Basie's more popular arrangements. The tune was written by Freddie Green and arranged by Basie tenor saxophonist Frank Foster. It became known also as *Until I Met You* when the lyrics were added. This live performance in 1962 is played by what is largely considered to be Basie's best Post-Swing Era band. This video features some of Basie's most celebrated sidemen: Thad Jones and Al Aarons on trumpet, Frank Wess on tenor sax, and Sonny Paine on drums. Freddie Green is still with the band and the Basie rhythm section plays with a hard-driving yet relaxed swing feeling.

SINGERS WITH THE BASIE BAND

Jimmy Rushing (1901–1972) Affectionately known as Mr. Five-by-Five because of his build, Jimmy Rushing sang with the Basie band from 1935 to 1950. He was characterized as a blues shouter who has a powerful voice that projected well over the band. He had a wide range and could sing both high and low. Although he thought of himself as more of a ballad singer, he is most associated with blues songs.

Figure 8.6: Jimmy Rushing.
Copyright in the Public Domain.

TAKE ME BACK BABY 1942

This was a 1942 Soundie. Soundies were the music videos of the day. They were shown at movie theatres and on video jukeboxes called Panorams. There is a plot is this Soundie that portrays Rushing as a sax player in the Basie Band who falls asleep and dreams about his girlfriend. The song is in a traditional Blues form.

Joe Williams (1918–1999) The successor to Jimmy Rushing, Joe Williams achieved great fame with the Basie band. Primarily known as a Blues singer, he also sang Pop standards. Williams presented an imposing figure, visually and vocally, as he stood in front of the band. His voice was deep, rich, and powerful. He continued his successful career on his own after leaving Basie and returned on special occasions to sing with the band.

Figure 8.7: Joe Williams.

Copyright © Richard Newhouse (CC BY-SA 2.0) at http://commons.
wikimedia.org/wiki/File:Joe_Williams.jpg

EVERYDAY I HAVE THE BLUES

Watch this later video of **_Everyday I Have the Blues_**. This is one of Williams' signature Blues songs with the Basie band. It is in a traditional Blues form. This is a live performance from the late seventies.

Chapter Nine

Duke Ellington

Edward Kennedy Ellington (1899–1974) was born in Washington D.C. As a boy, he took piano lessons from a Mrs. Clinkscales but learned to play jazz by watching his family's player piano play back piano rolls made by ragtime and stride pianists, including the "Father of Stride Piano," James P. Johnson. Ellington was a talented painter and received a scholarship to art school but decided on a music career. His interest in painting crossed over into his music and is evidenced by his unique blending of instrumental tone colors. He began leading bands in the 1920s and ended up leading the house band at the famous Cotton Club in the Harlem section of New York City. It is here that Ellington gained fame and developed his unique style. The style he performed at the Cotton Club is now referred to as Pre-Swing. There, Ellington got to experiment as a composer and arranger and had to continuously compose new music to accompany the elaborate floor shows presented at the club. Often these show were based on African motifs and Ellington invented music with exotic sounds and rhythms that he called **Jungle Music**. Ellington's style smoothly transitioned into the Big Band Swing of the 1930s and continued to lead a Swing big band until his death in 1974, well after the Swing Era had faded.

Ellington's bands were always in a category by themselves due in large part to unique styles and sounds of his individual sidemen. Ellington wrote for individual players, not for individual instruments. He exploited the unique talents of his musicians in such a way as to write parts that only they could play. Instead of writing the name of the instrument on a part, e.g., Trumpet 1 or Trumpet 2, he wrote the player's name, e.g., Bubber or Cootie. He also had extended loyalty from most of his players. Once hired, his musicians rarely left the band. Some were with him from the 1920s to the 1970s. On those rare occasions when someone left the band, Ellington would adapt his arrangements to the new player's sound and style. Although he was a good piano player, it was often said that Ellington's real instrument was his band. Since he had a continuously working band his whole adult life, he had the luxury of always being able to try out new ideas.

Ellington was a versatile and prolific composer. He wrote many songs that have become pop standards, dance music, sacred music, film score, and larger suites. All jazz musicians play at least several Ellington tunes, and because of his enormous and original contribution to jazz in regard to his own band's music, his compositions, and his arranging innovations, *Jazz Times* magazine named him the Jazz Person of the Century in 2000 when celebrating the first 100 years of jazz.

Figure 9.1: Duke Ellington.

Ellington is the second great arranger/composer in jazz history, chronologically, after Jelly Roll Morton. Most say that he is the single greatest. Below are some of his contributions.

CONTRIBUTIONS

1. **Sound and Tone Color**
   He emphasized and explored unique sounds and tone colors; this was his chief concern.
2. **Arranging and Orchestration**
   He invented a technique called **Scoring Across Sections** (Voicing Across Sections) that was an original arranging technique of blending instruments from different sections to create new sounds or tone colors, much like a painter blends colors to create new colors.
3. **Harmony**
   He enriched and advanced the harmonic and tonal pallet of jazz through the use of complex extended chords and chord progressions.
4. **Composer/Songwriter**
   He composed hundreds of songs, tunes, and larger extended works. He also is among the great songwriters of the Great American Songbook.
5. **Innovator**
   He is one of the great innovators in the Pre-Swing and Swing styles.

SCORING ACROSS SECTIONS

Ellington applied his talents as a painter to his music by blending different instrumental together to create new ones, much like a painter blends visual colors.

Watch and listen to scoring across section in the following clips

Mood Indigo—muted trumpet + muted trombone + clarinet

You Got to Cut a Rug—trumpet + valve trombone + clarinet + alto sax

Figure 9.2: Joe Nanton, muted trombone; Harry Carney, clarinet; Wallace Jones, muted trumpet, playing *Mood Indigo*.

EARLY PERIOD
Mid-1920s–Early 1930s
Pre-Swing, Jungle Music, Cotton Club

Pre-Swing is the label used for the larger jazz bands of the 1920s that combine elements of New Orleans–style jazz with some music played by the dance bands of the period. The music played by the more commercial dance bands of the period was referred to as *Sweet Music*. In the Fletcher Henderson chapter we noted the interesting evolution of 1920s Pre-Swing into 1930s Swing. Ellington led a Pre-Swing band that became famous playing at the Cotton Club in New York. Although everyone who worked there were Black Americans, Blacks were not allowed into the club as patrons—a segregationist policy that thankfully is lost on us today. The Cotton Club featured elaborate floor shows that often were based on African motifs. Ellington had to come up with new music to accompany the changing shows and it is here he got to experiment with exotic sounds to depict the African jungles. Ellington always had an interest in unusual tone colors and sounds and at the Cotton Club he was afforded a great opportunity in being able to explore and exploit their possibilities. The brass players in Ellington's band used a variety of mutes to change the sounds and inflections on their horns. Skillful manipulation of the plunger mute, wa-wa mute (Harmon mute with stem in), and hat mute created a vocal-like quality that gave the effect of talking or screaming horns, and wild jungle sounds.

EAST ST. LOUIS TOODLE-OO 1927

Duke Ellington Pre-Swing Band
Bubber Miley—Trumpet with plunger mute
Joe "Tricky Sam" Nanton—Trombone with plunger mute

This is one of Ellington's first famous records and a good example of Jungle Music. Notice the highly vocal-like quality that Miley obtains with the plunger mute. Miley was a master of the plunger mute and contributed much to Ellington's early sound. Joe Nanton does a similar solo on trombone.

BLACK AND TAN FANTASY 1929

Duke Ellington Orchestra
Arthur Whetsol—Trumpet with wa-wa mute

This is a scene from a short film Ellington made in 1929 featuring his Cotton Club Orchestra. The film shows some acts from the famous Cotton Club and has a plot centered on a dancer who falls ill while dancing and ends up on her deathbed. This segment is at the end when her dying request is to hear the **Black and Tan Fantasy**. Arthur Whetsol plays the muted trumpet solo. This is another example of Ellington's Jungle Music.

SWING ERA
Mid-1930s–Mid-1940s

Duke Ellington led one of the best and most important big bands of the Swing Era. Although the two dominant Swing styles were Eastern Swing, represented by Fletcher Henderson and Benny Goodman, and Southwest or Kansas City Swing, represented by Benny Moten and Count Basie, Ellington was really in a category by himself. While he fully transitioned from Pre-Swing to Swing, his uniqueness and fondness for unusual and exotic sounds and tone colors from his Jungle Music days remained with him, and as before, he wrote for and featured the unique playing styles of his sidemen. Considered to be a landmark year in Ellington's recorded output, 1940 was when some of his most famous tunes and arrangements were recorded. His bands at that time featured some all-time great players, including Johnny Hodges, Ben Webster, Barney Bigard, Harry Carney, Cootie Williams, Joe Nanton, and Jimmy Blanton. The three records represented here are a Swing standard, an exotic minor blues, and an anticipation of Bebop.

DUKE ELLINGTON ORCHESTRA 1940

Wallace Jones, Cootie Williams—Trumpets
Rex Stewart—Cornet
Joe Nanton, Lawrence Brown—Trombones
Juan Tizol—Valve Trombone
Barney Bigard—Clarinet and Tenor Sax
Jonny Hodges, Otto Hardwick—Alto Saxes
Harry Carney—Baritone Sax
Duke Ellington—Piano
Fred Guy—Guitar
Bass-Jimmy Blanton
Drums-Sonny Greer

Figure 9.3: Ellington horn section, 1943.
Copyright in the Public Domain.

IN A MELLOW TONE 1940

This is one of Ellington's most loved and often played tunes. It is an example of his pure Swing dance music. The chord changes were borrowed from an older tune called *Rose Room*. The 32-measure form is ABAC. Ellington created his tune from two catchy rhythmic motives. A rhythmic motive is an idea whose notes change while the rhythm remains constant. The tune begins with the first motive and is based mostly on that idea. The second rhythmic motive occurs mostly during the last C section. There are two classic solos here by Cootie Williams and Johnny Hodges.

rhythmic motive 1

Figure 9.4

rhythmic motive 2

Figure 9.5

What to listen for:

1. Call and Response between saxes and trombones during the first chorus
2. Cootie Williams' masterful use of the plunger mute during the second chorus, along with the Call and Response with the saxes
3. Johnny Hodges' silky smooth alto sax solo and his use of double-time during the third chorus

IN A MELLOW TONE

Duke Ellington Orchestra
Cootie Williams—Trumpet solo with plunger mute
Johnny Hodges—Alto Sax solo

Intro
Call   + Response
piano + bass
         8

	8	8	8	8
	A	B	A	C
Chorus 1	call + response———————————————————			
	Saxes + trombones——————————————————piano			
				2
Chorus 2	trumpet with plunger mute—————————————————			
	Williams |C+R with saxes			
Chorus 3	band	al sax——————break	al sax cont.————			
	Hodges			|call + response
	Band accomp——	|——————|band- al sax		
	4	4	6	2			

KO-KO 1940

This is one of Ellington's most acclaimed recordings from the Swing Era. This represents Ellington's original style and sound perhaps more than any other record of that period. *Ko-Ko* is a minor blues form. Minor blues is similar to traditional blues in form except the harmony comes from the minor scale rather than the major scale. The entire arrangement is based upon variations on a simple call and response pattern first heard in the intro. For the most part, the calls and the responses also act as riffs. The music gradually builds in intensity and reaches a climax in the last chorus. Ellington creates some very complex harmonic structures by scaffolding different chords on top of other chords (polychords). Ellington's long-time baritone saxophonist, Harry Carney, makes the call during the intro and coda. Juan Tizol plays the call during the first chorus on valve trombone. Joe Nanton then makes the call soloing on slide trombone with the plunger mute on the next two choruses along with brass punctuations responding while manipulating mutes in Ellington's "talking horns" style.

What to listen for:

1. The continuous variations on the opening call and response riffs
2. The vocal quality of Joe Nanton's trombone solo and the punctuating talking horns in the background during choruses 2 and 3
3. Ellington's glizzandi and dissonant piano chords in chorus 4
4. Jimmy Blanton's solo bass breaks in chorus 5
5. The gradual build and harmonic complexity throughout

KO-KO

Duke Ellington Orchestra
Harry Carney—Baritone sax
Juan Tizol—Valve Trombone
Joe Nanton—Trombone
Duke Ellington—Piano
Jimmy Blanton—Bass

INTRO	CH1	CH2	CH3
C+R riffs	C+R riffs	C+R riffs————————————	
bar sx - tbns	valve tbn - saxes	saxes-brass————————————	
Carney	Tizol	talking horns————————————	
		tbn solo-plunger mute————————	
		Nanton	

CH4	CH5	CH6	CH7	CODA
C+R riffs	C+R riffs	C+R riffs	C+R riffs	C+R riffs
saxes - brass	tpts - saxes+tbns	saxes-brass	brass-saxes	bar sx - tbns
piano- glizzando	complex sound	bass breaks	sxs-main mel	Carney

COTTON TAIL 1940

With this other great recording from 1940, Ellington seems to be anticipating Bebop, the next jazz style that really begins in 1941. The initial playing of the head is played in octaves by four instruments. The playing of the head in unison or octaves was the standard procedure for bebop combos. The head itself is Bebop-like in its angularity and rhythmic surprises. This is also a good example of Ellington's scoring across sections. A muted trumpet and alto saxophone play in unison with a trombone and baritone saxophone an octave below. Ben Webster then plays a two-chorus tenor sax solo—this was unusually long for this time period. This dramatic solo accompanied by a driving, swinging band is one the most acclaimed of the Swing era. The fifth chorus features the famous sax soli. A soli is a feature for one section of the band, usually for saxophones. Soli sections are typically written-out harmonized melodies that sound like an improvisation. This became a staple of future modern big band arrangements. Ellington looks toward the future here by using this technique and by the bebop-like melodic lines he wrote. A later group called Supersax made several recordings using this technique with transcribed Charlie Parker solos.

What to listen for:

1. The scoring across sections for the initial and final statement of the head
2. Cootie Williams' plunger mute trumpet solo during the first B section
3. Ben Webster's dramatic solo during the second and third choruses
4. The bebop-like sax soli section during the fifth chorus
5. The overall drive and intensity of the whole performance

COTTON TAIL

Duke Ellington Orchestra
Ben Webster—Tenor Sax
Cootie Williams—Trumpet with plunger mute
Harry Carney—Baritone Sax

	A	A	B	A
Chorus 1	al sx, bar sx, tpt, tbn———— in octaves (like bebop) band acc———		| C+R sxs-muted tpt Williams	| XXXXXXXXXX left out
Interlude band 4				
Chorus 2	ten sax solo——————— Webster		| C+R with band 6	| band 2
Chorus 3	ten sax solo cont——— bass pedal tone-|		| band accomp	|
Chorus 4	Brass———————————		| bar sx solo Carney	| Piano solo Ellington
Chorus 5	SAX SOLI—————————————— like a harmonized Bebop solo			
Chorus 6	C+R brass- saxes———————		|whole band——|	| al sx, bar sx, tpt, tbn | in octaves like beginning

IT DON'T MEAN A THING
IF IT AIN'T GOT THAT SWING

1943 FILM

This is one of Ellington's best-known tunes. This 1943 film version showcases several of his sidemen during this time: Ray Nance on violin and vocals, Taft Jordon on trumpet and vocals, Joe Nanton on trombone, and Ben Webster on tenor saxophone. The tune is in an AABA pop-song form. The A sections feature a four-measure call followed by a four-measure response. The calls are sung and the responses are repeated notes played by the brass in the talking horns style with plunger mutes. The actual lyrics mimic the talking horns.

It don't mean a thing, if it ain't got that swing.
Doo-ah, doo-ah, doo-ah, doo-ah, doo-ah, doo-ah, doo-ah, doo-ah,

---

What to listen for:

1. Classical-like violin rubato intro
2. Call and response during the head
3. Talking horns with plunger mutes
4. Joe Nanton's plunger mute trombone solo with riffs in the background
5. Ben Webster's tenor sax solo

IT DON'T MEAN A THING
IF IT AIN'T GOT THAT SWING

Duke Ellington Orchestra
Ray Nance—Violin and Vocal
Taft Jordon—Trumpet and Vocal
Joe Nanton—Trombone with plunger mute
Ben Webster—Tenor Sax

KEY PRE-SWING AND SWING ERA SIDEMEN

Bubber Miley (1903–1932) Trumpet
   Master of the plunger mute, growls, and exotic sound effects
   Associated with Ellington's Pre-Swing and Jungle Music
   Featured on *East St. Louis Toodle-oo*
   East St. Louis Toodle-oo Segment

Joe "Tricky Sam" Nanton (1904–1946) Trombone
   Master of the plunger mute, growls, and exotic sound effects Associated with
   Ellington's Pre-Swing and Jungle Music
   Played with Ellington from Pre-Swing through the Swing Era
   Featured on *East St. Louis Toodle-oo* and *Ko-Ko*
   C Jam Blues Segment

Cootie Williams (1910–1985) Trumpet
   Master of the plunger mute and growls and often played with a vocal-like quality
   Played with Ellington from 1929 to 1940 and 1962 to 1974
   Featured on *In a Mellow Tone* and *Cotton Tail*
   Concerto For Cootie Segment

Harry Carney (1910–1974) Baritone Sax
   "Father of the baritone saxophone"
   Played with Ellington from Pre-Swing until Ellington died.
   Deep, rich, full sound
   Featured on *Ko-Ko* and *Cotton Tail* and *East St. Louis Toodle-oo*
   You Got To Cut A Rug Segment

Johnny Hodges (1907–1970) Alto Saxophone
   One of Ellington's most important soloists
   Original style characterized by the bending of and sliding between notes
   As lead alto player of the sax section, he lent his style to the entire section
   Played with Ellington from 1928 to 1970
   Featured on *In a Mellow Tone*
   Don't Get Around Much Anymore Segment

Ben Webster (1909–1973) Tenor Saxophone
   One of Ellington's important soloists during the Swing Era
   Played tuneful and sometimes dramatic solos
   Had a full yet breathy sound
   One of the three major tenor sax players of the Swing Era

Played with Ellington from 1940 to 1943 and 1948 to 1949
Featured on Cotton Tail
C Jam Blues Segment

Ray Nance (1913–1974) Trumpet, Violin, Vocals, Dance
Multitalented instrumentalist and singer
played the famous trumpet solo on the original recoding of *Take the "A" Train*
Played with Ellington from 1940 to 1963
Featured on *It Don't Mean a Thing If It Ain't Got That Swing*
C Jam Blues Segment

Jimmy Blanton (1918–1942) Bass
"Father of Modern Jazz bass"
First great bass soloist
Virtuoso with bow and pizzicato
Often played melodic lines with horns
Played lines with varied rhythms as well as the standard quarter-note lines
Played with Ellington from 1939 to 1942
Featured on Ko-ko
Sophisticated Lady Segment

Barney Bigard (1906–1981) Clarinet and Tenor Saxophone
Featured as a clarinet soloist
Brought his native New Orleans flavor to the band
Played with Ellington from 1928 to 1942
C Jam Blues Segment

Sonny Greer (1903–1982) Drums
Adept at playing in Pre-Swing and Swing styles
Driving, assured sense of swing along with Jimmy Blanton was key for the great 1940 recordings
Played with Ellington from 1924 to 1951
C Jam Blues Segment

Billy Strayhorn (1915–1967) Composer/Arranger
Served as Ellington's alter ego
Wrote Ellington's theme song *Take the "A" Train*
Composed many other tunes for Ellington
Collaborated with Ellington on many compositions and arrangements from 1938 to 1967
Wrote music and lyrics for one of the all-time great jazz ballads,
Lush Life, at the age of 19
Take the "A" Train Segment

Chapter Ten

Singers from the Swing Era

All jazz singing stems from Louis Armstrong. He sang with all the characteristics and artistry that he played on his horn. He set a standard that each singer should be unique and each singer's performance of a song new and different each time. Through his singing Armstrong crossed over into the Pop world of entertainment and perhaps because of his universal appeal and commercial success, Louis Armstrong the entertainer eclipsed Louis Armstrong the innovative artist in the eyes of many.

There has always been debate on exactly what a jazz singer is. The majority of songs that jazz singers sing are Pop songs, so the material does not define a jazz singer, and much like jazz itself, it is the way the material is performed that makes it jazz. Yet some singers sing jazz sometimes and sometimes not. Superstar singers like Frank Sinatra and Tony Bennett have had many hits that would not be classified as jazz and still have recorded some great jazz performances. Some call the more modern singer Norah Jones a jazz singer, yet clearly much of what she sings is not jazz. During the Swing Era, jazz (Swing) was the dominant Pop of the day, so it is hard to distinguish the two. And the two have always been interrelated.

Pop singing changed drastically during the 1920s because of the microphone. The newly invented microphones made it possible for singers to be heard in larges venues without have to sing with a full voice. Singers no longer had to project their voices to the back of a theatre and older pre-microphone singers like Al Jolson and Sophie Tucker gave way to a new breed of singer, the crooners. **Crooners** were mostly tenor male singers who sang in a soft, intimate way. With amplification now possible, they could sing in a more natural way, essentially using their speaking voices while singing. There arose a real difference between traditional or Classical singing, opera singing, for example, and Pop singing. Crooners such as Gene Austin and Rudy Vallee, who became all the rage during the Roaring Twenties, appeared on radio, films, and records. The new singing style worked well on these new electronic media, as, for example, you probably would not want someone shouting at you while singing in your living room.

THE GREAT AMERICAN SONGBOOK

The vast majority of songs that jazz singers sing come from what is known as the **Great American Songbook**, which consists of the great Pop **Standards** written mostly during the twenties, thirties, and forties. These uniquely American Pop songs have served jazz singers and instrumentalists alike as endless sources of interpretation and improvisational fodder. Their typical 32-measure structure, like 90 feet between bases in baseball, seems to be just right. Since both jazz and pop performance rely on chorus repetition, anything shorter, other than Blues, would be too repetitive and anything longer would be too hard to remember. Remembering the initial tune leads to a greater appreciation of how the improviser is changing it. There are exceptions to the 32-measure pop song, but these usually rely on a vocal performance of the lyrics for continuity. Most of the songs of the Great American Songbook consist of four 8-measure periods in one of the following forms: AABA, ABAB[1], ABAC. The melodies of these songs are flexible and can interpreted and performed in many different ways; they are not too notey, as are many of the more contemporary songs, and there are plenty of spaces, either long held notes or rests, that can be filled. The chords and harmonic progressions give a sense of forward motion with subtle key changes that provide just the right amount of tension and release. The newer Pop songs and Pop song formats from the fifties on are more static and redundant with less room for interpretation and variation. These songs are not nearly as flexible since there are usually specifics built into them; bass lines and background parts, for example. The great standards can be performed in myriad styles, tempos, and arrangements. The lyrics for the Great American Songbook are usually witty and clever, containing some ingenious rhymes. They are almost always written in the first person, which enables the singer to assume a role and sing form their heart directly to someone, the audience or otherwise. Many of these great standards are still going strong, now going on one hundred years old.

The songwriters of the Great American Songbook are too numerous to mention here, but among them are Irving Berlin and Cole Porter who are two of the few who wrote both music and lyrics; the songwriting teams of George Gershwin, composer, and Ira Gershwin, lyricist; Richard Rodgers, composer, and Lorenz Hart, lyricist; composers Jerome Kern, Harold Arlen, Harry Warren, and Hoagy Carmichael; and lyricists Oscar Hammerstein II, Johnny Mercer, Dorothy Fields, and Yip Harburg.

BING CROSBY

Bing Crosby (1903–1977) became the dominant male Pop singer from the late twenties until the early forties when Frank Sinatra assumed that role. Crosby was essentially a crooner but one with a deep baritone voice who made good use of the microphone. Crosby sang "**sweet music**," which was corny, schmaltzy Pop of the day but he sang jazz as well. Influenced by Louis Armstrong, Crosby became the first successful White jazz singer. He began with a vocal group called the Rhythm Boys that sang with Paul Whiteman's band. Crosby had many hits during the Swing Era and was a successful movie actor as well. He was virtually the only major singer not associated with a band during the Swing Era.

Figure 10.1: Bing Crosby in *Road to Singapore*.
Copyright in the Public Domain.

VIDEOS of Bing Crosby

BLUEBIRDS AND BLACKBIRDS 1930

Clip from the movie **The King of Jazz**, featuring Paul Whiteman's Band
With the Rhythm Boys

Bing Crosby, Harry Barris, and Al Rinker

NOW YOU HAS JAZZ 1956

Clip from the movie **High Society**
With Louis Armstrong and his band
Written by Cole Porter

BIG BAND SINGERS

Although singers have dominated pop music for many years, this was not always the case. During the Swing Era the bands and their leaders dominated the jazz and Pop worlds. Almost all singers were associated with a band and many went from band to band as the musicians did. An exception was Bing Crosby who already had an established reputation before the Swing era. The typical vocal arrangements embedded the vocal in the middle of the performance. Usually the band starts the tune with the singer sitting off to the side of the band. When it is time to sing, he or she walks up to a microphone in front of the band to sing one chorus. After the vocal chorus, the singer walks back to their seat while the band finishes out the tune. Thus, the singer was not even standing up front to acknowledge the applause at the end of song; they were more or less incidental to the band as a whole. All this will change by the mid-forties when Frank Sinatra becomes such a sensation and breaks the mold by going it alone without a band.

HELEN FORREST

Helen Forrest (1917–1999) was one of the most popular "girl singers" of the Swing Era. Most bands had what was called a "boy singer" and a "girl singer; some even had vocal groups as well. She sang with three of the most popular band of the period: Benny Goodman, Artie Shaw, and Harry James. She was sometimes referred to as a female crooner.

VIDEO of Helen Forrest with Artie Shaw's Band

I HAVE EYES 1939

Clip from the short film *Artie Shaw's Class in Swing*

The rest of the chapter will focus on the three greatest singers to come out of the Swing Era who are also three of the greatest singers of the 20th century.

BILLIE HOLIDAY

Billie Holiday (1915–1959), born Eleanora Fagan in Philadelphia to teenage parents, weathered a very troubled life to become not only a great singer but a major influence as well. She had drug and alcohol problems and even resorted to prostitution for drug money. The abuses of her lifestyle got the better of her and she died at the young age of 43. She is widely considered to be the greatest jazz singer to come after Louis Armstrong (chronologically). She sang with several Swing bands, including Benny Goodman, Artie Shaw, and Count Basie. John Hammond, who discovered Goodman, Basie, and many others, also discovered her and paired her with Teddy Wilson for a number of recordings during the thirties. She was a life-long friend of Lester Young and the two of them shared a personal and musical bond that influenced each other's work. Her approach to singing like his to playing the saxophone was decidedly cool and she often lagged behind the actual tune when she sang. Her legacy continues to this day as she continues to inspire new generations of singers.

Billie Holiday did not have a great voice by any traditional standards: she had a relatively weak voice with a narrow range but she made up for these deficiencies with her great phrasing, feeling, and communication. What attracted her most to a song were the lyrics. When Billie sang a song, she wanted above all else to communicate the meaning of the lyrics. To do this she greatly altered the song's original melody, notes, and rhythm. But unlike Louis Armstrong, who also greatly changed things around, but much as in his trumpet playing, in order to make more interesting music, she did it to better communicate the words. Ironically by doing so she also made more interesting music. She was a great actor when she sang and like a great actor the listener believed her every word because she brought her personal experience to every song she sang.

Billie's greatest contribution to jazz was in the area of phrasing. Apart from changing notes and rhythms, phrasing involves subtle accents, dynamic shading, when to breathe, to connect or not connect notes, etc. For any musician, but especially for singers, there are countless ways to phrase a melody just as there are for actors reciting the exact same line in a play. In this area she influenced instrumentalists as much as singers, most famously Miles Davis. Intrinsically tied in with her phrasing was her inflection of notes. She bent notes, approaching them from above or below, slid from note to note, and sang in the cracks as a way of expressing the words.

Billie wrote several songs that have become standards; they include ***God Bless the Child***, ***Don't Explain***, and ***Fine and Mellow***.

Figure 10.2: Billie Holiday.

ALL OF ME 1941

This is one and the most famous of several recordings made of this well-known Pop Standard. It shows the young Billie Holiday at the peak of her powers as an interpreter and communicator of the Great American Songbook. Her good friend and kindred spirit, Lester Young, joins her on tenor saxophone, along with bandleader Eddie Heywood. She veers from the written melody of this song a lot and her second chorus is much different from the first even though the words are the same. Notice how she changes the first phrase of the song from the original music differently in each chorus she sings.

Figure 10.3

She ignores the motivic connection between the statements of "All of Me" and goes for a more dramatic gesture than musical one. In her second chorus she emphasizes the word "all" much more, as if she wanted to make herself clearer this time. An instrumentalist would never play this song that way, as it would make little sense without the words. She continues this way throughout both choruses of the performance, singing the words, not the notes.

What to listen for:

1. The laid-back intro with piano and band
2. Billie's scoop up to the first note on "All"
3. Billie's subtle interpretation of the lyrics and melody
4. Lester Young's solo's similarity to Billie's laid-back style
5. Billie's reinterpretation of the same lyrics during Chorus 2
6. Billie's heartfelt rendering of the lyrics

ALL OF ME

Billie Holiday—Vocal
Lester Young—Tenor Sax
Eddie Heywood—Piano, Bandleader

Intro
piano
8

	8	8	8	8
	A	B	A	C
Chorus 1	vocal—changes melody———			
Interlude—	Young improvises on C section			
Chorus 2	vocal—different interpretation			

VIDEOS of Billie Holiday

GOD BLESS THE CHILD 1950

Billie sings her popular original song with the Count Basie Band.

FINE AND MELLOW 1957

This famous clip is from a TV show and features an all-star group of musicians. In the order of their solos, they are Ben Webster, tenor sax; Lester Young, tenor sax; Vic Dickerson, trombone; Gerry Mulligan, baritone sax; Coleman Hawkins, tenor sax; Roy Eldridge, trumpet; and Doc Cheatham, trumpet. The rhythm section is Mal Waldron, piano; Danny Barker, guitar; Milt Hinton, bass; and Osie Johnson, drums. This is rare 12-bar Blues sung by Billie.

FRANK SINATRA

They still debate whether Frank Sinatra (1915–1998) was a jazz singer. He was a real phenomenon in the early forties and became the first superstar in Pop music history. His idol Bing Crosby was a big star but the world had never witnessed anything like Sinatra when he first achieved stardom. He became a bigger-than-life cultural icon. Everything he did and everything he said became news. He was constantly followed and hounded by the press. He performed in front of screaming young women and girls called "bobbysoxers" in much the same way later pop singers like Elvis Presley and The Beatles did. Indeed he was a Pop singer but was he a jazz singer? Most jazz historians don't seem to think so; he is rarely even mentioned in most jazz books. But ask most any jazz musician and they will tell you otherwise. James Kaplan, who wrote what is perhaps the definitive biography of Sinatra's early life and career, ***Frank the Voice***, said he was inspired to write the book when he was hanging out with a group of musicians who had played with him and they spoke in awe of Sinatra's artistry and musicianship. Much has been written about Sinatra's controversial personal life, some true, some not so true, but if you put down the tabloids for a minute and just listen to him sing, you cannot help being touched. Like Crosby, Sinatra also has a successful film-acting career, which places him more on the Pop category for some. The jazz intelligentsia seems to think that the more commercially successful you are, the less artistic or meaningful you must be. This was certainly not the case with Louis Armstrong, who enjoyed great commercial success as well. For much of the first half of the 20th century, jazz and Pop were related through shared repertoire and performance styles and Sinatra is arguably the best interpreter of the Great American Songbook. For that alone he is important to jazz. But he is more than that; he was an outstanding jazz singer in the truest sense of the word whose influence still resonates in the 21st century.

Sinatra first came to widespread attention in 1939 when he sang with Harry James' band and in 1940 received more exposure when he went with Tommy Dorsey's band. Dorsey led what was probably the most popular band at the time. In 1942 he left Dorsey to go out on his own; this was a risky venture since almost all singers were attached to bands. The move proved to be a wise one and he became bigger than ever, even causing riots at some appearances. One by one, other singers followed his lead and as WWII ended, the Big Bands declined and the singers rose to dominate the pop music market. By the early fifties most people thought he was washed up, as his career seemed to be in sharp decline. Then in 1953 with a new record deal with Capitol Records and an Academy Award for his role in the hit movie, *From Here to Eternity*, his career was resurrected and a more mature, bolder Sinatra emerged and contributed his most important work.

SINATRA'S INFLUENCES

Sinatra had several important influences:

Bing Crosby

Sinatra idolized Bing Crosby and emulated not only his singing but also his look and clothes. Crosby was the dominant male singer until Sinatra came along and influenced most male singers at the time. Crosby was essentially a crooner who sang in an intimate but detached manner. Sinatra went beyond crooning to a much more personal way of communicating with his audience. Sinatra's baritone voice was not quite as deep as Crosby's.

Tommy Dorsey

Dorsey, a trombone player, was known for his "seamless legato" playing, which referred to his ability to play very long lines without taking a breath. He could do this because he mastered the technique of circular breathing, which is a difficult-to-learn process that allows a wind player to take air into his lungs while blowing air into his horn at the same time. It is impossible for a singer to engage in circular breathing, but Sinatra, being fascinated by Dorsey's long lines, simulated the technique by singing long lines that might include several phrases in one breath. To do this he built up his capacity to breathe at larger intervals by running and swimming under water.

Billie Holiday

Sinatra always credited Billie Holiday as his biggest influence. Like Holiday, the most important part of a song for Sinatra was the lyrics and like her, he masterfully communicated those lyrics to his audience. Although not nearly as much as Holiday, he subtly changed notes and rhythms and even lyrics to better get the meaning of the lyrics across. He was like an actor when he sang and the listener believed every word; like Holiday, he brought his life's experience into every song. Frank was very fond of Billie and even visited her on her deathbed.

SINATRA'S CONTRIBUTIONS

Microphone

Sinatra is the first singer to fully exploit the microphone. Whereas singers during the twenties and thirties stood in front of the microphone to amplify their voices, Sinatra held the microphone and moved it closer or farther away from his mouth, depending on what he was singing. He realized that the audience was not hearing his voice coming out of his mouth but rather through speakers. He, thus, used the microphone as an extension of his voice; it was an important medium *through* which he sang rather than *into* which he sang.

Consonants

Sinatra had nearly flawless diction that made every word he sang understandable. He changed the manner of singing words by stressing consonant sounds rather than vowel sounds as was done in traditional singing. This technique aided his diction and his more direct, personal way of singing For example when singing ***I've Got You Under My Skin***, he holds out the "n" in skin not the "i," by singing "skinnnnnn" not "skiiin." He sometimes cut off words abruptly, emphasizing the final consonant in words like *bump* and *tramp*. The stressing of consonants made his singing more speech-like and thus more direct.

Swing

Although Sinatra mostly sang ballads during his early period, he turned into the ultimate swinger during his middle years. No singer other than perhaps Louis Armstrong swung harder than Frank. His series of swinging albums made in the fifties and sixties set a standard from which all other singers are measured. He was able to swing without sacrificing the meaning of the words. Swinging, in general, depends not only on when you start a note but also when you end it, when notes connect, when they don't, etc. Author Will Friedwald, who writes extensively on jazz and older Jazz/Pop singing, claims that no one can make quarter notes swing as much as Armstrong and Sinatra. Swing is intricately tied to phrasing.

Phrasing

Sinatra was a master at phrasing a lyric and like Billie Holiday he phrased to better communicate the lyrics. Like Billie he also influenced Miles Davis who in turn was known as a master phraser on the trumpet. No one disputes Frank's ability to get the heart of a lyric and extract its meaning better than anyone else. Related to his phrasing is his pacing of a song, he always spoke about a having climactic moment in each song and even if he sings through the song twice, the climax happens only once. His recording of *I've Got You Under My Skin*, described below, is a good example of this and his ability to produce and release tension. Like Billie Holiday, Sinatra inflected notes and slid between them as a way of highlighting the words. He was able to float rubato-like, unhampered by the beat at times, but also he could lock into the beat and swing as hard as any jazz instrumentalist.

Interpretation

All of the contributions listed here make Sinatra the master interpreter of the Great American Songbook. Once he recorded a song, that usually became the definitive version of it. When he changed notes, rhythms, or lyrics from the original written versions of songs, most people, including singers, assumed that that was the way the song was written.

Recording

Sinatra embraced the new recording technology of the 1950s and pioneered the production of record albums. The new 33⅓ RPM Long Playing record, the LP, could fit up to thirty minutes of music on one side of a record. This was considerably more than the four minutes on the older 78 RPM discs. While albums were not entirely new, now they were on a single disc. What were released as albums before the LP were collected discs packaged in separate sleeves of a binder, much like a photo album. Sinatra treated each album as a unique collection of songs with a common theme. The term *concept album*, associated with the Beatles during the sixties, was not used in the fifties, but that is exactly what Sinatra's albums were. He broke with the norm of placing a few hit singles on an album and filling it in with other material. In fact, his singles were never included on albums. The albums had two general themes of either all up-tempo happy love songs or all slow sad songs about lost love. The idea of a consistency of mood was something that jazz musicians emulated on their albums. Again, Miles Davis comes to mind.

Pop as Art

Much like Louis Armstrong turned jazz into an art form during the 1920s, Sinatra turned Pop music. The albums he made during the fifties and into the sixties are near-perfect forms of expression. For his albums Sinatra chose mostly older songs from the Great American Songbook and helped them achieve the level of standards that survive well into the 21st century. Of course, it is not just Sinatra but those he chose to work with him: the arrangers, the musicians, the engineers, and the producers. They all showed that Pop music, the songs and the performances of the songs, could be as artful as any other kind of music.

SINATRA'S EARLY PERIOD
1939–1952

Sinatra's work can be divided into three style periods. The early period takes him from his debut with Harry James's band until just before his famed comeback in 1953. During this time he was mostly a balladeer who made the bobbysoxers swoon to bent notes and long breathless phrasing.

I'LL BE SEEING YOU 1940
With the Tommy Dorsey Orchestra

I'll Be Seeing You was a big hit during WWII as the lyrics address the issue of separated loved ones. The arrangement is typical of the Swing Era with the vocal embedded within the fabric of the arrangement. Tommy Dorsey does a muted trombone solo in his seamless legato style before Sinatra enters with his vocal. Sinatra is tepid here compared to his later style but his direct personal approach to singing and his believability come through on this early record.

What to listen for:

1. How the vocal is only on the middle of the arrangement
2. The elaborate arrangement
3. Tommy Dorsey's seamless legato trombone solo
   Notice how long he plays before taking a breath
4. Sinatra's subtle but direct singing style
5. The sentimentality of the lyrics place in the context of WWII

I'LL BE SEEING YOU
Tommy Dorsey Orchestra

Frank Sinatra—Vocal
Tommy Dorsey—Muted Trombone
Sammy Fain—Composer
Irving Kahal—Lyricist

```
INTRO     A      C     Interlude   A B A C  Interlude  A        C
band————————————————|—————|vocal———|band—|—————————————
          | tbn solo  |                           |cl solo|
   8      16         8          32         8        8    |7
```

Figure 10.4: Frank Sinatra, 1947.
Copyright in the Public Domain.

SINATRA'S MIDDLE PERIOD
1953–1973

Sinatra essentially reinvented himself in 1953. Emboldened by his Academy Award and new record contract, he replaced the young fragile Frank with a mature brash Frank who clearly was in charge. The bobbysoxers had grown up with him and clearly liked what they saw and heard. Now known as the "Chairman of the Board," his new label, Capitol Records, let him call the shots and choose what he wanted to record and whom he wanted to record with, including arrangers, musicians, and others. Part of the reason for his decline was the inferior material he was forced to record with his former label, Columbia Records. Capitol took a chance on him, and with them, Sinatra recorded his greatest albums.

This is the period that Sinatra really begins to swing. Buoyed by his new collaborator, arranger, Nelson Riddle, Sinatra found the perfect complement to his new brash swinging style. Riddle knew exactly how to orchestrate and arrange for Sinatra in such a way that propelled the music without being overbearing. On the slower ballads, Riddle could capture the perfect mood and setting for Sinatra's poignant reading of tender sad love songs. During the fifties they pioneered the concept of a *concept album* by dividing the records into two general categories based on mood and lyrics: swinging happy love songs and slow, sad love songs. For the first time, songs were carefully chosen to match the theme and placed in a specific order on each side of the record. They thoughtfully considered which song should be first on side 1, which should be last on side 1, which should open the second side, etc. Sinatra was acutely aware that listening to recorded music in one's home was a very different experience from attending a live performance.

Figure 10.5: Frank Sinatra, 1960.

I'VE GOT YOU UNDER MY SKIN 1956

The most highly acclaimed of the Sinatra/Riddle swinging albums is **Songs for Swinging Lovers** and the highlight of that album is Cole Porter's **I've Got You Under My Skin**. This is generally regarded at their finest swinging recorded performance. This song is forever associated with Sinatra and he performed it in every live show. The arrangement is perhaps Riddle's finest and it is one that he hurriedly did as a last-minute addition to the album. Riddle took full advantage of the recording studio and often used instruments that were rarely used in the jazz/Pop worlds at that time, including flutes and bass clarinet.

This is an unusually long song that goes beyond the limits of a typical 32-measure Pop song form. It is 56 measures long in the form of A A^1 B C D.

The A sections are 16 measures and the other sections are 8 measures. The distinctive bass clarinet riff played during the intro to this cut sets the mood and adds buoyancy to the swinging underpinning. For the first chorus the bass plays in a "two feel," playing mostly on beats 1 and 3. After Sinatra sings the song through once, the band plays an interlude featuring superimposed trombone riffs that builds to a climax with an exciting trombone solo against the full orchestra beginning with the A^1 section. The bass now walks on all beats of the measure, adding to the intensity and build-up. The music calms down again as Sinatra reenters at the B section but builds tension again to another climax at the C section, which he sings with much more intensity than he did during the first chorus. He and the orchestra calm things down again at the end of the final D section. This is Sinatra at his best; he takes us on an emotional roller coaster ride as he tries in vain to resist his attraction for someone. The Sinatra/Riddle collaborations usually had the bass play with a two feel for the first chorus and walk all four beats during the second chorus of the swinging songs. This became standard procedure for many singers and instrumentalists; Miles Davis again comes to mind.

What to listen for:

1. The classic Nelson Riddle intro featuring a bass clarinet
2. The way Sinatra floats above the beat during the whole first chorus
3. The trombone riffs that crescendo during the interlude
4. The first climax when the trombone solo starts after the interlude
5. The way the music calms down again when Sinatra reenters
6. The way Sinatra builds the music back up for his climax at the start of the C section: "Don't you know little fool…"
7. The final calming down and release of the tension at the end
8. The overall pacing and ups and downs of Sinatra's performance along with the arrangement

I'VE GOT YOU UNDER MY SKIN

Frank Sinatra—Vocalist
Cole Porter—Composer
Nelson Riddle—Arranger

Intro	A	A¹	B	C	D
bs cl	vocal————————————————————————				
6	16	16	8	8	6

Interlude	A¹			B	C	D		Tag
band————	|tbn solo|	band		|vocal ——————————————————				
crescendo—	|climax |	riffs		| cresc	|climax————	|soft————		
12	|8	| 8		| 8	| 8	| 4	| 4	| 4

ONE FOR MY BABY 1958

Sinatra called this type of song a saloon song and this particular song the granddaddy of all saloon songs. These were sad songs about lost love. Sinatra made many albums of nothing but sad songs. He would never do that in a live performance but as mentioned earlier, he knew that someone perhaps alone at home might very well be in that kind of a mood. This cut comes from Sinatra's most acclaimed ballad album and his personal favorite, *Frank Sinatra Sings for Only the Lonely*, usually called *Only the Lonely*. Two of the great contributors to the Great American Songbook collaborated to write *One for My Baby*: composer Harold Arlen and lyricist Johnny Mercer. Again this is an unusually long song, 56 measures, in the form of A A¹ B A¹. There is a key change written into the song at the A¹ section that continues for the remainder of the song. Not only is this a saloon song, the settings is actually in a saloon; a man walks into a bar late at night and tells the bartender his sad tale of love.

Nelson Riddle subtly arranges the music that consists mostly of a solo piano recorded in the distance to give the ambiance of an empty bar late at night. Sinatra makes the listener the bartender and he assumes the role of one who had one too many in an effort to forget. Again he reaches a climax toward the very end that makes us believe that he is actually experiencing what he is singing: *This torch that I found, it's gotta be drowned or it soon might explode.*

What to listen for:

1. How the piano in the distance sets up the ambience of the scene
2. Sinatra's conversational way of singing to the bartender
3. Sinatra assuming the role of the tipsy lover
4. The key change at A¹
5. The effect of the strings and saxophone entering at the last A¹ section
6. Sinatra's emotional climax toward the end
7. The implication of walking away as his voice fades during the tag

ONE FOR MY BABY

Frank Sinatra—Vocal
Harold Arlen—Composer
Johnny Mercer—Lyricist
Nelson Riddle—Arranger
Bill Miller—Piano

Intro	A	A¹	B	A¹	Tag
piano	vocal with piano——————— strings + sax				fades
Eb:		G:			
4	16	16	8	16	6

SINATRA'S LATE PERIOD

As Pop music changed during the sixties with Rock and Soul dominating the charts, Sinatra retired briefly in 1971, feeling no longer relevant in that modern world but came back in 1973 and settled into a role of an elder statesman of the music of the great American Songbook. His voice had aged and declined in quality, but once again, as he reinvented himself, he sang with a more assertive declamatory manner. He focused more on live concerts than on recordings and continued to perform well past his prime till he was eighty years old. Although the voice was not what it once was, his phrasing and communication were still intact as they adjusted to his aging instrument.

VIDEOS of Frank Sinatra

I'VE GOT YOU UNDER MY SKIN 1970

Frank is older in this video but still is in full command of his voice and the song.

FLY ME TO THE MOON

This is a 1965 performance with the Count Basie Band. Frank's recording with the Basie Band was played by Apollo astronauts when they went to the moon.

ELLA FITZGERALD

The aptly named "First Lady of Song," Ella Fitzgerald (1917–1996) was born in Newport News, Virginia, and raised in Yonkers, New York. After winning a talent contest at the famous Apollo Theatre in New York City, she was hired by Swing bandleader, Chick Webb. Her recording of *A-Tisket, A-Tasket* with Webb was a huge hit in 1938. When Webb died in 1939, Ella took over leadership of the band and it was renamed Ella Fitzgerald and Her Famous Orchestra. In 1946 she signed with the famous manager and impresario Norman Grantz, who catapulted her career and turned her into an international star. Ella recorded extensively in both studio and live settings. Her Songbook series in the fifties of albums of songs by individual songwriters was highly acclaimed and serves as a recorded encyclopedia of the Great American Songbook. Her three albums with Louis Armstrong are among the best vocal jazz albums ever made. It is on her live albums, however, that Ella shines most when the audience inspires her performance. Like Sinatra, Ella did her best work during the fifties and sixties.

Ella possessed an amazing instrument in her voice, which is by most opinions the purest, most natural voice ever. Ella certainly made good on her natural talent and developed an original approach to singing that appealed to jazz and non-jazz listeners alike. She had an enormous range of three octaves that meant she could sing very high, very low, and everywhere in between. Unlike Billie Holiday and Frank Sinatra, Ella approached singing more like an instrumentalist: she was more interested in making interesting music than conveying the lyrics; in this regard she was more like Louis Armstrong. Also like Armstrong, she was a great scat singer; neither Holiday nor Sinatra scat sang. Ella's scat solos rank up there with some of the great instrumentalists' improvised solos. Her scat solos incorporate elements of the newer Bebop style as well as Swing and have served as models for all later scat singers. Ella's instrumental approach to singing does not mean she did not convey the meaning and emotion of a song's lyrics; especially on ballads, she could evoke tenderness, real feeling, and empathy with the words. Ella did not really sing Blues and like Sinatra and Holiday, the bulk of her songs came from the Great American Songbook. Having come along at the same time, Ella was often contrasted to Billie Holiday; Ella seemed sweet and innocent compared to Billie's traveled and weathered lifestyle.

A-TISKET, A-TASKET

Watch this 1942 clip of a young Ella singing her first hit in the movie *Ride 'Em Cowboy* with Abbott and Costello.

Figure 10.6: Ella Fitzgerald.

THEY CAN'T TAKE THAT AWAY FROM ME 1956

The album ***Ella and Louis*** is a jazz vocal classic. The contrast between Ella's pure natural voice and Louis's rough, gravelly voice is startling but the combination is magical. The whole album and its sequel ***Louis and Ella Again*** are relaxed, spontaneous, and swinging. With just rhythm section accompaniment, they both sing freely and creatively, unencumbered by arrangements. Ella always did her best singing in this format. ***They Can't Take That Away from Me***, written by George and Ira Gershwin, is one of the great standards and Ella and Louis give it one of its most memorable treatments. They both freely play with the melody, yet are clearly aware of lyrics. Louis also plays a trumpet solo that makes variations on the melody. The form of the song is AABA[1] Tag; the four-measure tag repeats the words of the title. Ella and Louis are ably supported by the Oscar Peterson Quartet.

What to listen for:

1. The relaxed but swinging accompaniment of the rhythm section
2. The purity and precise intonation of Ella's voice
3. Ella's effortless singing
4. The stark contrast of Louis's rough gravelly voice
5. Louis' playful singing on the words off key
6. Louis' trumpet solo entrance—classic Armstrong swinging of repeated notes
7. Ella's reentrance on the bridge of the last chorus—she drastically changes the melody of the original song
8. The playful ending on the tags

THEY CAN'T TAKE THAT AWAY FROM ME

Ella Fitzgerald—Vocal
Louis Armstrong—Vocal, Trumpet
Oscar Peterson—Piano
Herb Ellis—Guitar
Ray Brown—Bass
Buddy Rich—Drums

Intro
4

	8	8	8	8	4
	A	A	B	A^1	Tag
Chorus 1	Ella ———————————————————————————				
	trumpet fills like call and response				
	bass in 2———————————————————————				
	Key of Bb:				
Chorus 2	Louis ———————————————————————————				
	bass in 4				
	Key change to Eb:				
Chorus 3	tpt solo———————————| Ella + Louis———————————Extra tag				
	bass in 4———————————| in 2- | in 4—————— | in ———————				

ELLA AND FRANK MEDLEY

Watch this medley of songs from a 1967 TV show. Ella does a great scat solo on **Stompin' at the Savoy**. It is preceded by **The Song Is You** and **They Can't Take That Away from Me**.

Chapter Eleven

Transitional Figures

ART TATUM

Art Tatum (1909–1956) was born in Toledo, Ohio, and became one of the most astounding virtuosos of the twentieth century. He became the envy of not only jazz pianists but classical pianists as well. All the more remarkable, he was essentially blind with very limited vision in one eye. Some very good pianists refused to play in front of him and many simply gave up playing after hearing him. Many musicians could not believe what they heard on records was possible and had to witness his playing in person to believe it. The famous Russian classical pianist Vladimir Horowitz was in awe of Tatum and even tried to learn to play what Tatum played by transcribing some of his records to music notation. Charlie Parker, the great Bebop saxophone player, took a job as a dishwasher at a club that Tatum played in, just so he could listen to him every night. While Tatum's virtuosity was a great part of his appeal, his harmonic sense was unparalleled by anyone else during the 1930s. Although he was technically a Swing player coming out of the Stride tradition, his amazing technical and harmonic skills put him in a category by himself. He had a huge influence on the next generation of jazz musicians, the bebop players, by inspiring them to become as fluent on their instruments as possible and by setting precedents for further explorations of complex chords and chord progressions. As awesome as Tatum's records were, his best playing was done at informal settings, typically at late-evening private parties, etc. There are some bootlegged recordings that attest to this and back up these clams made by those that heard him in those settings. There are some who have criticized Tatum for being all flash with little substance. They claim he did not really improvise on the tunes he played but merely ornamented and decorated them with a lot of runs going up and down the keyboard. While it is true he stuck mostly within the framework of Pop standard songs, he used them more as a sculptor uses clay to mold original unpredictable objects of beauty.

Most Swing piano players played fast runs with their right hand. (See Teddy Wilson, p.114.) Tatum played runs with his right and left hand and sometimes with both at the same time. He fingered these runs not in the typical way and often using only three fingers—the thumb, index, and middle fingers.

Tatum used a variety of left-hand techniques, including basic striding, alternating bass notes and chords, Swing walking tenths, and Earl Hines–like random jabbing chords. His tenths were often filled in with one or two notes, creating a thick complex texture. While chording with both hands he often played very complex altered and extended chords.

For the most part the art of solo jazz piano died with Tatum in 1956. He took as far as it could go or at least as far as anyone until now can imagine it going. There are some isolated solo recordings, including some notable ones by Thelonious Monk and Bill Evans, but no major pianists have dedicated themselves so completely to the art of solo jazz piano. Keith Jarrett revised solo jazz piano somewhat during the 1970s but his approach was to play pure unprepared improvised music with no underlying tunes or structure rather than play on tunes as Tatum and others before him did.

Figure 11.1: Art Tatum.
Copyright in the Public Domain.

TEA FOR TWO

Tea For Two is a Pop standard written by Irving Caesar and Vincent Youmans. This, along with *Tiger Rag*, is one of the remarkable recordings Tatum made in 1933. Tatum dazzles with runs and reharmonizations in this amazing display of virtuosity. The form is ABAC; the B section is similar to A but in a different key. Tatum added many chords to the original song, often playing a new chord on every beat.

What to listen for:

1. The sureness and cleanness of Tatum's technique
2. The quick runs throughout
3. The almost constant reharmonization
4. The solid tempo and swing of the music despite the flourishes

---

TEA FOR TWO 1933

Art Tatum — Piano

Intro
4

0:06   A   B   A¹   C
Chorus 1   Head with some fills———————————————

0:53
Chorus 2   improvisation — many runs————————————

1:39
Chorus 3   more runs and new chords- reharmonization

2:24
Chorus 4   Head with variations and runs——————————

YESTERDAYS 1954

Watch this video of Tatum performing the Pop standard *Yesterdays*, written by Jerome Kern and Otto Harbach. Seeing is believing!

CHARLIE CHRISTIAN

Charlie Christian (1916–1942) is the first notable jazz musician to play the electric guitar. The instrument was new in 1939 and Christian popularized it in the jazz world when he famously played with the Benny Goodman Sextet. He grew up in Oklahoma City and was discovered by John Hammond who urged Goodman to hire him. While some were drawn to the novelty of the amplified guitar, it was his new advanced solo style that impressed jazz musicians. In many ways he is proto Bebop player.

Figure 11.2: Charlie Christian.
Copyright © Charlie Christian
Family Archives (CC BY-SA 3.0) at
http://commons.wikimedia.org/wiki/
File:Charlie_Christian.jpg

He approached soloing more like a saxophone player than earlier guitarist; using amplification made this possible and electric guitarists could now be heard as well as horn players. His lines were harmonically and rhythmically akin to those of the new generation of jazz players and he served as an influence on and inspiration to them. His melodies tended to emphasize the upper extensions of chords and his phrases were often uneven and unpredictable in length. These practices became common from the Bebop period on. It is instructive to compare his solos next to Goodman's on the same recordings; Goodman's solos are typical of the Swing style with mostly clear-cut even phrases of two and four bars, while Christian's sound much more modern.

Christian, unfortunately, died young from tuberculosis but left a lasting influence on jazz guitarists as well as other instrumentalists.

I'VE FOUND A NEW BABY 1941
Benny Goodman Sextet

Charlie Christian plays one of his classic solos on this recording with an all-star ensemble led by Benny Goodman. The other solos are true to the swing style but Christian played in a way that was new at the time but wouldn't be for long, as the Bebop players of the early forties soon emulated what Christian was doing.

What to listen for:

1. The relaxed Swing feel of the band
2. Goodman's Swing style varied interpretation of the head
3. Christian's newer style of soloing with extended chord tones and uneven phrase lengths
4. The typical way Basie solos—light and sparse
5. The trumpet and tenor sax swing style solos
6. The New Orleans style at the very end
7. The riffs behind the solos

I'VE FOUND A NEW BABY 1941
Benny Goodman Sextet

Benny Goodman—Clarinet
Charlie Christian—Electric Guitar
Cootie Williams—Trumpet
George Auld—Tenor Sax
Count Basie—Piano
Artie Bernstein—Bass
Jo Jones—Drums

		8	8	8	8
		A	A	B	A
Chorus 1	Clarinet- plays head with variations———————————				
	Band riff 1——————————|			|riff 1————
0:44					
Chorus 2	Guitar———————————————————				
1:22					
Chorus 3	Piano—————————————————————				
	Band riff 2————————————| C+R with cl | band riff				
1:58					
Chorus 4	Trumpet———————————| ten sax————————————				
	Band riff 3———————————|				
2:35					
Chorus 5	xxxxxxxxxxxxxxxxxxxxxxxx| Drums———| head————				
	Left out |band C+R | New Orleans style				

COLEMAN HAWKINS

Coleman Hawkins (1904–1969) is considered to be the Father of the Tenor Saxophone. He is the first great tenor player and one of the first great saxophone players in jazz history. The saxophone was relatively rare in early jazz and Hawkins helped to elevate it to an important jazz instrument. He was born in St. Joseph, Missouri, and studied music at Washburn College in Topeka, Kansas. His music training is evident in his schooled approach to harmony. He first came to public attention when he played in Fletcher Henderson's band from 1923 to 1934. He gradually developed from a stiffer Pre-Swing style to a smoother, swinging style as Henderson's band evolved Pre-Swing to Swing. In 1934 he moved to Europe and returned to New York in 1939 where he recorded his highly acclaimed version of *Body and Soul*. Hawkins' approach to improvisation was very influential on most tenor sax players. His was the *vertical* approach that relied on arpeggiating chords. In this way he is considered to be opposite of Lester Young who was a *horizontal* player. Hawkins was hot while Young was cool. Hawkins tended to climb up and down chord tones as he created his melodic lines. Greatly inspired by Art Tatum, he would play extended and altered chord tones as well as employ substitute chords and reharmonization. In these areas he served as a model for the next generation of Bebop players but his phrases and accents were regular and consistent with the more predictable Swing style. Young's phrases were supple and unpredictable and his melodies often were constructed around the chords rather than from the chords. A listener can usually discern the chords of a tune by listening just to what Hawkins played independent of any accompanying chords, whereas this would not be the case with Young. Both Hawkins' and Young's approach influenced younger players with some emulating one or the other, or some incorporating elements of both.

Figure 11.3: Coleman Hawkins.
Copyright in the Public Domain.

BODY AND SOUL 1939

After spending several years in Europe, Hawkins returned to the United States and tried to reclaim his status as the greatest tenor saxophonist. His recording of *Body and Soul* did just that in the ears of many. This is one of the most famous recordings in all of jazz history and Hawkins' solo is regarded as one of the greatest. We have already listened to the Benny Goodman Trio's 1935 recording of this song (see Chapter 7). In this recording, Hawkins climbs up and down the chords as they change and reharmonizes the song in ways that would become standard practice in the future. He barely even plays the melody of the song and chooses to improvise almost immediately with only briefly referring to rather than playing the head. This song was so well known at the time that playing the melody of the song was unnecessary. There is small back-up band that plays sustained chords during the second chorus. This recording was very influential on the Bebop players and was even a hit record. Singer Eddie Jefferson put words to this famous solo, a practice known as **vocalese**. The Manhattan Transfer has an excellent recording of it.

What to listen for:

1. Hawkins' hot sound with much vibrato
2. The vertical up and down direction of his lines
3. The sequencing of ideas at the beginning of the second chorus
4. The background horns during the second chorus
5. The climactic last A section when Hawkins' tone get courser, his notes get higher, and his volume increases

BODY AND SOUL
Coleman Hawkins and His Orchestra

Coleman Hawkins—Tenor Sax

Intro - Piano
  4

	8	8	8	8
	A	A	B	A

0:09
Chorus 1   Tenor sax———————————————————————————————
            Var of mel | improv———————————————————————

1:30
Chorus 2   Tenor sax continues————————————————————————
            Sequences ideas————| | climax
                                          louder, higher

            Horns in background———| | horns——————————

ROY ELDRIDGE

Trumpeter Roy Eldridge (1911–1989) was a transitional Swing player who evolved the art of jazz trumpet player from the New Orleans style of Louis Armstrong to the Bebop style of Dizzy Gillespie. Unlike most Swing trumpet players, he modeled his playing on saxophone players rather than on Louis Armstrong. He extended the range of the trumpet and played both higher and lower notes than Louis Armstrong. His use of altered chord tones led the way to the Bebop style (see Chapter 12). His unique style was characterized by sudden changes in register and a raspy tone. He was a featured soloist in Gene Krupa's band during the early forties.

WILLOW WEEP FOR ME 1957

Watch this film of Roy Eldridge playing the Pop standard *Willow Weep for Me*. Notice the raspy tone and extended range of his playing. He is accompanied by the Oscar Peterson Trio (see Chapter 16) with Oscar Peterson on piano, Ray Brown on bass, and Herb Ellis on electric guitar.

PART 3

What is usually thought of as modern jazz begins in the early forties with a revolution of sorts. Swing was mainstream jazz from the mid-thirties until the end of WWII and Swing was also Pop during this time. There was a small group of jazz musicians who thought that jazz was in a rut and that it had become too commercial. They attempted to redefine jazz as an art music, not as entertainment and not as dance music. The birthplace of this revolution was Minton's Playhouse in the Harlem section of New York City. Minton's was an afterhours club that featured all-night-long jam sessions. The handful of musicians who worked there in the house band and a few of those who sat in set out to change the direction of jazz and that is exactly what they did. They called it Bebop and Bebop spawned most of the new jazz of the forties and fifties. The new jazz was nearly as popular as Swing and most of those brought up on Swing music never took to Bebop.

The Bebop revolution was a conscious attempt to not only change jazz but to advance it in every way beyond the jazz that preceded it. That meant more complex melody, harmony, and rhythm. The emphasis was on improvisation and not written arrangements, so we see a return to smaller groups. Most Bebop musicians approached the music intellectually with theories of chords and harmony. Most of them tried to intimidate those whom they thought were inferior players without such theoretical knowledge.

By the fifties, Bebop settled into mainstream jazz and branched off into Cool Jazz and Hard Bop. These were natural evolutions of Bebop and emphasized different aspects of it. Cool Jazz formalized and intellectualized jazz and appealed in part to college audiences while Hard Bop emphasized the Black American roots of jazz by bringing in more Blues and Gospel music. Both Cool Jazz with its laid-back lyrical style and Hard Bop with is down-home earthy quality enjoyed more popularity than Classic Bebop and some of the greatest jazz and jazz musicians of all time occurred and played during the fifties.

Modern Jazz

Advances in recording technology greatly improved the jazz listening experience at home. Recordings were made on magnetic tape beginning in 1948, which meant editing and overdubbing were possible for the first time. First high fidelity and then stereo records became available by the late fifties. The LP, the long-playing record, was also new in the early fifties. This made jazz on records truer to a live jazz performance since recordings were no longer restricted by time constraints. Previously, records were limited to about four minutes per side; now, up to thirty minutes was possible and the musician could stretch out as they normally would in live performance. It is from this time that the history of jazz is told from its important albums, not isolated singles (see Chapter 10 for more on recording during the fifties). While Rock 'n' Roll was overtaking the Pop world, jazz albums, from ***Birth of the Cool*** to ***Kind of Blue***, were literally making jazz history.

Chapter Twelve

The Bebop Revolution—Dizzy Gillespie and Charlie Parker

I n many ways Bebop was an active revolution against the commercial aspects of Swing. It was started by a handful of players who sought to change the course of jazz by changing it from a popular dance music to a purely listenable art music. Bebop began to form around 1941 in the Harlem section of New York and blossomed during after-hours jam sessions at Minton's Playhouse and Monroe's Uptown House. A few musicians began to tire of Swing music and, inspired by the playing of Art Tatum, Charlie Christian, Coleman Hawkins, Lester Young, Roy Eldridge and others, sought to modernize jazz. The early Bebop players intellectualized the music with advanced ideas of harmony and rhythm. The jam sessions at Minton's spotlighted these innovations and the new generation felt an air of superiority about them. They often delighted in showing up those who they considered to be inferior or old-fashioned musicians by playing very fast tempos, and unusual keys and chords.

Many Swing musicians would play at Minton's after their regular gigs were finished and these jam sessions would go on into the early morning hours. The *Founding Fathers of Bebop* who played in the house band at Minton's or regularly sat in there included Dizzy Gillespie, Charlie Parker, Thelonious Monk, and Kenny Clarke. These players originally developed their new ideas on their own but soon discovered the others who had similar notions. The roots of Bebop were in the air during the Swing Era but the beboppers turned the exceptions into the rules of a new jazz language. Many Swing players adapted to and adopted the new harmonic language but none really were able to incorporate Bebop's rhythmic complexity.

The sound of the earliest Bebop is unknown since it was not recorded until 1945. A Musicians Union strike against the record companies lasted from 1942 to 1944 and virtually no new records were made during that time. New Swing records were still being released, however, from previously recorded unissued sessions. There are a few recordings made at Minton's Playhouse that have since surfaced and somewhat document the emerging new style. The first Bebop records were made in 1945 just as the swing Era was ending and thus Bebop seemed to have an abrupt beginning to those hearing it for the first time. Freed from the need to supply music for dancers, Bebop tunes, compared to Swing, were played faster for the up-tempo tunes and slower for the slower tunes. Fast or slow, Bebop was a virtuosic music that featured a lot of fast notes during fast or slow tempos. By the mid-forties, most bebop musicians had moved downtown to play at several clubs on 52nd Street, which became the main center for the new music.

Figure 12.1: Thelonious Monk, Howard McGhee, Roy Eldridge, and Teddy Hill in front of Minton's Playhouse in 1947.

BEBOP COMBOS

Bebop bands were smaller than Swing bands, composed of three to six players usually referred to as combos. The typical (Classic) Bebop combo consisted of five players, usually trumpet, saxophone, piano, bass, and drums. Noticeably absent is the guitar, which was deemed no longer necessary for reasons described below. The emphasis was on improvisation and a big band ensemble would only stifle the limit of the new players' creativity and flexibility. Big bands incorporating Bebop's innovation do emerge later but the new style was more suited to a return to smaller groups. The roles of the players changed from Swing and are described below.

RHYTHM SECTION

As before, the rhythm section supplies the chords and keeps the beat but the beat is played less emphatically and other rhythms are overlaid on it. Thus the rhythmic complexity of Bebop begins with the rhythm section and it is widely acknowledged that drummer Kenny Clarke was really the first Bebop player, since, as early as 1937, he functionally changed what drummers would typically play while accompanying the other musicians. The swing drummers kept the pulse going by playing every beat on the bass drum while playing the ride rhythm on the hi-hat as they opened and closed it on every other beat. Clarke no longer played the bass drum on every beat and transferred the main time-keeping role to the ride cymbal by playing the ride rhythm on it. With the other hand and bass drum, he was now free to randomly play whenever he felt like doing so and thus created other layers of rhythm over the basic pulse. The random accentuations were referred to as "dropping bombs" and became the standard way of playing jazz drums to this day. The drummer could now interact with the soloists rather than strictly keep time and this in turn allowed for a more fully integrated music with less structured instrumental role-playing. The piano finally sheds its Ragtime roots and no longer plays a bass note or chord on every beat but rather comps by playing random-like chords instead. Count Basie comped chords during the Swing Era but was virtually alone in doing so; in Bebop it became the norm and continues to this day. Much like the drummer's random-like accents, the random comping of chords adds new layers to the rhythmic complexity. The bass continues to play on every beat, keeping the pulse, but inspired by Jimmy Blanton and Walter Page, does so in a more aggressive way with more forward-moving step-wise lines.

HORNS

The typical Bebop combo is often referred to as the Classic Bebop Quintet and contains two horn players, usually trumpet and saxophone. As complex a music as Bebop was compared to Swing, it was simpler as far as arrangements were concerned. There really were no arrangements for the most part or essentially there was only one arrangement technique used for most tunes. Typically the horns play the head in unison (or octaves) then various instruments take solos before returning to the unison head. Occasionally the horns played in harmony but the heads were usually complex enough that no other parts were feasible or necessary. The focus of a Bebop performance was on the improvised solos and the heads were more or less just vehicles to set up and get to the solos.

HARMONY

The harmonic language of jazz grew more complex with each new style and Bebop musicians embraced the advances of Art Tatum, Lester Young, and Coleman Hawkins, and extended them into all facets of their playing. Melodies focused on the upper extensions of chords became the norm. Altered notes, especially the flatted fifth, became common, and superimposed or substitute chord changes and reharmonization became standard operating procedure. As with Art Tatum, these reharmonizations were either preplanned or improvised during performance. The harmonic palette was now virtually complete, comprising the full harmonic spectrum. Beboppers also preferred more complex chord progressions with quicker harmonic rhythm—changing chords more often. They challenged themselves by playing tunes that changed keys often and modulated to distantly related keys—keys whose scales have fewer notes in common.

MELODY/RHYTHM

Bebop melodies were usually angular with unexpected changes of direction and sudden cut-offs. Swing melodies tended to have smoother up and down contours. The accents with the melodic line were often unpredictable and varied. Accents could come on or in between any beat. This greatly contrasted to Swing's more even accentuation usually occurring on strong beats: beats 1 and 3. Phrase lengths varied greatly compared to Swing's even and predictable two and four measure groupings. In Bebop, a two-measure phrase could be followed with a three-measure phrase and then a two-and-a-half-measure phrase with a five-measure phrase, etc. Pairs of eighth notes were typically played more evenly than the long–short swing eighth notes of the Swing players. All of these rhythmic aspects, although anticipated by some during the Swing Era, were never fully applied by the Swing players during the Bebop Era.

The harmonic, melodic, and rhythmic differences between Swing and Bebop are demonstrated below by contrasting a segment of a Benny Goodman solo with one by Charlie Parker.

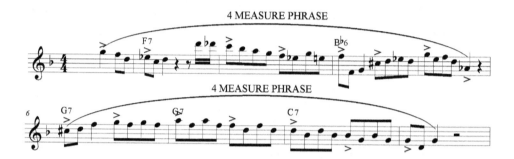

Figure 12.2: Typical Swing improvised melodic line—Benny Goodman

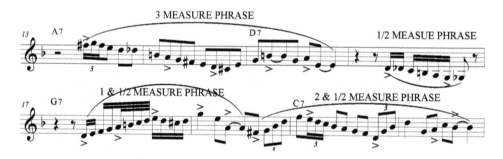

Figure 12.3: Typical Bebop improvised melodic line—Charlie Parker

BEBOP TUNES

The Bebop musicians generally played three types of tunes: Blues, Pop songs, and original tunes that were usually based on pre-existing Pop songs. The original melodies had all of the characteristics of Bebop improvisations. In fact, many were originally improvised lines that were later written out. The newly written Blues tunes tended to be through-composed, i.e., had a continuous melody with no repeats. The evolution of jazz Blues tunes went from the traditional AAB form to mostly AAA forms during the Swing Era, employing a single riff for the melody, to through-composed ABC forms during the Bebop period. Charlie Parker's **Billie's Bounce** is a good example of a Bebop Blues tune. The beboppers also frequently embellished the standard 12-bar chord changes with many added and substitute chords. Charlie Parker's **Blues for Alice** and **Au Privave** are good examples of this process. Pop songs have been a mainstay of the jazz repertoire from the beginning and Bebop musicians used many of the great Pop standards from the Great American Songbook as springboards for their improvisations.

Other than the Blues tunes, many of the Bebop newly written tunes were based on the forms and chord progressions of Pop songs. Basically, this means they took a song that had a chord progression they liked to improvise on, removed the melody, and wrote a new melody on the pre-existing chord progression of the song. In essence they "stole" the chord progression. There is nothing unethical about this practice since chord progressions cannot be copyrighted; as we have already seen, there are countless numbers of Blues songs using the exact same chord progression. This practice of "borrowing" a song's chords was not new in the Bebop Era but was more rampant then than in any other style period of jazz history. A favorite song to borrow chords from was George and Ira Gershwin's **I Got Rhythm**. It was used so much that musicians usually simply refer to the chord progression as "rhythm changes." The term is just a shortened way of saying "the chord changes to *I Got Rhythm*": the word "rhythm" having no reference to the element of music called *rhythm*. There are literally thousands of tunes based on rhythm changes, including Charlie Parker's and Dizzy Gillespie's **Anthropology** and **Shaw 'Nuff**, and several earlier tunes, including Duke Ellington's **Cotton Tale** and Lester Young's **Lester Leaps In**. As with the Blues tunes, there were many variants on the original chord progression. The practical aspect of writing new melodies on a pre-existing song's chord progression was copyrights did not have to be paid to the song's original writers.

DIZZY GILLESPIE

John Birks Gillespie (1917–1993) was born in Cheraw, South Carolina, and moved to Philadelphia as a teenager. He earned the nickname "Dizzy" for his mischievous personality and on-stage antics. In 1937 he replaced his idol, Roy Eldridge, in Teddy Hill's band and then played with Cab Calloway's band in 1939. He began sitting in at Minton's Playhouse in 1941 and it is there that he with a few others invented Bebop. In 1943 he played in Earl Hines' band along with Charlie Parker and in 1944 they both played in Billy Eckstein's band. Along the way Dizzy played with several other small groups and big bands. Dizzy used Roy Eldridge as a point of departure from which he learned to play higher and faster than anyone before him. He was able to play very fast notes that were previously thought to be possible only on reed instruments. He is the first Bebop music theorist who not only worked out new ides of harmony, melody, and rhythm but codified them as well. Although Bebop musicians were often thought to be aloof and standoffish to their audience, Dizzy put a more human face on Bebop and was able to entertain and well as impress his audience. Dizzy was, however, first and foremost, a serious musician who greatly advanced the jazz language and formed the modern jazz movement.

The name *bebop* came from a tune Dizzy wrote called ***Bebop***. "Bebop" or "rebop" were scat syllables the musicians used to sing the two-note cut-offs that typically ended their phrases. Along with being a great player, Dizzy also was an outstanding arranger/composer who wrote many of the jazz standards in the repertoire today. Dizzy Gillespie pioneered the concept of a Bebop Big Band in 1947 and although the band did not last long, he proved that such a thing was possible and big bands need not limit themselves to the Swing style. Also in 1947 he developed Afro-Cuban Jazz, which was a hybrid of Bebop and Afro-Cuban Latin music. He collaborated with Cuban conga drummer Chano Pozo to merge the two styles and left a lasting legacy of Latin Jazz that continues to this day. Dizzy continued to lead various bands remaining true to his Bebop style until his death in 1993.

Figure 12.4: Dizzy Gillespie with his famous bent trumpet.

Copyright in the Public Domain.

CHARLIE PARKER

Charlie Parker (1920–1955) grew up in Kansas City, Missouri, and became, perhaps, the most influential jazz musician of all time. He was one of the inventors of modern jazz and inspired a generation of jazz musicians during the forties and fifties. He was a troubled genius who became the personification of Bebop and the precarious lifestyle often associated with it. He came to be known as "Bird," which is short for "Yardbird," a name he purportedly received from musicians when he wanted to eat a chicken after a band car they were traveling in accidentally ran over it. The name stuck as it also symbolized his virtuosic soaring musical flights of fancy. By the time he was 17 years old he was addicted to heroin and drank heavily. His substance abuse led to his early death. He died while watching television alone at a friend's apartment. The local coroner estimated him to be a man in his mid-fifties, indicating the toll his lifestyle took on his not-quite-35-year-old body. When playing with Jay McShann's band, a Swing band from Kansas City, he decided to leave the band and settle in New York. He started sitting on at Monroe's Uptown House and then Minton's Playhouse, the birthplace of Bebop, in 1941. It was there he met up with Dizzy and Monk and discovered they were thinking alike. According to Dizzy, Bird was more rhythmically advanced than he was even though they were similar in their harmonic thinking. Parker was the most influential Bebop player in the areas of displaced phrasing and unpredictable accents and it is his rhythmic approach that is the most radical aspect of Bebop, in general. Essentially he thought at twice the speed of earlier jazz musicians; for Parker the eighth note was the point of departure, whereas for previous players the quarter note was. The implication here is Parker played many sixteenth note and even faster note values, depending on the tempo.

Parker had a sociopathic personality. He was loved by almost everybody but he often abused that love. His lifestyle led to his unreliability and he was often late for gigs and he often hocked his horn for drug money. But Charlie Parker got away with this behavior because not only was he such a great player but also people just liked him and liked being around him. He was equally at home participating in highly intellectual discussions as he was in hanging out with low-life junkies. The downside to Bird's influence was others were so enamored with his playing that they took to heroin, believing that was the secret to his astounding ability to play music. Many wanted to be like Bird but to his credit, he never encouraged anyone to be like him in that regard. In he his quoted as saying, "Any musician who says he is playing better either on tea, the needle, or when he is juiced, is a plain, straight liar. When I get too much to drink, I can't even finger well, let alone play decent ideas. ... You can miss the most important years of your life, the years of possible creation."

Figure 12.5: Charlie Parker.

SHAW 'NUFF 1945
Dizzy Gillespie All-Stars

This is one of the first recorded Bebop performances and features two of Bebop's inventors, Dizzy Gillespie and Charlie Parker. The listener is first struck by the very fast tempo and the even faster notes that are played by the soloists. This is Bebop at its raw early stage and the vitality and enthusiasm of the player clearly comes through on this recording. The tune, composed by Gillespie and Parker, is based on rhythm changes (the chord progression to *I Got Rhythm*) as many Bebop tunes were, and the head is played in unison and octaves, as was typical at the time. There is also an introduction and coda added to the head. Intros and codas were neither standard nor typical but were used from time to time. The horns even play in harmony during the middle of the intro when they enter, which also was not typical. The head typically sounds like a Bebop improvisation with convoluted shapes and chromatic notes. The soloists play in the typical Bebop style, as well, with all its unpredictability and uneven accents. The rhythm section also plays with random accents and *dropping bombs* from the drummer and random-like comping from the pianist, **Al Haig**. Haig was one of the first pianists playing in the new style.

What to listen for:

1. The unsettling rhythm played by the rhythm section during the first part of the intro
2. The horn entrance in harmony and the quick stops and starts that are typical of Bebop during the last section of the intro
3. The angular quick moving head played by the horns in unison
4. The characteristic Bebop solos by Parker, Gillespie, and Haig
5. The return to the unison head
6. The coda that is the same as the intro

SHAW 'NUFF

Dizzy Gillespie—Trumpet
Charlie Parker—Alto Sax
Al Haig—Piano
Curly Russell—Bass
Sid Catlett—Drums

INTRO	piano, bass, drums 2-measure pattern 8	tpt and sax in harmony 8	tpt and sax in unison 6	piano 2

	8 A	8 A	8 B	8 A
CHORUS 1	tpt and sax unison or octaves head———————			
CHORUS 2	sax solo———————			
CHORUS 3	trumpet solo——————— dramatic high note at start			
CHORUS 3	piano solo———————			
CHORUS 4	tpt and sax unison or octaves head——————— same as chorus 1			
CODA	piano, bass, drums 2-measure pattern same as Intro	tpt and sax in harmony	tpt and sax in unison	

KOKO 1945
Charlie Parker's Re-Boppers

Charlie Parker's solo on *Koko* is one of the most celebrated in jazz history. Like Armstrong's **West End Blues**, Beiderbecke's **Singing the Blues**, and Young's **Lester Leaps In** solos, musicians have learned this solo note for note from the record. There really is no tune or head for *Koko* but only a written intro and coda. The chord changes that Parker improvises on are from *Cherokee*, a tune written by Ray Noble and made famous during the Swing Era by Charlie Barnett's Band. *Cherokee* is a 64-measure-long tune, twice the usual length, and the B section of the AABA form was considered to be a real challenge to improvise on. Many players shied away from doing so, but Parker loved the challenge and played *Cherokee* often to display his prowess at improvisation. In *Koko* he dispenses with the melody of *Cherokee*, renamed it, and added an intro that also served as a coda. At this time a young Miles Davis was playing trumpet in Charlie Parker's band, but because the tune proved to be too difficult for him, Dizzy Gillespie plays both trumpet and piano on this cut. *Koko* should not be confused with Duke Ellington's **Ko-Ko**, which is an entirely different tune. The bass/drums rhythm section is probably the best of the early Bebop period: Curley Russell on bass and Max Roach on drums. Max Roach was the best of the Bebop drummers and they both appear together on many historic recording of the period.

What to listen for:

1. The written opening of the intro that leads to improvised trumpet and sax sections before going back to a written part
2. The sureness and assertiveness of Parker's playing during his solo
3. The ease that Parker plays with during the difficult B sections
4. The sequential pattern during the second B section
5. Max Roach's aggressive Bebop drumming and drum solo.

KOKO

Charlie Parker—Alto Sax
Dizzy Gillespie—Trumpet and Piano
Curley Russell—Bass
Max Roach—Drums

INTRO	tpt + sax (A) octaves drums (brushes)—	tpt solo improv	sax solo improv	tpt + sax (A¹) harm then octaves
	8	8	8	8
	16	16	16	16
	A	A	B	A
0:25	Chord changes to Cherokee————————			
CHORUS 1	sax solo————————————————————			
1:16				
CHORUS 2	sax solo cont.—————————————————			
2:06				
DRUM SOLO				
16				
2:35				
CODA	tpt + sax (A) octaves drums (brushes)—	tpt solo improv	sax solo improv	tpt + sax (A²) harm
	8	8	8	4

PARKER'S MOOD 1948
Charlie Parker All-Stars

Parker's Mood is an interesting mixture of traditional Blues and Bebop. Parker plays some down home kinds of Blues licks, but offsets them with very fast Bebop lines. The slow tempo of this 12-bar Blues form does not deter him from playing at lightning speed when he wants to. His uneven phrase lengths can clearly be heard during his solos as he soars like a *bird* on top of the music underneath him. He also plays a great variety of rhythms. Like **Koko**, there is really no tune here; just fanfare-like intro that is used also as the coda. Bird is backed up by an all-star rhythm section of John Lewis, Curly Russell, and Max Roach.

What to listen for:

1. The fanfare intro that really is the tune
2. The soulful Blues passages
3. The fast Bebop lines that are interspersed
4. John Lewis' simple but effective piano solo
5. Parker's emphatic reentry after the piano solo
6. The return of the fanfare for the coda

PARKER'S MOOD 1948

Charlie Parker—Alto Sax
John Lewis—Piano
Curly Russell—Bass
Max Roach—Drums

INTRO		Ch1	Ch 2	Ch 3	Ch 4	Coda	
sax - piano		sax———————|	piano——|	Sax——|	sax - piano	
2	4	12	12	12	12	2	2

HOT HOUSE 1952

Dizzy Gillespie –Trumpet
Sandy Block—Bass
Charlie Parker—Alto Sax
Charlie Smith—Drums
Dick Hyman—Piano

Watch this video from a TV show of Bird and Diz playing Dizzy's tune *Hot House*, which is based on Cole Porter's *What Is This Thing Called Love*. This is one of only a couple of known videos of Charlie Parker performing.

Chapter Thirteen

Bebop Pianists—Bud Powell and Thelonious Monk

I t is during the Bebop revolution that jazz piano finally sheds its Ragtime roots. With few exceptions, most notably, Count Basie, jazz pianists from the beginnings of jazz kept one foot in Ragtime by keeping the beat going in their left hands. By the 1940s jazz was well enough established that the beat no longer had to be pounded out by the entire rhythm section. Basie showed that by comping, the piano could add a new layer of rhythm that was flexible and unpredictable; this concept suited the beboppers well and it became the norm. With Bebop, the real revolution was rhythmic with rhythms and accents placed unpredictably within the flow of the music, making for a playing *with* the beat rather than *on* it. Just as the guitar's strumming chords on every beat was no longer necessary, so were the pianist's playing bass notes or chords unnecessary on every beat. Comping chords in a random-like manner begins in earnest with Bebop and continues to this day. But that is not all that changed with Bebop; the way they played chords also changed. Chord voicings (the way notes are positioned) were different as well. Thelonious Monk was the first Bebop pianist but as we shall see later, he never really played in a pure Bebop style. It was his student Bud Powell who serves as the model Bebop pianist.

BUD POWELL

Bud Powell (1924–1966), born and raised in Harlem, was a real prodigy and was playing professionally as a teenager. Thelonious Monk tutored him when he was quite young and he quickly made a name for himself in modern jazz circles. He was influenced by Art Tatum and could on occasion sound a lot like Tatum. It was Charlie Parker, however, who turned the young Powell toward Bebop and he set out to do on the piano what Parker did on the saxophone. In many ways Bud Powell was to the piano what Charlie Parker was to the alto saxophone. He was able to play extremely fast notes at fast tempos. Unfortunately, Powell suffered from mental problems that were apparently brought on by a police beating when he was twenty years old; he was in and out of mental hospitals the rest of his life. He was also unreliable because of his problems and apparently not well liked among musicians. Powell's influence, however, is enormous and all modern jazz pianists owe much to him.

SHELL VOICINGS

A **shell voicing** refers to a way of playing a chord without playing all the notes in that chord. This usually means the root and seventh, which would be the outer notes, thus the shell, but it also could be the root and third or sometimes the third and seventh. Although Thelonious monk is the pianist who pioneered the use of shell voicings, they are most associated with Bud Powell and sometimes referred to as "Bud Powell" voicings. The example below shows typical left-hand shell voicings.

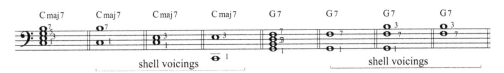

Figure 13.1

Shell voicings can be ambiguous and only imply chords rather than state them; this is desirable for Bebop players and leaves room for harmonic substitution in melodic lines. The sounds of these voicings are very different from the ones Swing pianists used and can be very dissonant.

Notice in the excerpt below how Powell comps in his left hand with shell voicings while play Bebop angular lines.

Figure 13.2

A NIGHT IN TUNISIA 1951
Bud Powell Trio

During the 1940s, Dizzy Gillespie explored the use of Afro-Cuban music in jazz. Written in 1942, *A Night in Tunisia* is one of his first ventures in combining Bebop with Latin music. Powell's version adheres to the usual format of playing the first six measures of the A section with a Latin feel and the second four measures of the A section in a "swing feel." (*Swing feel* here means the bass walking all four beats, typical of Bebop, not in a Swing Era style.) The solos are played with the swing feel throughout. The form of the tune is AABA, but there is an interlude that Dizzy wrote that is played only after the first head, which consists of a repeating riff with slight modifications. After the interlude there is a four-measure solo break that has served as a place for the first soloist to dazzle the listeners. Most solo breaks are two measures long, so this four-measure break gives the soloist more time to show off; there a several famous recorded breaks on this tune, including an amazing one by Charlie Parker. Powell does not disappoint on his solo break on this recording.

Like Charlie Parker, Powell frequently plays several short phrases separated with rests before unleashing a longer line with very rapid notes. The tensions created by the starts and stops are released by the longer lines. Once again the bass/drums combination of Curley Russell and Max Roach appear on this historic Bebop recording. For some reason they skip the A section at the end of the first solo chorus on this recording.

What to listen for:

1. The Latin groove during the intro
2. The changing from Latin to swing feels during the head
3. The riff-like interlude
4. Powell's very fast notes during his solo break
5. Powell's virtuosic playing during his solo
6. Roach's use of wire brushes and his interactive drumming throughout

A NIGHT IN TUNISIA

Bud Powell—Piano
Curley Russell—Bass
Max Roach—Drums

```
            4        4       4
Intro       Latin———————————————
            drums ——————————————
                      bass ——————————
                            piano ————————

            8            8           8          8
0:17        A            A           B          A
Chorus 1    head——————————————————————————————————————
            Latin  swing  | Lat    sw|—————————| Lat      sw
               6      2      6     2  8            6        2

0:50        12                      |   4
Interlude ——————————————————————————| break –piano

            8            8           8          8
            A            A           B          A
1:24
Chorus 2    piano improvisation———————————————| xxxxxxxxx
            swing feel——————————————————————   left out
1:57
Chorus 3    piano continues—————————————————————————————

2:43
Chorus 4    piano continues—————————————————————————————
            refers to head | improvises ————————————————
3:30
Chorus 5    piano—variation on head   | xxxxxxxxxxxxxxxxxxxxxx

3:52
Cadenza     piano
```

ANTHROPOLOGY
1962 VIDEO

Bud Powell—Piano
Neil-Henning Orsted Pedersen—Bass
Jorn Elniff—Drums

Watch this video from Copenhagen, 1962 of the "Amazing Bud Powell," as he was often called. As several other jazz musicians did during the late fifties and early sixties, Bud Powell lived and worked in Europe. In Europe they were better paid and more appreciated as artists. This clip shows Powell in top form with Danish musicians Neil-Henning Orsted Pedersen on bass and Jorn Elniff on drums. ***Anthropology*** is a classic Bebop tune written by Charlie Parker and Dizzy Gillespie based on rhythm changes. Powell plays the head in octaves with two hands.

THELONIOUS MONK

Although he was one of the inventors of Bebop, Thelonious Sphere Monk (1917–1982), veered off into his own unique direction that makes him really hard to classify as a musician and composer. Even though his personal playing style is far removed Bud Powell's, he essentially played with Bebop musicians and his music is usually classified as Bebop. He was born in Rocky Mount, North Carolina, and raised in New York City. In the early forties, as a member of the house band at Minton's Playhouse, he got together with Dizzy Gillespie to work out harmonic, melodic, and rhythmic ideas that gave birth to Bebop. Like Bud Powell, Monk suffered from some mental problems throughout his life. Monk was not widely known outside of jazz circles until he appeared on the cover of *Time* magazine in 1964; from then on he was in demand all over the world and became an intentional jazz star, something he was never really comfortable with, being a very shy person.

Monk is the **third great composer in jazz history**, chronologically, after Jelly Roll Morton and Duke Ellington. Unlike Morton and Ellington Monk was not really an arranger as most of his output was with small groups. His playing and his composing are similar and both are extremely unorthodox. He is truly one of the most original and unique musicians of the 20th century.

MONK'S PIANO PLAYING

Other than Monk, no one sounds like Monk. Even though he pioneered the use of shell voicings, he developed a unique way of playing chords and striking the keys on a piano that distinguish him from all other pianists. His chords can be extremely dissonant and they may sound to some like wrong notes at times, but Monk knew exactly what he was doing. He struck the keys with such a percussive attack that some criticized him for banging on the piano, but Monk's ears were so sensitive he did this purposefully to coax higher overtones from the strings. He playing in general was lean and spare with lots of space between notes that came in odd unexpected places. He did not play a lot of fast notes like Bud Powell but was able to get maximum effect from the notes and chords he did play. Some criticized Monk for his lack of technique because he did not play many notes, but his technique was subtler than that; he could, for instance, play a seven note chord and control the individual volume of each note. This is mainly why no one else sounds like Monk. The term classical pianists use for this is *voicing a chord*, meaning playing each note at different dynamic levels, which is different from the way jazz pianists use the term to mean positioning notes of a chord. Voicing a chord in the Classical sense of the term is extremely difficult to do and Monk did it so well that only he could make chords sound the way they did when he played them.

Another subtle aspect of Monk's technique was his seeming ability to bend notes on the piano. One cannot really bend notes on the piano, of course, but Monk gave the illusion of notes actually bending. He did this by crushing notes a half-step apart together then gradually releasing one of them. His timing was just right and the listener could almost swear that the notes were bending.

Monk also liked to play **whole-tone scales**, often for no apparent reason other than he just liked them. A whole-tone scale is a scale that is composed of all whole steps, unlike diatonic scales that include major and minor scales that are composed of whole steps and half steps. He usually played these as descending scales and often at the end of a tune, but also in the middle of a solo.

Monk did not always accompany in the standard way, which from Bebop on was to comp chords behind a soloist. He did that sometimes but also might play counter-melodies, random-sounding notes, or nothing at all by laying out completely. He often stood up and did a little dance when he laid out during another solo.

Monk did not really swing in the conventional sense; his rhythms were not part of the swing lexicon, but the music around him always swung. Monk juxtaposed his oddly placed notes and chords onto a swinging underpinning and made it work extremely well.

MONK'S COMPOSITIONS

Monk' s tunes are as unique as his playing. They are true compositions rather than tunes, in the sense that they contain inner relationships and a unity that are found in the most well-crafted Classical compositions, and unlike most Classical compositions, Monk does this within the confines of a 12-bar Blues or a 32-measure Pop song form. Most of Monk's tunes contain just one or two ideas and like, let's say Beethoven, he gets the most mileage from them. When working with two ideas, he usually ingeniously combines them at some point in the tune. Some tunes serve more as abstract structures than tunes in the conventional sense of the term. Monk's melodies and harmonies are as quirky as his piano playing, and melody and harmony are so intricately bound together that it is virtually impossible to improvise on a Monk tune unless you know both—on most other tunes one can get by knowing one or the other. His chord progressions are unorthodox and difficult to make sense of without the melody.

MISTERIOSO 1948
Thelonious Monk Quartet

Misterioso is one of Monk's many tunes based on a 12-bar Blues form. It is based on a single idea of "walking sixths." He takes the interval of a sixth and walks it up and down on each chord change. It is more of an abstract structure than a tune since the process and rhythm, a constant stream of eighth notes, never changes.

Figure 13.3

Copyright in the Public Domain.

The process continues this way through the 12-bar form. Milt Jackson plays vibraphones on this recording. He is considered to be the best Bebop vibraphonist and went on in the fifties to play with the famous Modern Jazz Quartet. The contrast of styles is obvious between Jackson's and Monk's solos. Jackson plays in a typical Bebop manner but Monk plays like Monk. Monk, during his solo, plays around with a few different ideas that have subtle connections to the theme, including playing upward arpeggios (broken chords) as extensions of the original broken sixth idea. He also bends notes and interjects whole-tone scales. During Jackson's solo, Monk does not comp but rather plays broken sevenths as an extension of the broken sixths idea of the theme. He also bends the sevenths. For the last chorus while Jackson plays the head, Monk plays broken intervals in a seemingly random manner that develops the broken sevenths idea he played during Jackson's solo.

What to listen for:

1. Monk's percussive attack during the intro
2. The theme made from walking broken sixths
3. Jackson's Bebop style solo
4. Monk's playing of broken sevenths during vibes solo
5. Monk's unorthodox solo with silences breaking up the continuity
6. Monk bending notes and playing whole-tone scales
7. Monk's random-like broken intervals during last head

MISTERIOSO

Thelonious Monk—Piano
Milt Jackson—Vibraphones
John Simmons—Bass
Shadow Wilson—Drums

Intro
4

Chorus 1	head—walking broken 6ths vibes and piano
Chorus 2	vibes solo—bebop style Monk plays broken sevenths to accompany
Chorus 3	piano solo bends notes, whole-tone scales
Chorus 4	piano solo continues upward arpeggios (broken chords) whole-tone scales, bends notes
Chords 5	head—vibes Piano plays broken intervals in background

BLUE MONK
1957 VIDEO

Thelonious Monk—Piano
Ahmed Abdul-Malik—Bass
Osie Johnson—Drums

Watch this video of another Monk Blues tune; this one is based on two ideas. This clip is from the now-famous TV show, **The Sound of Jazz**. Monk plays with a trio here and an apparently amused Count Basie looks on, sitting in front of the piano. Monk is as much fun to watch as to listen to and you can clearly see his unorthodox piano technique (everything your piano teacher told you not to do) as well as his fancy footwork.

Chapter Fourteen

Cool Jazz

Bebop evolved into two main branches during the 1950s: Cool Jazz and Hard Bop. Unlike the transition from Swing to Bebop, neither of the new trends was revolutionary but rather evolutionary. Cool and Hard Bop took certain elements of Bebop and refined or extended them into a more modern fifties jazz. Cool Jazz came first during the late forties and in many ways Hard Bop was a reaction against Cool jazz. Cool Jazz emphasized a lighter, more subtle, more laid-back approach than Classic Bebop. The primary model was Lester Young who became known as the "Father of the Cool." Bix Beiderbecke might then be called "Grandfather of the Cool." Whereas Lester and Bix were relatively rare cool players in an otherwise hot world of jazz, the fifties formed an entire Cool school of jazz musicians.

Much of Cool Jazz has its origins in Claude Thornhill's band of the mid-forties. This band consciously sought to give a new sound to big band jazz. Some called it *Impressionistic* since it had similarities to the music of French Impressionist composers Claude Debussy and Maurice Ravel. Like Ellington, the band endeavored to broaden the tone color palette of jazz but did so by using new instruments, voicings, and textures. The instruments and arrangements favored the middle to low end of the pitch spectrum. Virtually new to jazz was the use of flutes, French horns, and tubas, which was used here as a low melody instrument, not a bass instrument as it was in early jazz. They also embraced Bebop and played several Charlie Parker tunes and had soloists playing in the Bebop style. Several musicians and arrangers in Thornhill's band went on to become major players in the Cool Jazz movement; they include Gil Evans, Gerry Mulligan, and Lee Konitz. Gil Evans, a Canadian arranger, had a unique arranging and orchestration concept that would set Cool in motion and keep it viable for years to come.

Lennie Tristano, (1919–1978) a pianist from Chicago who was blind, developed an alternative approach to Bebop that would also become influential on the Cool movement. He took bebop, intellectualized it, and formalized some of its rhythmic practices, turning them into more conscious subdivisions and metric superimpositions on the basic four-beat meter. His tunes were melodically, rhythmically, and harmonically complex and his approach never became accepted by mainstream jazz musicians. He performed and recorded rarely but had an influence as a teacher. The whole concept of jazz education was something new and many thought jazz could be learned but not taught. Jazz education has grown over the years from this time and has become an accepted discipline in schools around the world. Tristano's work is most reflected in the playing of some of his famous students, most notably alto saxophonist Lee Konitz, but also tenor saxophonist Warne Marsh, and guitarist Billy Bauer.

Figure 14.1: Lennie Tristano, 1947.

CHARACTERISTICS OF COOL JAZZ

In general, when compared to Classic Bebop, Cool jazz is subtler, softer, more intellectual, more detached, more laid back, less emotional, and less intense. It is characterized by a dry sound with little or no vibrato and lyrical, tuneful, more singable improvised melodies. They tend to favor the middle to lower registers of their horns. More arrangements were used than in Classic Bebop and also polyphony, usually referred to as **counterpoint**, was occasionally employed as part of an arrangement of improvisation between or among players. Rhythm sections tend to be more neutral and less interactive than in Classic Bebop or Hard Bop. Drummers used brushes more to go along with the lighter approach and while they still dropped bombs, they did so less often and pianists generally comped but usually less prominently. Elements of Classical music were sometimes incorporated into Cool Jazz as jazz was moving away from being a dance music to a more pure listening art form.

BIRTH OF THE COOL

Birth of the Cool is an album of collected recordings done by the Miles Davis Nonet that was issued in 1957, long after the individual recordings were made. The original recordings were made between 1949 and 1950 and some were released as singles. The album is aptly named as the original records were among the first in the new Cool style and many of the young players on the recordings went on to become major players of the Cool School. The initial idea for the Miles Davis Nonet was to continue with a smaller group some of what Claude Thornhill's band started a few years earlier. The project began as informal gatherings in 1947 at Gil Evans' apartment in New York. Evans had arranged for Thornhill and the gathering included former Thornhill musicians Gerry Mulligan and Lee Konitz. Miles Davis, John Lewis, and John Carisi also joined the group. As with Thornhill's band, the focus was on a new sound. Although these young players were coming from Bebop, they desired a more laid-back, less frantic kind of Bebop.

Miles Davis (1926–1991) was a trumpet player who had played with Charlie Parker since 1945 and assumed leadership of this group by default. He had the only recognizable name and assumed responsibility for organizing rehearsals, gigs (not many), and eventually a record deal. Miles, who had been playing in Dizzy Gillespie's shadow, was evolving his own understated style that relied on fewer notes and focused on the middle to low range of the horn. The *Birth of the Cool* sessions were predicated on these premises and this nonet is the first of many important Miles Davis bands.

Unlike a big band, the size and instrumentation of the band were unique: trumpet, trombone, French horn, tuba, alto and tenor saxophones, and three rhythm section instruments: piano, bass, and drums. Each instrument has a unique tone color and there were no homogeneous sections. This was not a big band but it was not a combo either, being somewhere in between.

The arrangements were not like Swing band arrangements; there were generally no riffs or call and response, back and forth among sections. The solos were often embedded into the fabric of the arrangement—sometimes they emerge or end in the middle of a phrase. A common arranging device was stating the melody in parallel block chords. These are thick five- or six-part chords that underscore the main melodic line where all notes move in the same direction. The tuba, however, often moves in contrary motion by going in the opposite direction of the others. Simultaneous melodic lines (polyphony or *Counterpoint*) were also explored. The key players on the recordings are Miles Davis, trumpet; Gerry Mulligan, baritone sax; Lee Konitz, alto sax; John Lewis, piano; and Kenny Clarke and Max Roach on drums. The arrangers are Gerry Mulligan, Gil Evans, John Carisi, John Lewis, and Miles Davis.

BOPLICITY 1949
BIRTH OF THE COOL
Miles Davis Nonet

Boplicity, from *The Birth of the Cool* sessions, was written by Miles Davis and Gil Evans, and arranged by Gil Evans. The sound and feel of the music is ultra cool and this cut is a good representative of the early Cool mindset. Solos are dovetailed into the written parts and all are very laid back and economical compared to Classic Bebop solos. Gerry Mulligan on baritone saxophone, Miles Davis on trumpet, and John Lewis on piano take solos on this track. The arrangement features mostly parallel block chords with a trumpet lead; the tuba sometimes plays in contrary motion. The tune is in a standard AABA form but the arrangement veers from this during the second chorus. The rhythms of the head melody are very varied, more so than typical Swing or Bebop melodies. This most likely comes from Lennie Tristano's influence.

What to listen for:

1. The overall unique sound of the band and how it differs from Bebop and Sing bands
2. The overall laid-back, cool feeling of the music
3. Gerry Mulligan's very laid-back solo
4. Miles Davis' cool sound and economical solos
5. John Lewis's sparse light solo
6. The parallel voicings of the melody

BOPLICITY

Miles Davis —Trumpet
J. J. Johnson—Trombone
Lee Konitz—Alto Sax
Gerry Mulligan—Baritone Sax
Sandy Siegelstein—French Horn

Bill Barber—Tuba
John Lewis —Piano
Nelson Boyd—Bass
Kenny Clarke—Drums

	8	8	8	8
	A	A	B	A
Chorus 1	head————————————————————
	mostly parallel block chords

	8	8	10	8
0:57	A	A	B¹	A¹
Chorus 2	Bar sax solo————————band————
			Tpt—	

	8	8	8	8
1:58	A	A	B	A
Chorus 3	tpt————————————	piano————	band
	band————————		head

WEST COAST JAZZ

Several Cool Jazz musicians settled in California during the early fifties and a sub-category of Cool Jazz emerged known as West Coast Jazz. The terms *Cool* and *West Coast* are often erroneously taken to be synonymous. Not all Cool Jazz is West Coast Jazz although much of it is. The laid-back quality of the music is considered to be indicative of the laid-back Southern California lifestyle and the term *West Coast* was used to set the music apart from the more hectic New York Bebop and lifestyle. West Coast Jazz focuses on pure melody, even at the expense of the accompanying rhythm section, which functions more or less as a blank canvas upon which to paint pastel-like melodic lines. Many West Coast Jazz musicians found good-paying day gigs playing for Hollywood film scores and commercial records that in turn freed them up for less lucrative but more artistically satisfying jazz gigs at night. Some West Coast musicians like Gerry Mulligan and Shorty Rogers formed mid-sized *Birth of the Cool* type bands from time to time as well as smaller groups and Big Bands. Much West Coast Jazz was used in film scores during the fifties and film composer Henry Mancini famously scored the television series *Peter Gunn* using this style exclusively while using many major West Coast players. Famous West Coast players include Gerry Mulligan Chet Baker, Shorty Rogers, Shelly Mann, Chico Hamilton, Bud Shank, Lou Levy, Stan Levy, Conte Candoli, and Dave Pell.

GERRY MULLIGAN
THE PIANOLESS QUARTET

Gerry Mulligan (1927–1996) was born in New York and is one of the founders of Cool and West Coast Jazz. He is the most well-known baritone saxophone player in jazz history and among only a handful of major baritone soloists. He was playing in and arranging for Claude Thornhill's band when he was just 19 years old and was a key soloist and the chief arranger for the *Birth of the Cool* sessions. He led groups of various sizes throughout his career as well as collaborated on records with some of the most legendary players in jazz history. Mulligan is a major contributor to jazz as a player, bandleader, composer, and arranger. His tuneful, lyrical improvisations are among the best in all of jazz and the epitome of Cool.

In 1951, when he moved from New York to Los Angeles, he essentially started the West Coast sound, which was derived from his work on *Birth of the Cool*. In 1952 he formed a quartet that became known as the "Pianoless Quartet" because the rhythm section consisted of only bass and drums. The absence of a piano or a guitar or any instrument to supply chords was virtually unheard of at this time. The absence of audible chords forces the players as well as the listeners to focus on the **contrapuntal** relationship between the melodies and the bass lines. It also adds to the dryness of the sound and challenges the players and listeners to play on and "hear" the chords even though they are not audibly present. The music is still based on chords and chord progressions but no instruments are playing them. They can only be implied and inferred by the melodic and bass lines played. In the original Pianoless Quartet was Mulligan on baritone saxophone, Chet Baker on trumpet, Red Mitchell on bass, and Chico Hamilton on drums. In lieu of a chord instrument, Mulligan and Baker often played countermelodies or suggested the harmonies by playing slow-moving accompanying notes derived from the chords. The group had a couple of minor hits with *My Funny Valentine* and *Moonlight in Vermont*.

CHET BAKER

Chet Baker (1929–1986), born in Yale, Oklahoma, gained attention when he played trumpet with Charlie Parker in 1946 and again in 1951. He became a key member of the Gerry Mulligan Pianoless Quartet in 1952. He had a notorious drug habit and was arrested several times in the U.S. and Europe. He became somewhat of a matinee idol and his looks were compared to the actor James Dean. His trumpet playing was similar to that of the young Miles Davis but was even cooler and more detached, almost fragile. His playing was very lyrical and vocal-like. Baker also sang and his singing was similar to his trumpet playing. He was similar to Louis Armstrong in that regard, although their styles were quite different, and like Armstrong, he was also a great scat singer. He is probably more remembered as a singer today and has enjoyed resurgence in popularity in recent years. His mysterious death was ruled accidental; he was found dead apparently having fallen from a second-floor hotel room. Baker's struggles with heroin and cocaine put his career on hold many times and his great promise, as a young player, was never fully realized.

Figure 14.2: Chet Baker, 1983.

LEE KONITZ (b. 1927)

Alto saxophonist Lee Konitz (b. 1927) was born in Chicago and became one of the leading players of the Cool School. He studied with Lennie Tristano and became his most famous student. He played with Claude Thornhill's Band in the forties and was a key player on the ***Birth of the Cool*** sessions. He was considered to be the most viable alternative to Charlie Parker during the fifties and while he was certainly influenced by Parker to some extent, he developed his own style based on Tristano's ideas of rhythm and melody. He often superimposes uneven and unpredictable meters on the existing meter, creating shifting metric units that go against the grain of the tune. For example, while the rhythm section keeps the pulse, 1234, 1234, etc., Konitz might be playing as if the meter were 123,123,12,123,12, etc. He was as agile and quick as Parker but his lines tended to be longer and straighter. His tone was lighter and dryer and typical of cool playing in general. In later years Konitz's playing became less slick and more abstract. He developed a way to improvise while trying to discover the "essence" of each tune he played. He has played and recorded with many great jazz artists over the years in various combinations, including some novel duets with virtually every instrument.

Figure 14.3: Lee Konitz, 2012.

I CAN'T BELIEVE THAT YOU'RE IN LOVE WITH ME
LEE KONITZ PLAYS WITH GERRY MULLIGAN QUARTET 1953
Gerry Mulligan Quartet plus Lee Konitz

I Can't Believe That You're in Love with Me is a Pop standard written by Clarence Gaskill and Jimmy McHugh. Lee Konitz joined the Pianoless Quartet to make this classic Cool Jazz album. Mulligan and Baker play in their typical lyrical, cool style while Konitz is much more abstract and angular. Notice how singable Mulligan and Baker's solos are compared to Konitz's solos. Lee Konitz displays his Lennie Tristano influence by superimposing cross-meters on the existing four-four meter; in essence he keeps shifting the bar lines around so that his phrases seem to be composed of changing meters. While listening to Mulligan and Baker play, it is easy to hear why they were so popular. Their lines are clear, simple, and above all they swing. The absence of a piano or guitar brings out the contrapuntal lines between the soloists and the bass and lets the listener focus on walking bass lines in general. The horns play the head polyphonically; this is obviously arranged and not collective improvisation à la New Orleans style.

What to listen for:

1. The drummer playing with wire brushes during the intro and throughout
2. The 3-way polyphony during the head with the trumpet playing the main melody
3. Mulligan's lyrical solo
4. Baker's lyrical solo
5. Konitz's more angular solo with cross-rhythm effects of changing meters
6. The bass solo during the bridge of the last chorus head

I CAN'T BELIEVE
THAT YOU'RE IN LOVE WITH ME

Gerry Mulligan—Baritone Sax
Chet Baker—Trumpet
Lee Konitz—Alto Sax
Joe Mondragon—Bass
Larry Bunker—Drums

INTRO - Bass and Drums
   4

	8	8	8	8
	A	A	B	A
CHORUS 1	3-way Polyphony (arranged) - trumpet-main melody			
				bar sax break
				2
CHORUS 2	Baritone Sax Solo (Mulligan)———————			
CHORUS 3	Trumpet Solo (Baker)———————			
CHORUS 4	Alto Sax Solo (Konitz)———————			
CHORUS 5	3-way Polyphony (arr)——————| Bass + drums	| Horns continue		

VIDEOS

AS CATCH CAN

Gerry Mulligan Quartet in Rome 1959
With Art Farmer—Trumpet, Bill Crow—Bass, Dave Bailey—Drums

MY FUNNY VALENTINE

Chet Baker in Torino, Italy 1959
Lars Gullin—Baritone sax, Glauco Masetti—Alto Sax, Romano Mussolini—Piano,
Franco Cerri—Bass, Jimmy Pratt—Drums

SUBCONSCIOUS-LEE

From *The Subject Is Jazz* TV Show 1957
Lee Konitz—Alto Sax, Warne Marsh—Tenor Sax, Eddie Safranski—Bass,
Ed Thigpen—Drums

DAVE BRUBECK QUARTET

Dave Brubeck (1920–2012) was born in Concord, California, and his quartet became the most popular jazz group of the 1950s and for much of the sixties. With popular success, however, came much critical disdain, perhaps jealousy, from other jazz musicians. He is erroneously called a Classical pianist who started playing jazz. Brubeck was never a classical pianist but did study classical composition with French composer Darius Milhaud and briefly with famed Austrian composer Arnold Schoenberg. He led an octet in the late forties that experimented with harmonies, orchestrations, and textures similar to and even predating the Miles Davis Nonet on **Birth of the Cool**. In 1951 he formed a quartet featuring alto saxophonist Paul Desmond, which began playing on college campuses and soon was selling records of some of these live concerts. The Dave Brubeck Quartet's popularity soon spread so much that in 1954 he appeared on the cover of *Time* magazine—only the second jazz musician, after Louis Armstrong in 1949, to do so.

Brubeck and Desmond were perfect foils—Desmond played gently and lyrically, Brubeck was often heavy handed and rhythmic. The contrast proved to be part of the appeal of the group and each solo took on a different mood, much like contrasting themes or movements in a symphony. The two often engaged in improvised counter-point. Their repertoire consisted of Pop standards and original tunes mostly written by Brubeck. With the addition of Joe Morello on drums in 1956, the group began to explore more rhythmic possibilities and different meters. Virtually all jazz had been played four-four time or quadruple meter with four beats in a measure or bar. A notable exception was *Jitterbug Waltz* by Fats Waller. Brubeck and a few others, including Max Roach, began to explore the use of triple meter, the so-called jazz waltz, in the mid-fifties. But Brubeck, under the influence of Morello, also started experimenting with other meters using groupings of five, seven, nine, etc. In 1959 they recorded **Time Out**, the first album dedicated to these unusual meters, and what seemed to be a risky endeavor proved to be immensely popular. The album soon sold over a million copies and *Take Five* from the album, written by Paul Desmond, became a top-forty hit. In the ensuing years, jazz waltzes have become commonplace and other meters, although much rarer, are no longer considered off-limits or unplayable. Although the quartet originated out of California and is often considered a West Coast group, their music was unique to themselves and not emblematic of West Coast Jazz.

BRUBECK'S PIANO PLAYING

The contrast between Brubeck and Desmond's styles is reflected in Brubeck's own piano playing. He tended to play either long passages in single notes with little or

no left-hand accompaniment, or passages using thick, complex block chords in repetitive or quasi-repetitive cross-rhythms. His chords and melodies were often polytonal and polymetric and did not swing in the traditional way, and although he was often criticized for not swinging, his fans loved his forays into new time dimensions, and his climactic, fortissimo rhythmic iterations. In his solos, Brubeck clearly developed ideas that casual jazz fans could understand and follow despite his lack of Swing or Bebop clichés or mannerisms. After the Quartet broke up in 1967, Brubeck continued to perform with various players, including his sons, and composed large and small works for various size ensembles and choruses.

Figure 14.4: Dave Brubeck, 1954.

PAUL DESMOND

While critics often panned Brubeck, his alto saxophonist, Paul Desmond, (1924–1977)

was almost universally admired. His solos were always lyrical and imaginative, yet logical and full of surprises. At times he seemed to exhaust all possibilities of a single idea by continually finding new ways to vary it. He often seemed to play duets with himself by changing registers in a Call and Response–like patter. He sound was light, unique, and immediately identifiable; a sound Desmond, himself, likened to a dry martini. He favored the high (altissimo) register of the horn and played at a slower pace than Lee Konitz and Charlie Parker. Although stylistically very different, like Brubeck, his playing showed little influence of Swing or Bebop and his ideas were easy for the casual jazz listener to follow. Although he was miles apart from him in approach, sound, and style, Charlie Parker's favorite alto sax player was Paul Desmond. Desmond even interviewed Parker on a radio show.

Figure 14.5: Paul Desmond, 1954.

TAKE FIVE 1963
THE DAVE BRUBECK QUARTET AT CARNEGIE HALL
Dave Brubeck Quartet

Take Five may be the most popular jazz tune ever, which is remarkable since it is played in the unusual meter of five-four. It was written by Paul Desmond and had become the quartet's most popular tune. The opening piano and bass **vamp** (an open-ended repeating part) is infectious and immediately recognizable. The five beats per measure are divided into units of 3+2. The idea for this came from drummer Joe Morello, who was the first drummer to master and play in unusual meters. Morello was crucial for the group's metric explorations. The tune is in a standard AABA Pop song form but the solos do not follow the form of the tune. Instead, Desmond, Brubeck, and Morello improvise on the vamp only. This was quite different in 1959 when the group first recoded *Take Five*. The concept of letting go of the tune, itself, as a basis for improvisation is something that became more commonplace during the sixties. Here, by soloing only on the vamp, they are actually improvising modally. The idea of improvising on modes (scales) is credited to Miles Davis for his album, ***Kind of Blue***, also recorded in 1959. This whole modal idea and concept are described in Chapter 17 on Miles Davis. As we will see later, 1959 was a landmark year for jazz records.

This version of ***Take Five*** was recorded at Carnegie in 1963. By this time this group played in these unusual meters with ease and they play this tune with an obvious abandon that was not quite there on the more cautious first recording. Desmond plays lyrically and rhythmically and even "engages in duets with himself." Brubeck starts his solo by playing a simple melody against his pulsating left-hand chords. He soon plays right-hand chords against the left-hand chords and then in typical fashion plays thick two-handed chords in quasi-repetitive rhythms. Morello follows with a brief drum solo before the final head.

What to listen for:

1. The famous opening vamp—try to count 1-2-3-4-5 to it
2. The vamp continuing during the A sections of the head
3. The change that occurs on the B section
4. Desmond's solo and his playing "duets with himself"
5. Brubeck's solo that build from its simple beginning
6. Morello's virtuosic drum solo
7. The incessant five-four vamp with variations during the solos
8. The return of the head and form

TAKE FIVE

Dave Brubeck—Piano
Paul Desmond—Alto Sax
Eugene Wright—Bass
Joe Morello—Drums

	4	4		
Intro	drums ———————————————			
	Piano and bass vamp			
	8	8	8	8
0:10	A	A	B	A
Head	sax———————————————			
Solos	improv only on vamp, not the form			
0:43	Sax solo			
3:03	Piano solo			
4:55	Drum solo			
5:30				
Head	sax———————————————			

BLUE RONDO A LA TURK

Watch this video from the early sixties of the quartet playing the other famous tune from the *Time Out* album. The head is very complex and is in nine-eight meter, another unusual meter. The meter subdivides into units of 2-2-2-3 or 3-3-3. The improvisations are not based on the head, however, but on a 12-bar Blues progression. Both Brubeck and Desmond solo true to form. Notice Brubeck building a solo that climaxes with thick block chords played in quasi-repetitive rhythms. This video is from a TV show called *Playboy After Dark*.

MODERN JAZZ QUARTET
MJQ

Like the Dave Brubeck Quartet the MJQ was a band unique to itself. They are also the longest lasting small jazz group in history. They began in 1952 and played together on and off into the 1990s. Their personnel remained intact since 1954 when drummer Connie Kay replaced the original drummer, Kenny Clarke, and joined pianist John Lewis, vibraphonist Milt Jackson, and bassist Percy Heath. John Lewis, the leader of the group, like Brubeck, studied Classical music but unlike Brubeck, was a trained classical pianist with degrees in music. Lewis wanted a jazz band that would play music that was more refined, more intellectual, and more like Classical chamber music. Their name itself, the tuxedos they wore, their dignified stage presence, and the concert venues they performed in enhanced this sophisticated image. Like Brubeck's group, they performed mostly in concert halls around the world as opposed to in clubs where most jazz music was played in at the time.

Like some other Cool groups, the MJQ sought to tame some of the wildness of Bebop and explore alternative ways of performing modern jazz. John Lewis, who composed most of the original material for the group, tried to expand the formal scope of jazz. As we have seen in this book, jazz can be a complex music but it was always relatively simple in regard to form. Jazz musicians usually play on simple 12-bar Blues forms, Pop songs, or original tunes that almost always are based on Pop song forms— AABA, ABAC, etc. There are good reasons for this: the simpler and familiar forms help the improviser and the listener more easily relate the improvisations to the material on which it based. Classical music, on the other hand, makes use of complex but also familiar forms since the music is a playing "of" rather than "on" something. John Lewis came up with workable compromises between the two and thus was able to expand the formal aspect of jazz without sacrificing its comprehensibility. He composed suites with separate movements and pieces with mood and tempo changes. The MJQ took this flirtation further and was the most prominent group involved in an attempt to merge jazz with Classical music called *Third Stream*. (See below.) The MJQ was a huge popular success that stood the test of time and, like the Dave Brubeck Quartet, appealed to the casual jazz fan. Also like Brubeck's quartet, Milt Jackson and John Lewis played in contrasting styles that held the listener's interest as changing scenes in a movie might. Drummer Connie Kay and bassist Percy Heath were crucial rhythm section members of this group who provided a rock-steady sense of time, swing, and feel to support the two main soloists.

JOHN LEWIS

Pianist John Lewis (1920–2001) was raised in Albuquerque, New Mexico. He studied Classical music and received a master's degree in music from the Manhattan School of Music in 1953. He played with Charlie Parker and Dizzy Gillespie, and the Miles Davis Nonet on *Birth of the Cool*. He became the de facto leader of the MJQ and wrote most of

Figure 14.6: John Lewis, 1957.

Copyright © Verhoeff, Bert / Anefo (CC BY-SA 3.0) at http://commons.wikimedia.org/ wiki/File:John_Lewis_1977.jpg

their original tunes. His love of Classical music is apparent in his jazz playing, and his touch and melodic concept has a distinctly Baroque flavor. His reverence for Bach can be seen in his compositions as well as his playing through his use of written or improvised counterpoint, and even well-crafted fugues. His playing is derived from Bebop and Blues as well as Bach, and the certain elegance he brought to his playing, he also imparted to the band. He played with a clearly defined sense of melody and rhythm that was always light, logical, and economical. Count Basie served as a model for his light, understated approach and Basie's band served as a model for the tight cohesive ensemble the MJQ became. Lewis' concept of jazz was one that is coherent and interdependent, one where all the parts contribute to the whole, one where planning and improvisation meld into a cohesive yet flexible unity. Other than the normal background comping he would often accompany Jackson's solo with counter melodies that further integrated the parts toward the whole.

MILT JACKSON

Figure 14.7: Milt Jackson, circa 1947.

Copyright in the Public Domain.

Milt Jackson, (1923–1999) the best and most representative of the Bebop vibraphonists, had a soulful, bluesy, free-wheeling style that offset Lewis' more staid, spare playing. He played with Dizzy and Monk during the forties and turned the vibes away from Lionel Hampton's approach to a more modern one based on Bebop's innovations. Although it is a percussion instrument, Jackson could make the vibes "sing" and he was able to play with the subtle inflections and phrasing of a wind player. "Bags," as he was often called, famously slowed down the tremolo motor speed on his instrument to impart a warmer sound than had been used in jazz. The motor opens and closes the resonator tubes under the mallet bars and simulates a wind or string instrument's vibrato—thus the name vibraphone.

DJANGO
EUROPEAN CONCERT
The Modern Jazz quartet

Django is dedicated to the memory of Django Reinhardt who died in 1953; it is the group's most well-known tune. Reinhardt was a Belgian Gypsy guitarist who developed a unique style of playing Swing guitar during the Swing Era. Upon his death, John Lewis wrote this tune in his memory. It is a good example of Lewis' interest in expanding the formal scope of jazz. The tune starts as a slow funeral march until the solos, which are twice the tempo and not based on the funeral march tune; instead, Lewis wrote a different chord progression to improvise on. There is brief interlude based on the opening theme between solos and the slow funeral march returns at the end. Since Lewis does not use the tune as a basis for the solos, he places some reference points in the arrangement to guide the listener. The first is a pedal point played by the bass. A **pedal point** or **pedal tone** is a held or repeated note that remains constant while other note and/or chords change. In this case the bass repeats the note F on every beat for 8 measures during the B section of the solos. During the D solo section, the bass plays a Blues-like riff the same way every time.

The contrasting solo styles of Milt Jackson and John Lewis are evident in this recoding, Jackson is bluesy and boppish, while Lewis is delicate and light. There is slowing down of the tempo at the end of Lewis' solo to bring the funeral march back at the slower tempos. The influence of classical music is evident here but this is clearly straight-ahead swinging jazz.

What to listen for:

1. The sad quality of the opening theme (funeral march)
2. The tempo increase during the solos
3. Milt Jackson's bluesy Bebop-like solo
4. The bass pedal point and riff sections during the solos
5. The light delicate piano playing of John Lewis during his solo
6. The deaccelerando (slowing down) at the end of the piano solo
7. The return to the opening theme at the slower tempo

DJANGO

John Lewis—Piano
Milt Jackson—Vibraphones
Percy Heath—Bass
Connie Kay—Drums

Head		Vibes Solo	Interlude		Piano Solo		Head
slow		fast ———	———		———slows down		slow
funeral march		3 choruses	|from head		2 choruses		funeral march
20		|32 x 3		4	|32 x 2		20

FORM FOR SOLOS

	A		B		C		D
				pedal point				blues riff	
		12		8			4		8

DJANGO
VIDEO

Watch the MJQ in this TV performance of *Django* on the TV show, *Night Music*, from the late eighties. The quartet was still going strong after many years together. The elegance of the group comes through when you watch them play as well as listen.

THIRD STREAM

As some Cool jazz musicians were beginning to use Classical music techniques, such as counterpoint and extended forms during the fifties, it became inevitable that an attempt would be made to merge the two idioms. A movement emerged called **Third Stream**. Classical composer and French horn player **Gunter Schuller** coined the term. The attempt by Schuller and others was to create a new music that was neither jazz nor Classical music but a new, "third" kind of music that combined the two into something unique. Although Schuller played French horn on the *Birth of the Cool*, he is not really a jazz musician. He is, however, an avid champion of jazz who has collaborated with several jazz musicians, including the Modern Jazz Quartet, and has written on jazz, including two scholarly texts on the history of jazz: *Early Jazz* and *The Swing Era*. The attempt to merge jazz and Classical music was not new in the fifties; George Gershwin famously did so during the twenties, as did famous composers Igor Stravinsky, Bela Bartok, and Darius Milhaud, among others. Third Stream was different because it attempted to merge contemporary Cool jazz with the contemporary experimental Classical music of the time. It was not meant to be a jazz-influenced Classical music or a Classical music–influenced kind of jazz, but a brand new musical idiom that had elements of both. For the most part, Third Stream was not generally well received by the public or most musicians. For most, it seemed to be too artificial with "swing," that intangible element of jazz being literally caught in the middle. Third Stream efforts continue to this day, although not as a full-fledged movement. What one calls successful attempts at Third Stream music might depend on what one defines as Third Stream. Some would consider *Sketches of Spain*, a Third Stream album, a collaboration between Miles Davis and Gil Evans, while others might not. Either way, the important thing is the quality of the music, not the stylistic label one puts on it, and in that particular case, few would argue the merits of this music. Beside the MJQ, the Dave Brubeck Quartet, among others, engaged in Third Stream music.

Figure 14.8: John Lewis and Dave Brubeck, 1977.

Chapter Fifteen

Hard Bop

As Bebop matured during the early fifties, it splintered into two opposing directions. While Cool Jazz evolved the more intellectual, softer, laid-back side of Bebop, Hard Bop developed its more dynamic, intense, spirited side. In some ways Hard Bop was also a reaction against Cool Jazz, which was thought to be too pretentious and uninspired. Hard Bop musicians tended to be more aggressive in their playing and simpler in their overall approach to melody and harmony. Some Hard Bop musicians desired to focus on the Black American roots of jazz and let Black Gospel music and Blues color much of what they played. Some historians divide Cool Jazz and Hard Bop along racial lines: Cool=White jazz, Hard Bop=Black jazz. This is not entirely true; although most Hard Bop players were Black, many Cool players, including Miles Davis and the Modern Jazz Quartet, were Black as well.

Cool preceded Hard Bop and thus Hard Bop consciously steered in the opposite direction, striving for a simpler music than both Cool and Classic Bebop. Some of this simplicity as well as the harder edge to the music were influenced by Rhythm & Blues, which was gaining popularity during the late forties and early fifties. Some Hard Bop players, especially the saxophonists, had experience playing in R&B bands and brought some of that influence into the jazz world. Jazz on the whole had been losing popularity since the end of World War II and the decline of Swing. The average fan of Swing music did not embrace bebop and when jazz musicians stopped playing for dancers, the dancers stopped listening. Much as some Cool groups like the Dave Brubeck Quartet and the MJQ attracted a non-Bebop audience, many of the Hard Bop groups did as well with their more direct, more tuneful, less chaotic approach.

The heyday of Hard Bop was the mid-fifties to the mid-sixties and its practitioners included some of the all-time great jazz musicians. Most historians cite 1954 as the year Hard Bop was born with the releases of *Horace Silver and the Jazz Messengers* and *Walkin'* by Miles Davis. Miles Davis, who ushered in Cool Jazz a few years earlier, was now instrumental in creating Hard Bop. **Soul Jazz** is an offshoot of Hard Bop and became popular during the 1960s. The style and feeling of Gospel Music and R&B are prevalent and obvious from the titles as well as the music itself. Cannonball Adderley's group of the sixties is a major exponent of Soul Jazz and had several hits including ***Mercy, Mercy, Mercy***, and ***Work Song***.

CHARACTERISTICS OF HARD BOP

Hard Bop was a more full-bodied music than either Classic Bebop or Cool Jazz. All registers were used and the musicians played with an aggressive "on top" feeling. While some beboppers (Dizzy Gillespie excepted) seemed aloof and detached from their audience, and some Cool musicians seemed almost too formal and erudite, the hard boppers sought to entertain as well as perform art music. The down-home unpretentious music as well as the informal ambience of their performances made for a more inclusive experience for their audience. One can clearly garner this image by listening to any of Cannonball Adderley's live recordings. The inclusiveness is indicative of the Black Gospel music that inspired some Hard Bop and the services that it accompanies. Blues colors much of Hard Bop and the influence of newer Rhythm & Blues elements helped to popularize the music.

Minor keys were more prevalent in Hard Bop than in previous jazz and Minor Blues became common. Whereas traditional Blues bases its chords from the major scale, Minor Blues uses the minor scale. The form is the same but the minor scale chords darken the mood. Duke Ellington wrote his *Ko-Ko* as a minor Blues. There tend to be more arrangements in Hard Bop than in Classic Bebop. Rather than the standard Bebop procedure of *unison head-solos unison head*, there are often parts written in harmony, background riffs, and shout choruses. The repertoire for Hard Bop consists of Blues, standards. and original tunes, but the original tunes are not as commonly based on standards as in Bebop and vary in length and form. Along with the aggressive nature of the music come louder dynamics and more interaction between the rhythm section and the soloists. The pianists comp prominently and the drummers come much more to the foreground than Cool and even Classic Bebop drummers. Pianist Horace Silver and drummer Art Blakey exemplify this interactive approach. The tone and sound of the wind players are rounder, fuller, and darker than their Bebop and Cool counterparts.

HORACE SILVER

Pianist Horace Silver (b. 1928), born in Norwalk, Connecticut, is one of the first and most representative players of the Hard Bop style. He played on two of the formative Hard Bop albums, *Walkin'* with Miles Davis and *Horace Silver and the Jazz Messengers*. The name *Jazz Messengers* was first used by drummer Art Blakey in the late forties and used again when Blakey essentially co-led a quintet with Silver in 1954. Silver left the group in 1956 to form his own quintet and Blakey retained the name Jazz Messengers for the rest of his life. Silver continued to lead various groups, mostly quintets, throughout his career.

Silver developed a unique "funky" piano style and is among the greatest and most prolific of jazz composers. Funky piano is rooted in Blues and Gospel music. It is characterized by crushed seconds, slides from black to white keys, and catchy almost Boogie-woogie-like rhythmic figures. Silver used the term *funky* to describe his playing and it should not be confused with the term, *Funk*, a subcategory of Soul music invented by James Brown during the 1960s. Silver's playing is direct, unassuming, and accessible. He purposely tried to make his music simple but not simplistic. His solos like his tunes consist of catchy riff-like figures that are memorable and appealing. His left hand is very percussive and he often plays dissonant clusters of notes that have more of a drum effect than any harmonic value. His comping for others is very aggressive and the listener is well aware of his presence. This is in stark contrast to most Cool pianists who typically comped lightly in the background. Many of Silver's tunes have become standards of the jazz repertoire; they include **The Preacher, Doodlin', Senior Blues, Nica's Dream, Song for My Father, Peace**, and **Sister Sadie**. Silver arranged many of his tunes and they might include horns in harmony, background riffs, interlude-like sections, and shout-like out choruses. Silver was always in control of his music through his arrangements and comping that dictated the flow of the music. His band's alumni include Kenny Durham, Hank Mobley, Junior Cook, Blue Mitchell, and Joe Henderson.

Figure 15.1: Horace Silver, 1977.

THE PREACHER 1955
HORACE SILVER AND THE JAZZ MESSENGERS
Horace Silver and The Jazz Messengers

After this album Horace Silver would no longer be associated with the Jazz Messengers and Art Blakey went on to lead the groups with that name. This is one of the first Hard Bop albums and features five musicians associated with the style. The most popular tune from the album is *The Preacher*, written by Horace Silver. It represents the side of Hard Bop that sought a more direct connection with the African American roots of jazz. The Gospel influence is evidenced by the title and the down-home unpretentious quality of the music clearly comes through to the listener. The record producer did not want this tune on the album because it was "too old-timey" but Silver and Art Blakey insisted on it, and the producer reluctantly included it. It became an immediate hit in the jazz world.

The tune is very simple and a far cry from some of the slicker Cool Jazz repertoire. The chord progression is actually derived from the old folk song *I've Been Working on the Railroad.* It is only 16 measures long, as many Hard Bop Original tunes were, and typically for the shorter tunes, the head is played twice. Also consistent with Hard Bop, the horns are arranged in unison or harmony. Silver is very aggressive in his comping, as usual, and is prominently heard during the horn solos. His own solo is typical as well, consisting of catchy repetitive riff-like figures. During the last two choruses of the piano solo, the horns play a quasi-riff in the background that Silver interacts with in a Call and Response manner. Art Blakey is a little more subdued on this recording than he usually was known to be.

What to listen for:

1. The simple Gospel-like melody and harmony of the tune
2. The arrangement for the horns in unison or harmony
3. The bass playing with an old-fashioned-style 2-feel during the head then walking during the solos
4. The more assertive Hard Bop style of the horn players compared to Cool Jazz and simpler style compared to Classic Bebop
5. Silvers prominent aggressive comping
6. Silver's catchy repetitive figures during his solo
7. The riff-like horn part during the last two choruses of the piano solo

THE PREACHER

Horace Silver—Piano
Art Blakey—Drums
Doug Watkins—Bass
Kenny Dorham—Trumpet
Hank Mobley—Tenor Sax

	4	4	4	4
	A	A^1	A^2	B
Chorus 1	Head - trumpet and sax in octaves and harmony			
	Bass in old style "2 feel"————————————			
	Piano - comping counter melodic-rhythmic figures			
0:23				
Chorus 2	same as Chorus 1————————————dr roll			
1:27				
Chorus 3 + 4	Trumpet solo with prominent piano comping———			
	Bass in 4			
1:27				
Chorus 5 + 6	Sax solo with prominent piano comping————			
2:09				
Chorus 7 + 8	Piano solo - catchy repetitive rhythmic figures———			
2:50				
Chorus 9+10	Piano solo continues with horn riff - C+R horns + piano			
3:31				
Chorus 11+12	Head - same as chorus 1 and 2————————			

SEÑOR BLUES

Horace Silver—Piano   Gene Taylor—Bass
Blue Mitchell—Trumpet   Louis Hayes—Drums
Junior Cook—Tenor Sax

Watch this video of one of Silver's great quintets playing his original tune, Señor Blues. It is a 12-bar blues with an interesting six-eight Latin feel.

ART BLAKEY
AND THE JAZZ MESSENGERS

Art Blakey (1919–1990) epitomizes Hard Bop drumming and was one of the first drummers categorized as Hard Bop. He came up playing with various Swing and Bebop bands. After co-leading The Jazz Messengers with Horace Silver from 1954 to 1956, he continued to lead the group after Silver's departure and maintained the name as Art Blakey and the Jazz Messengers for the rest of his career. He was an aggressive, forceful drummer who continually interacted with his soloists. He often directed the flow of a solo through his drumming by controlling dynamics and intensity. He famously introduced new solos by playing a press roll to transition from the head or a previous solo. He studied African drumming in Africa and occasionally used some African techniques such as hitting the side of the drum and changing the pitch of his tom-toms by tightening the heads with his elbow. He became known as "Papa" Blakey because he continually hired young talented players and nurtured them along. He updated his band every few years to do this and his alumni read like a Who's Who of jazz who went on to illustrious careers of their own. His band members included Wayne Shorter, Benny Golson, Lee Morgan, Bobby Timmons, Freddie Hubbard, Clifford Brown, Hank Mobley, Keith Jarrett, Wynton Marsalis, and Branford Marsalis. His bands played in the Hard Bop style long after it was fashionable.

Figure 15.2: Art Blakey, 1985.

MOANIN' 1958

ART BLAKEY AND THE JAZZ MESSENGERS

Art Blakey and the Jazz Messengers

After Horace Silver left the band, Art Blakey was the sole leader of The Jazz Messengers. The name of this album was simply the name of the band but *Moanin'*, written by pianist Bobby Timmons, became so popular that reissues of the album often title it *Moanin'*. Like Horace Silver's *The Preacher*, *Moanin'* comes right out of church. This is in a minor key; minor keys were very common in Hard Bop. The A sections of this AABA tune feature a call and response pattern; the piano makes the call and the horns give an "Amen" response. The rhythm section plays "time" only during the bridge of the head. The bass plays in 2 during the A sections of the solos and in 4 for the B sections. For the solos, the A sections use a different chord progression from the one used for the head, and Blakey plays a *shuffle rhythm* with a strong *backbeat* on the snare drum on beats 2 and 4.

Figure 15.3 A shuffle rhythm is a variation on the Swing ride rhythm.

Both the shuffle rhythm and backbeat show the influence of Rhythm & Blues on Hard Bop. Both trumpeter Lee Morgan and tenor saxophonist Benny Golson are key Hard Bop players and their playing here is representative of the style; it is aggressive yet simpler than most Classic Bebop playing.

What to listen for:

1. The church-like Call and Amen response of the head
2. The minor key color of the tune
3. Blakey's typical press roll into the first solo
4. The shuffle feel on the drums during the solos
5. The bass plays in 2 for the A sections and in 4 for the B sections during the solos
6. Bobby Timmons' prominent piano comping
7. The typical Hard Bop aggressive but relatively simple solos compared to Classic Bebop
8. Blakey's control of the music with his sturdy drumming

MOANIN'

Art Blakey—Drums
Lee Morgan—Trumpet
Benny Golson—Tenor Sax

Bobby Timmons—Piano
Jymie Merritt—Bass

	8	8	8	8
	A	A	B	A
Chorus 1	Head ————————————————————————————
	Piano—Horns——————————| Horns ——| piano + horns
	Call + Response—————————| bass in 4 | C + R
1:00
Chorus 2+3	Trumpet solo————————————————————————
	Drums play shuffle rhythm with backbeat for all solos
	Bass in 2————————————| bass in 4 |in 2 -for all solos
3:01
Chorus 4+5	Tenor Sax solo———————————————————————
5:03
Chorus 6+7	Piano solo———————————————————————————
7:02
Chorus 8	Bass solo———————————————————————————
7:58
Chorus 9	Head- same as Chorus 1

Coda—based on B section
 12

DAT DERE

Art Blakey—Drums
Lee Morgan—Trumpet
Wayne Shorter—Tenor Sax

Bobby Timmons—Piano
Jymie Merritt—Bass

Watch this video performance of another Bobby Timmons tune, **Dat Dere**, 1961. As in **Moanin'**, there is a heavy Gospel music and Blues influence. Wayne Shorter is now in the group and will become a major player in the 1960s.

THE CLIFFORD BROWN-MAX ROACH QUINTET

CLIFFORD BROWN

Clifford Brown (1930–1956), born in Wilmington, Delaware, was the most promising of the trumpet players associated with Hard Bop. Although, tragically, he died young in a car accident, he left a lasting legacy. "Brownie," as he was often called, was one of the few jazz musicians of the time who did not indulge in drugs or alcohol, yet still died at a young age, while others died young because of their lifestyle choices. His sound and tone came more from Bebop trumpeter Fats Navarro than from Dizzy Gillespie. It was a warm, yet full-bodied tone that was rounder and more powerful than that of Chet Baker or Miles Davis. Brown was as technically adept as any trumpeter in jazz history and more creative than most. His improvisations were lyrical, yet powerful and logical. He often played sequences and developed motives. He sometimes constructed longer lines from shorter patterns of notes, and was able to play extremely fast notes and at extremely fast tempos. He was always in full control of his horn and his playing, overall, was as disciplined as his lifestyle. In 1954 he formed the Clifford Brown-Max Roach Quintet and although short-lived because of Brown's untimely death, it became one of the best groups in jazz history. Roach seemed to perfectly complement Brown's playing by cushioning the time, allowing breathing room, and interjecting at just the right moments. Brown's influence from their recordings can still be heard in today's jazz world. Clifford Brown wrote several tunes that have become jazz standards, most notably: *Joy Spring, Jordu, Daahoud*, and *Sandu*.

MAX ROACH

Max Roach (1924–2007), born in Newland, North Carolina, was one of the best Bebop and Hard Bop drummers. Although Kenny Clarke was the first Bebop drummer, Roach soon became the most prominent and influential drummer of the 1940s. He had played with virtually all the great Bebop players, including Charlie Parker, Dizzy Gillespie, Thelonious Monk, and Bud Powell. In 1954 he formed the legendary Clifford Brown-Max Roach Quintet, one of the great groups in jazz history. He was an exceptionally "musical" as well as technical drummer and also studied Classical percussion. He carefully tuned his drums, which made his playing melodic as well as rhythmic. His solos were usually based on the tunes themselves and approached them as a melody instrumentalist would by playing around the pitch and rhythmic structure of the tune. He sensitively accompanied soloists with an aggressive, yet reserved flow of time, and interacted with them complementary rather than interruptive accents and fills. His career extended into the 21st century and he remained active to the end of his life.

Figure 15.4: Max Roach, 1977.

SONNY ROLLINS

Sonny Rollins (b. 1930) is one of the great tenor saxophonists of all time. Born in New York City, he continues to perform into his eighties. He benefited from growing up with mentoring neighbors who included Bud Powell and Thelonious Monk, and Rollins would jam with them as a teenager. He played with several important players before leading his own bands over the years; these include Miles Davis, Thelonious Monk, Clifford Brown, Max Roach, and Bud Powell. He was very self-critical and stopped performing several times in order to improve his playing. He famously used to practice on the Westminster Bridge over the Hudson River in the middle of the night so as to not disturb his neighbors. He kicked his heroin habit in 1955 by hospitalizing himself and emerged as a better, more productive player.

Whereas most great players develop their own sound, Rollins used several different sounds and used them in structural ways that became as important as the notes and rhythms he played. He also used articulation structurally through varying his attacks by playing long passages legato (connected notes) or staccato (separated notes). Rollins is one of the supplest rhythmic players in jazz history. He often phrases in tempos that are different from the prevailing beat or in a free rubato against the steady beat that the rest of the band plays, giving the effect that he is in a different time dimension. His improvisations often employ the technique of thematic or motivic development. That is to say, he often takes an idea from the tune and explores it during his solo. A motive is a short musical idea that has a strong melodic and rhythmic identity, one that is easily remembered. When the idea comes from the tune or theme itself, it is referred to as thematic development; when it is not from the tune itself, it is called motivic development. The process is the same either way. Rollins is a master at doing this and often ingeniously gets the most mileage out of a single idea. His solo on *Blue Seven* was analyzed in this regard by Gunther Schuller for the *Jazz Review*, a scholarly jazz journal, in 1958. Rollins, after reading the article, said that he had no idea that he was doing such things and that by thinking about it while he played messed him up. He took one of his famous hiatuses at that time to straighten himself out. Rollins, however, has continued to engage in thematic and motivic development during his solos. Rollins often chooses material than many consider simplistic or banal. He has recorded, for example, Kurt Weil's ***Moritat (Mack the Knife)*** and Johnny Mercer's ***I'm an Old Cowhand***. He proves that you do not need complex material to produce artful, complex, intriguing improvisations. Many of his original tunes are harmonically and melodically simple, as well, and part of Rollins' great art relies on extracting surprisingly subtle and exciting performances from them. The fewer obstacles in his way seems to unleash the creative force within him, and much like his ability to separate his playing from the pulse at times, he is able to separate himself from the tunes themselves and interpolate masterful improvisations that are more *above* the tunes than *on* the tunes.

Figure 15.5: Sonny Rollins, 1982.

PENT-UP HOUSE 1956
SONNY ROLLINS PLUS 4

The band here is really the Clifford Brown-Max Roach Quintet. Sonny Rollins had just replaced Harold Land on tenor saxophone in the quintet but recorded this album under his own name. *Pent-Up House*, written by Sonny Rollins, features great solos by Rollins and Clifford Brown. Max Roach also does some great Call and Response trading 2-measure units back and forth with them (*trading 2's*) toward the end of the tune. He follows this with a typical "melodic" drum solo where he plays off the melody and rhythms of the tune. The tune is only 16 measures long, as many Hard Bop tunes were, and is in an AABA[1] form with four 4-measure sections. It is slightly arranged but the horns play mostly in octaves. The chord progression, which is relatively simple, is characteristic of Rollins' tunes; he preferred simple, sometimes even banal, chord progressions to improvise on.

Brown's solo is characteristically lyrical and logical. His complete command of the trumpet is evidenced in this solo. He plays off ideas and often sequences them. Rollins characteristically works from motives taken from the tune and develops them along with other ideas. His rubato-like phrasing, use of different sounds, and fast double-time passages are all used in this solo. Pianist Richie Powell, who is Bud Powell's younger brother, plays a simple Horace Silver–like solo. Max Roach interacts with the players throughout their solos.

What to listen for:

1. The disjunct and off-rhythmic character of the head
2. Brown's use of sequences and repeating idea
3. Rollins' development of the theme and other ideas
4. Powell's simple Horace Silver–like solo.
5. The trading 2s between the horns and drums
6. Roach's "melodic" drum solo
7. Roach's aggressive, interactive drumming throughout

PENT-UP HOUSE

Sonny Rollins—Tenor Sax
Clifford Brown—Trumpet
Richie Powell—Piano
Doug Watkins—Bass
Max Roach—Drums

	4	4	4	4
	A	A	B	A^1
Chorus 1–2	head —mostly in octaves———————			
Chorus 3–8	trumpet solo———————			
Chorus 9–14	tenor sax solo———————			
Chorus 15–20	piano solo———————			
Chorus 21–22	trumpet and sax trade 2's with drums			
Chorus 23–24	drum solo			
Chorus 25–26	head			

A WEAVER OF DREAMS 1959

Sonny Rollins—Tenor Sax
Henry Grimes—Bass
Joe Harris—Drums

Watch this video of Sonny Rollins, with just bass and drums, play the Pop standard. Notice the many different sounds he evokes from his horn and how he improvises off the opening motive of the tune.

WES MONTGOMERY

Wes Montgomery (1923–1968), from Indianapolis, Indiana, was the most influential Post-Swing electric guitarist. He was influenced and inspired by Charlie Christian and taught himself to play by listening to Christian's recordings. He developed a unique style, sound, and technique. By using his thumb instead of a pick to strum the strings, he imparted a warmer, mellower tone to his sound. His solos typically progressed from single-note lines to lines in octaves to melodies in full chords. Fast-moving octave melodies are difficult to play on guitar, but Montgomery devised an unorthodox way of fingering them that facilitated their playing. He also could play fluid chord melodies by using a unique fingering. In these ways he was somewhat similar to the Belgian Gypsy Swing guitarist Django Rheinhardt, who had to devise unique ways of fingering due to a physical deformity in his left hand. Montgomery could play Bebop, Hard Bop, and Soul Jazz, and could swing as well as anyone on any instrument, and even when many thought he sold out in the mid-sixties by recording popular hits of the day, his musicianship and artistry were never questioned. Among Montgomery's pure jazz albums, *Smokin' at the Half Note* with pianist Wynton Kelly, bassist Paul Chambers, and drummer Jimmy Cobb, who all were members of Miles Davis' rhythm section from 1959 to 1963, is the most highly regarded.

FOUR ON SIX 1965

Wes Montgomery—Electric Guitar
Stan Tracey—Piano
Rick Laird—Bass
Jackie Dugan—Drums

Watch this live performance of Wes Montgomery's jazz standard, **Four on Six**, a tune that is based on George Gershwin's **Summertime**. The tune begins with a vamp played on bass and guitar that continues while changing along with the chord progression. The guitar then states the head as the bass continues as before. Wes does a typical solo by starting with mostly single notes and building the solos by then playing octaves. Notice how he plays with his right-hand thumb, which is highly unorthodox, but produces a cushioned mellower sound without losing any drive and forward momentum. His phrasing is masterful and an often-overlooked aspect of Montgomery's art.

SOUL JAZZ

Soul Jazz is an offshoot of Hard Bop that incorporates elements of Rhythm & Blues and sixties Pop Soul along with traditional Gospel and Blues. Soul Jazz is more groove oriented than pure Hard Bop and relies more often on repetitive background figures from the rhythm section. Soul music was an outgrowth of R&B that became the dominant Black Pop music of the sixties. Motown and Atlantic Records were the major producers of this music and just as these labels marketed equally to Black and White audiences, Soul Jazz had a universal pop-like appeal.

The first true Soul artist was Ray Charles, an eclectic performer who crossed over in the worlds of R&B, Jazz, Pop, and even Country music. Charles is the first performer to bring the soulful, ecstatic, inspired singing of the Black churches into the mainstream world of popular entertainment. In Charles' case, *soul* was a manner of performance rather than a style of music. But he clearly set the precedent for sixties Soul music with his fifties hits from ***I Got a Woman*** in 1954 to ***What'd I Say*** in 1959. Both of these records have clearly defined background rhythms that help define the song itself.

Although one can quibble about what exactly is Soul Jazz as opposed to Hard Bop, the term *Soul Jazz* is thought of here as a more groove-oriented music with more or less specific background rhythms and/or heavy backbeat (emphasis on beats 2 and 4). Therefore, whereas *The Preacher* and *Moanin'* have clear Gospel associations during the heads, the solos are more in a straight ahead, swinging traditional jazz feel, making them Hard Bop. On the other hand, Lee Morgan's ***The Sidewinder*** and Herbie Hancock's ***Watermelon Man***, both recorded during the early sixties, begin and continue with the R&B-like groove throughout the performance.

Soul Jazz was a popular alternative to the more esoteric and difficult-to-understand jazz of the 1960s (see Part IV). While his former band mates Miles Davis and John Coltrane were losing many fans while exploring new domains, Cannonball Adderley had several hits during this time with ***Work Song, Jive, Samba***, and especially ***Mercy, Mercy, Mercy***, a tune that introduced the Fender Rhodes electric piano to most of the jazz world. During the fifties, the organ had come out of church and became a mainstay of Soul Jazz and Jimmy Smith dominated a field of talented jazz organists.

JIMMY SMITH

Organ trios proliferated during the fifties and sixties and Jimmy Smith (1925–2005) reigned supreme among the players of the Hammond B-3 electric organ. Smith grew up in Norristown, Pennsylvania, just outside of Philadelphia, which became a mecca for jazz organ music in those days. The Hammond electric organ was designed as a less expensive alternative to church pipe organs. Smith set the tone bars in such a way to produce a percussive attack that was more suitable for jazz playing. This sound and his astounding virtuosity inspired a whole generation of jazz organists. He could glide on the keys or pound on them to produce percussive effects. Unlike pianos, dynamics on the organ cannot be controlled by the fingers but only by a foot pedal. Organists use all four limbs as the other foot plays bass pedals for bass lines while both hands play on two keyboards. Because the organist usually plays bass lines, organ trios usually consist of organ, electric guitar, and drums. Other than drums, the organ trios are the first electric ensembles in jazz history and their performances are usually hard driving and electrifying, filled with energy. The organ can produce a very full-sounding texture with a full dynamic range that can rival that of a big band. Jimmy Smith's trio served as a model for many other famous organists, including Richard "Groove" Holmes, Johnny Hammond Smith, Jack McDuff, Jimmy McGriff, Shirley Scott, Trudy Pitts, and more recently another Philadelphian, Joey DeFrancesco, who more than anyone current is keeping the tradition alive. Smith also made several albums with big bands arranged by Oliver Nelson that crossed over into the Pop charts.

As electric keyboards and synthesizers became common during the seventies, the Hammond B-3 fell out of favor, but as much as electronic keyboards tried to simulate the B-3's sound and feel, players eventually realized that much like an acoustic piano, the impersonators pale in comparison.

THE SERMON 1964

Jimmy Smith—Hammond B-3 Organ
Quintin Warren—Electric Guitar
Billy Hart—Drums

Watch this 1964 live performance from BBC-TV. The title clearly relates to the Gospel music influence. *The Sermon* is swinging Blues, written by Smith that makes use of a shuffle drum feel with a backbeat that was typical of Rhythm & Blues. This music is danceable and highly infectious; one cannot help move to this music, if only to tap your foot, clap your hands, or snap your fingers. Watch Smith as he acrobatically uses all four limbs in a highly coordinated manner to produce this soulful, exciting performance. Notice his foot plays the bass line. Toward the end of his solo he holds on to one note (an F) with his right-hand thumb for seven full choruses while he plays melodic figures with his other fingers. Notice how that tension is released with the return of the head.

Chapter Sixteen

Great Piano Trios

For the first fifty years of jazz, the piano functioned, for the most part, as a solo instrument or as a rhythm section instrument. The piano was rarely a featured instrument within a group situation. During the 1950s piano trios became numerous and popular. During the 1940s, Art Tatum played occasionally with a trio but it was the **Nat "King" Cole Trio** that served as the model for the modern jazz piano trio. Cole's trio, as Tatum's trio, consisted of piano, bass, and guitar. All three pianists covered in this chapter began with similar trios but replaced the guitar with drums during the 1950s. Cole was an innovative piano stylist who during the forties, let go of the striding left hand but never really played in a Bebop style. He played middle register chords in his left hand that lightly accompanied swinging right-hand lines. This type of chording anticipated the later left-hand playing of modern jazz pianists. Cole is an important transitional figure who, by sidestepping Bebop, seemingly provided a direct link from Swing to modern jazz piano. Because he achieved great success and popularity as a singer, his contribution to jazz piano is often overlooked. At a time when most pianists were under the spell of Bud Powell, the 1950s gave birth to several great piano trios that seemed to defy current trends and instead, took advantage of and featured each pianist's unique style and approach. As previously noted, the art of solo jazz piano died with Art Tatum, for the most part, and it was now in the trio format that pianists could best express themselves and explore the full possibilities the keyboard had to offer. The three pianists discussed in this chapter are the ones who most prominently developed this format during the fifties and sixties. Bill Evans, who also led an important trio during this time, will be discussed in Chapter 18. All of them pioneered the use of rootless voicings in the left hand, which was the modern way of playing chords without their roots. These rootless voicings lighten up the texture of the music and give more leeway to the bass player to construct bass lines that do not clash with the piano (see Chapter 18). All of them developed unique styles that are readily identifiable to jazz piano fans.

ERROLL GARNER

Erroll Garner (1923–1977), born in Pittsburgh, Pennsylvania, was a self-taught pianist who played in a highly original style. Although he had played in some bands and as a solo pianist, he is best known for his astounding work with his trio. Garner had a masterful technique that took advantage of the entire keyboard. He typically strummed middle register chords with his left hand on every beat, much like a Swing guitarist would play. His right hand would play either fast single-note Bebop-like lines or chordal melodies. Part of his unique approach was characterized by his right hand lagging behind the beat at times. This created a laid-back kind of phrasing that was at odds with his strumming left hand. The effect is quite stimulating and the tension it creates gets released by getting back in sync with the left hand. He frequently articulated certain notes by sliding octaves from black to white keys. Garner continually interrupted the flow of his music with cross-rhythmic interjections and other surprises. His playing featured many dynamic and textural contrasts by abruptly switching from full two-handed chordal, orchestral-like passages to soft single-note segments. Garner's musical language comes from equal doses of Swing and Bebop. He famously played long introductions that disguised the tune from the audience and sometimes even from his players. His ballads were often filled with flowery arpeggios and rolled tremolo chords. His original song, *Misty*, has become one of the most-often performed standards from the Great American Songbook. His 1956 album, *Concert by the Sea*, became a best seller and stayed on the Jazz charts for decades.

Figure 16.1: Erroll Garner.
Copyright in the Public Domain.

HONEYSUCKLE ROSE 1964

Eddie Calhoun—Bass   Kelly Martin—Drums

Watch this vintage performance of Fats Waller's *Honeysuckle Rose*.
Notice how Garner's introduction keeps the listener and the band in suspense. This is a high-energy performance filled with typical Garner interjections and surprises.

OSCAR PETERSON

Oscar Peterson (1925–2007), from Montreal, Canada, was considered by many to be the heir to Art Tatum. He had a technical mastery of the piano that rivaled Tatum's and could do a convincing imitation of his playing. Peterson claimed he was so intimidated by Tatum when he first heard his record of *Tiger Rag* he could almost gave up playing. Peterson studied classical piano and seems to have reaped technical benefits from it. He gives us the impression that he could play anything he can think of. His technique is not just about fast notes; he can control subtle gradations of dynamics over long periods as well as individual phrases. Like Erroll Garner, he often contrasted passages of thick complex block chords with softer, lighter swinging single-note lines. Peterson swings as much as any pianist and his style contains elements of Swing, Bebop, and Post-Bop piano. Although he sometimes was dismissed by critics as all "chops" and no substance, he had a hugely successful career and following. These critics obviously could not hear the underlying beauty of his touch, the subtlety of his phrasing, and the unabashed swing of his playing. Peterson performed solo at times, especially in his later years, and one can clearly hear the Tatum influence in his dazzling runs and surprising and sophisticated reharmonizations. Peterson's early trio was with **Ray Brown** on bass and **Herb Ellis** on guitar. In 1959 he replaced the guitar with drummer **Ed Thigpen**. Ray Brown has achieved legendary status among bass players and is one of the best, most admired, and most imitated bassists of all time. Peterson formed several other trios during his life.

Figure 16.2: Oscar Peterson.
Copyright © Tom Marcello (CC BY-SA 2.0) at http://commons.wikimedia.org/wiki/File:Oscar_Peterson.jpg

C JAM BLUES

Ray Brown—Bass   Ed Thigpen—Drums

Watch this incredible performance of Duke Ellington's C Jam Blues.
Oscar begins with just drums and shows his solo piano ability with no bass. The music continues to swing even harder when Ray Brown comes in on bass. Oscar's virtuosity is on full display here.

AHMAD JAMAL

Ahmad Jamal (b. 1930), like Erroll Garner, is from Pittsburgh, Pennsylvania. His playing, however, is a world apart from Garner. Jamal invented a style that relied on understatement, few notes, space, and silence. He possesses an imposing technical facility but unlike Garner and Peterson, he rarely displays it. Rather, he saves it and uses it as dramatic contrast to his otherwise delicate, sparse figures and lines. Like Oscar Peterson he originally led a trio with bass and guitar, but replaced the guitar with drums in 1957. This trio with **Israel Crosby** on bass and **Vernell Founier** on drums in 1958 recorded *But Not for Me*, which became one of the best-selling jazz albums in history. Jamal's trio structured their music around flexible arrangements that relied on cues. Vamps were a common feature. Vamps are short repetitive sections that repeat until cued to continue to the next section. Vamps are typically used as introductions but Jamal used them anywhere during a performance: as intros, after choruses, and as endings. He used hand gestures, even shoulder shrugs, to cue the band.

Figure 16.3: Ahmad Jamal.
Copyright © Brianmcmillen (CC BY-SA 3.0) at http://commons.wikimedia.org/wiki/File:Ahmad_Jamal_KK.jpg

This group played extended turnarounds, not only at the end of tunes, where they typically are used to delay endings, but also between choruses, which served to enlarge the formal aspect of the tune. Jamal, thus, takes a standard tune and expands on its limited formal dimension by interrupting its continuous repetitiveness with interludes and extensions in original and surprising ways. He sometimes plays nothing at all for several measures. When he does this, the bass and drums come to the foreground and as the tune still continues, the listener, consciously or unconsciously, fills in the gap. Jamal's unique approach is a nonlinear one, where the tune acts like a road over which he flies silently and randomly touches down on with melody and chords. Crosby's bass lines become melodies themselves and Fournier's crisp rhythms underpin the structure in such a convincing way that Jamal is free to plug in and out the tune as he sees fit, often going against the grain of the tune's form and phrase structure. Essentially Jamal plays over a groove set up by the bass and drums. This was very different from other jazz at the time that relied on the pulse, or beat, on which to play. The ramifications of this will have huge effects on Miles Davis and others later on. Like Peterson and Garner, Jamal contrasts full orchestral-like chordal passages with lighter single note lines but offsets the two with silence rather than going right from one to the other.

DARN THAT DREAM 1959

Israel Crosby—Bass
Vernell Fournier—Drums

This performance is from a 1959 TV show. This is Jamal's "classic" trio with Israel Crosby on bass and Vernell Fournier on drums. Notice the light swinging groove they achieve and the interspersed interludes that break the flow of the music from time to time. They seem like endings but Jamal keeps the music going by releasing the tension they produce. *Darn That Dream* is a Pop standard written by Jimmy Van Heusen and Eddie DeLange.

Ahmad Jamal is known for his unique treatment of **Poinciana**, a Pop standard written by Nat Simon and Buddy Bernier in 1936. He recorded it several times and continues to play it at each performance. The feel is hard to categorize or describe but it is undeniably infectious and appealing.

POINCIANA 2005

James Cammack—Bass
Idres Muhammad—Drums

Watch this later version of Jamal's signature tune. There are parts that are consistent with his original 1950s version but he always adds new and surprising elements each time he plays it. Notice the spaces that he leaves and how, when he does, the bass and drums come to the foreground. Notice, also, the infectious groove that is established and maintained throughout.

Chapter Seventeen

Miles Davis in the Fifties

Miles Dewey Davis (1926–1991) is perhaps the most seminal figure in all of post-1950 jazz. Never one to rest on his laurels, he continually reinvented himself and his style of jazz. He went from Bebop to Cool Jazz to Hard Bop to Modal Jazz to Freer jazz to Fusion within a span of twenty-five years. He remained on the cutting edge of jazz invention and stylistic evolution and led some of the greatest jazz bands of all time. Miles, born in East St. Louis, Illinois, came from a relatively affluent family. Miles arrived in New York in 1944 to study at the famous Juilliard School of Music. His real music education, however, occurred on 52nd Street listening to Charlie Parker and Dizzy Gillespie. Parker took him under his wing and soon Miles was playing and recording for him.

Figure 17.1: Miles Davis.
Copyright © Tom Palumbo (CC BY-SA 2.0) at http://commons.
wikimedia.org/wiki/File:Miles_Davis_by_Palumbo.jpg

We last left Miles with his innovative ***Birth of the Cool*** project in the late 1940s (see Chapter 14). Miles abandoned the mid-size band concept after *Birth of the Cool* and, as was his wont, he went on to explore new territory. He mostly played in and led small groups in the earlier fifties. Besides being one of the key participants of the Cool movement, Miles also was instrumental in starting Hard Bop. In 1954 he sought to make a music that was simpler, more direct, and more Black in nature. His album **Walkin'** is a major contribution to the Hard Bop movement. We pick him up here in 1956 with the first of his great quintets. This group is often referred to as the "Classic" Miles Davis Quintet, but since Miles also led another great quintet during the 1960s that is sometimes referred to a "classic quintet," this 1950s group will referred to as the 1950s Quintet. Both combos are, indeed, classic. Part of Miles Davis' great talent was not just playing the trumpet but also assembling great bands that contained not just great individual players but players who played extremely well together. The 1950s Quintet contains what is considered by most jazz historians to be the second great rhythm section in jazz history (chronologically after Count Basie's 1930s rhythm section). Most jazz groups of the 1950s are categorized as Cool or Hard Bop and many historians place this quintet in the Hard Bop category. The opinion here, however, places this group in a category by itself and we can hear elements of Cool Jazz and Hard Bop.

Contributions

1. Developed a unique lyrical trumpet style
2. Merged Cool Jazz with Hard Bop to create a unique 1950s sound and style
3. His Classic 1950s Quintet featured the second (chronologically) great rhythm section in jazz history
4. His Quintet and Sextet were two of the greatest bands in jazz history
5. Created and developed modal jazz that influenced the way jazz musicians improvised
6. Led the way to freedom in 1960s jazz
7. Recorded the most influential and, perhaps, best jazz album of all time

MILES DAVIS' TRUMPET STYLE

Miles' 1950s trumpet style can be described as cool, mellow, economical, and lyrical. He made much use of space and silence during his solos. He would often let several beats or even measures go by without playing anything. This creates an interesting effect that lets the rhythm section come to the foreground; he was influenced by the pianist Ahmad Jamal in this regard. His sound was unique and almost the opposite of Louis Armstrong's brilliant and brassy sound. Miles had a mellow, understated and laid-back approach and he played with little or no vibrato. He was very influenced by singers, especially Billie Holiday and Frank Sinatra, and like them he was a master at phrasing melodies. Miles' frequent collaborator, arranger/composer Gil Evans, called Miles "a great singer of songs." Also, like those singers, Miles carefully articulated and placed every note he played, and without playing a lot of notes he made every note count. Phrasing involves the rhythmic placement of notes and the shaping of a melody with dynamics and accents. Miles "sings" as he plays and freely floats over the beats rather than being confined by them. Miles created a unique sound by the way he used the Harmon mute. The Harmon mute is made from aluminum and makes the trumpet very soft. It comes with two parts: the main mute and the stem, which can be removed from the main mute. Miles removed the stem and played right into a microphone like a singer. The use of the microphone amplified the soft muted sound and created a unique sound that immediately became associated with Miles Davis.

Figure 17.2: Miles Davis playing with a Harmon mute. Excerpt from Bye, Bye, Blackbird 1956.

THE "CLASSIC" 1950s QUINTET

This quintet featured five of the greatest players in jazz history. As with all Miles Davis bands, they were not only great individual players but also played extremely well together. The fact that the three main soloists played in contrasting styles made for changing moods and variety within the performance of each tune. Miles liked musicians whose styles foiled his lyrical cool approach.

JOHN COLTRANE

John Coltrane (1926–1967), tenor saxophonist, was almost the complete opposite of Miles Davis. He had a dark, penetrating, serious sound and whereas Miles seemed to play the fewest number of notes to get his point across, Coltrane seemed to play the most humanly possible. One critic described his playing as "sheets of sound." Much of his playing with Miles had a searching, exploring character to it. In his recordings with his own band he seemed much more self-assured and virtuosic. Coltrane and his bands are described more fully in Chapter 20.

Excerpt of John Coltrane playing So What in 1959

RHYTHM SECTION

This is one of only three great rhythm sections in jazz history. The first chronologically was the Count Basie rhythm section of the 1930s (see Chapter 8). What makes for a great rhythm section? Obviously, the role of the rhythm section has changed since the 1930s and the standards that applied to Basie's band no longer apply here. While the Swing big band rhythm section's main function was to give the pulse or beat as steadily and evenly as possible, the rhythm section in a 1950s combo was more concerned with interaction with the soloist and each other, rhythmic and harmonic comping, and textural underpinning. This rhythm section was remarkable in the way they adapted to very different styles of Miles and Coltrane. During Miles' simple, lyrical heads and solos, the rhythm section is locked into a more or less consistent groove. Garland, on piano, comps mostly by playing on the "and after 2" and the "and after 4," essentially anticipating beats 1 and 3. Philly Joe Jones, on drums, plays either with brushes, mostly on heads, or simply with sticks. This consistency departs as soon as Coltrane enters when his more complex, aggressive, random-like style is matched by much busier, more interactive piano and drums. When Garland solos after Coltrane, things calm down and swings with Jones sometimes playing the stick against the rim of the snare drum on the fourth beat of every measure The groove is always present and this rhythm section swung more consistently during this time period than, perhaps, any other.

RED GARLAND

Red Garland (1923–1985) was one of the great piano accompanists to emerge out of bebop. His comping was light and swinging and he always seemed to know just what the music needed at any particular moment. He was one of the first pianists to use rootless voicings in the left hand (see Chapter 18 on Bill Evans for more on rootless voicings) and this allowed his left hand to voice chords with upper extensions in the middle register of the piano, which significantly lightened up the texture compared to how the earlier bebop pianist voiced chord shells lower on the piano. (See the previous page on his comping for the Quintet.)

His solos usually followed a general procedure: light, buoyant single-note lines, often in a high register, accompanied with middle-register left-hand chords anticipating beats 1 and 3 for the most part followed by a climactic ending with thick block chords. Garland had a unique way of playing block chords; he would play a full chord or rootless voicing on the left hand in rhythmic unison with the right-hand melody played in octaves with another note a fifth above the lower octave. Some of his playing with Miles, at Miles' urging, was influenced by Ahmad Jamal, the same pianist who influenced Miles' own trumpet playing.

Excerpt of Red Garland playing Bye, Bye, Blackbird 1956

PAUL CHAMBERS

Paul Chambers (1935–1969) was one of the best bassists of all time. Although the primary role of the bass player during this time period was to play quarter notes (on every beat), there are an infinite number of ways of doing it. No one seemed to do it better than Paul Chambers. He subtly inflected certain notes with quick grace notes and often pushed beats ahead a little, which added rhythm impetus to the music. Chambers seemed to make almost perfect note choices in his lines, playing melodically and complementarily to the soloists, and often dramatically with sudden shifts of register. Chambers was an outstanding soloist himself and one of the first jazz bassists to play solos with the bow.

Excerpt of Paul Chambers playing *So What* in 1959

PHILLY JOE JONES

Philly Joe Jones (1923–1985), from Philadelphia, went by that name to distinguish himself from Jo Jones, Count Basie's great drummer. He is one of the best drummers associated with Hard Bop and could play as aggressively as that style demanded, but could also lay back and just groove behind a Miles or Red Garland solo. Jones swung as much as any drummer in jazz. He was equally adept with brushes as with sticks and often superimposed polyrhythms (polymeters) and cross-rhythms while playing. Jones was also a great drum soloist who played interesting inventive solos with precision and finesse.

Excerpt of Philly Joe Jones playing *Nardis* in 1978

1956 CLASSIC QUINTET RECORDINGS

In 1956 Miles was signed with Prestige Records but had an offer from Columbia Records. Columbia offered Miles much more exposure, distribution, and money, but under his contract with Prestige, he owed four more albums before he could release an album with anyone else. Remarkably, he recorded four albums for Prestige and one for Columbia within a year's time. Miles never liked to rehearse, preferring the music to sound fresh and spontaneous, and usually chose first takes from recording sessions for that reason even if there were mistakes on them. The Prestige albums were titled *Cookin'*, *Steamin'*, *Workin'*, and *Relaxin'*, all followed by *With The Miles Davis Quintet*. The album for Columbia was *'Round About Midnight*. These are all great classic albums that still sound fresh and spontaneous even today.

IF I WERE A BELL 1956

RELAXIN' WITH THE MILES DAVIS QUINTET

This is a good example of how the Quintet performed pop standards. Miles plays the head by himself and essentially sings the song. The influence of Billie Holiday and Frank Sinatra is evident here. During the 1950s, most groups with two horns would play the heads in unison, octaves, or in some simple arrangement. While Miles plays the head, Paul Chambers plays a "two feel" on bass and Philly Joe Jones plays with brushes. Miles then solos for the next two choruses while the bass now plays "in four" and the drums are played with sticks. A unique procedure with this band was to play a tag at the end of each solo. A tag is an extension put on the end of a tune. Tags are typically played at the end of a performance and could be for just a few measures or extended a bit more. The purpose of a tag is to suspend the ending, building tension until the final chord. Miles, as he does here, often liked to use tags at the end of each solo. These tags were open ended and each determined how long he would play his tag and would then cue the band to end it. In this performance a solo break follows each solo tag. *If I Were a Bell*, one of several great songs written by Frank Loesser for the Musical *Guys and Dolls*, is in a ABAC 32-measure Pop song form.

What to listen for:

1. Miles' famous soft, raspy voice talking to the producer at the start
2. Red Garland's doorbell intro
3. Miles "singing" the song while playing with the Harmon mute along with the bass in 2 and brushes on the drums
4. Miles' lyrical solo with few but well-placed notes and his use of silence and the bass now "in 4" and the drums with sticks
5. The rhythm section's light, swinging accompaniment and how the rhythm section comes to the foreground during Miles' silences
6. The extended tags after Miles' and all the solos
7. The way John Coltrane's solo contrasts with Miles' solo
8. Coltrane's more aggressive sound and style and the rhythm section's more aggressive, random-like accompaniment
9. Red Garland's light, buoyant solo with consistent left-hand comping and block chord playing during the A sections of his last chorus
10. The final head played similarly to the opening head
11. The overall performance in how the mood changes for each solo and swings throughout

IF I WERE A BELL

Miles Davis—Trumpet
John Coltrane—Tenor Sax
Red Garland—Piano
Paul Chambers—Bass
Philly Joe Jones—Drums

Miles speaks

Intro—Piano doorbell
  8

	8	8	8	8
0:20	A	B	A	C

| Chorus 1 | Head - trumpet with Harmon mute————————tpt br |
| | Bass in 2, drums-brushes————————————2 |

| 1:01 |
| Chorus 2 | Trumpet solo——————————————————————— |
| | Bass in 4, drums- sticks————————————— |

1:42	2:18
Chorus 3	Trumpet solo continues————————————————TAG sax br
	10 2

| 2:38 |
| Chorus 4 | Sax solo———————————————————————————— |
| | Rhythm section more active———————————— |

3:18	3:57
Chorus 5	Sax solo continues——————————————————TAG pno br
	18 2

| 4:25 |
Chorus 6	Piano solo———————————————————————
	RH single notes - Consistent LH comping,
	drums -cross stick on rim on 4th beat of each bar

| 5:07 |
| Chorus 7 | Piano solo continues———————————————— |

5:49	6:26
Chorus 8	Piano solo continues——————————————TAG tpt break
	block chords		block chords	18 2

5:57	7:38
Chorus 9	Head - trumpet with Harmon mute————————TAG END
	Bass in 2, drums-brushes———————————— 18 2

KIND OF BLUE 1959
MILES DAVIS SEXTET

In 1958 Miles Davis formed a sextet by adding Cannonball Adderley on alto saxophone to his 1950s classic Quintet. This group recorded another one of Miles' great albums, **Milestones**. The tune **Milestones** on this album presented a whole new approach to jazz. The tune was based on modes, instead of major or minor scales, and the improvisations were based on these modes, instead of chord progressions. The success of this initial experiment in playing on modes, in 1959, sparked a whole album devoted to this approach. That album is **Kind of Blue**. Most jazz historians, critics, and fans would agree that **Kind of Blue** is the single greatest, most important, most influential jazz album of all time. It is now the best-selling jazz album of all time. It has been selling steadily and continuously since it first was released over fifty years ago. Miles made a few changes to his original Sextet before the recording of **Kind of Blue**. John Coltrane, Cannonball Adderley, and Paul Chambers remained but newly added were Jimmy Cobb on drums and most importantly, Bill Evans on piano. Evans was an equal partner to Miles in forming and implementing the unique concept of this entire project. One might ask why this album is such a big deal. Other than the great playing from everyone, this album was revolutionary because it changed the way jazz was approached and played for much of the 1960s and for much jazz played to the present day.

HISTORIC SIGNIFICANCE

There are two revolutionary aspects to *Kind of Blue*:
1. **The music is based on modes.**
    The term *mode* is used for diatonic scales that are neither major nor minor. Most Western music from around 1600 was based primarily on two scales: major and minor. Modes are actually nothing new. For various reasons these modes were mostly discarded and replaced with the major and minor tonal system. The reasons for this are beyond the scope of this book but, suffice it to say, this change was monumental in the evolution of Western music, and the so-called tonal system still controls most music we hear to this day. Almost all jazz harmony before *Kind of Blue* was based on the traditional tonal system with blues being a unique American addition to it. The music on *Kind of Blue* is written with modes, rather than major or minor scales. These particular modes are often referred to as Church Modes and actually go back to the music of the early Christian church that was

used for Gregorian chants. These modes were explored also by some turn-of-the-twentieth-century classical composers. So, the use of these modes was nothing new when Miles Davis used them, but they were new to jazz and we will see in later chapters how this expanded the tonal possibilities of future jazz musicians.

2. **The improvisations were based on modes rather than chords and chord changes.**

   As noted in earlier chapters, jazz improvisation evolved from simple embellishment, ornamentation, and variation to more complex, newly invented melodies based on chords and chord progressions. The bebop musicians carried this procedure to the extreme with increasingly complex chords and progressions. Oddly enough this concept reached its ultimate manifestation in the music of John Coltrane. (Coltrane's late-1950s music is described in Chapter 20.) Miles Davis steps in at this time and essentially puts an end to it by getting rid of pre-set chord changes and replacing them with scales or modes. This does not mean that chords won't be played. Chords are played throughout this music but the difference is they are not predetermined by the tune, and are freely improvised and derived from the modes or scales themselves. This entire process is radical at the time because it puts less emphasis on a predetermined structure (the tune), and more on the freedom to improvise within less restricting parameters. Freedom becomes an important term and attitude in 1960s and the culture in general. We will see various responses to the challenge of freedom in jazz in subsequent chapters. *Kind of Blue* announces to the world that the 1960s are dawning and a new era is about to arrive. For jazz, that era can be lumped under the term *Post-Bop*. *Kind of Blue* marks the end of Bebop and its offspring, Cool Jazz and Hard Bop, and all that came before, and ushers in the Post-Bop era that for many was the beginning of the end of jazz as they knew it.

MODES

Modes can easily be thought of and played on just the white keys on a piano. Just as a major scale can be played from C to C an octave higher and a minor scale can be played from A to A an octave higher on just white keys, modes can be derived by starting on the other white keys. Below are some examples of modes with their whole-step, half-step patterns indicated by W and H. Even a major scale (Ionian) can be used modally.

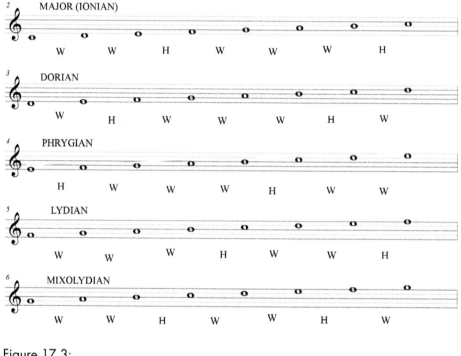

Figure 17.3:

DORIAN = D to D
PHRYGIAN = E to E
LYDIAN = F to F
MIXOLYDIAN = G to G

CANNONBALL ADDERLEY

Alto saxophonist Cannonball (Julian) Adderley (1928–1972) was considered by many to be the heir apparent to Charlie Parker. He was as technically facile as Parker and had strong roots in Bebop and Blues. Cannonball was the one leading Hard Bop saxophonists and formed his own successful group with his brother Nat, which played

Soul Jazz and was also rooted in Gospel and traditional African American music. His recording of *Mercy, Mercy, Mercy* in 1967 became a top-forty hit and introduced the Fender Rhodes electric piano to the jazz and Pop worlds. Some of Cannonball's best playing was during the 1950s and his tenure with Miles Davis.

Excerpt of Cannonball Adderley playing Brother John in 1963

BILL EVANS

Pianist Bill Evans (1928–1980) is the "Father of Modern Jazz Piano." He revolutionized the way jazz pianists played in many ways. (See Chapter 18 on Bill Evans for a fuller description of his work.) His unique way of playing the piano was crucial to the making of *Kind of Blue*. It is almost impossible to think of *Kind of Blue* without him. He was an equal partner with Miles Davis in the album's conception and manifestation. His unique way of voicing chords gave the whole project its ambience and coloration. His recording of **Peace Piece** in 1958 is a modal improvisation that predates *Kind of Blue* and served as the model for one of the tunes on the album **Flamenco Sketches**. Although the album **Blue in Green** is credited to Miles, Evans always claimed that he really wrote it. Evans also wrote the liner notes for the album that beautifully described the process used on the album.

Excerpt of Bill Evans playing Elsa in 1965

JIMMY COBB

Drummer Jimmy Cobb (b. 1929) comes from a hard bop tradition and remains active to this day. He played with Miles Davis for four years and later, among many others, with Sarah Vaughn for nine years. He is most noted for his contribution to *Kind of Blue*.

SO WHAT 1959

Much has been written on **Kind of Blue** and the making of *Kind of Blue*. The album contains five tunes that treat modes in various ways. The tune that we will focus on is **So What**. *So What* is based on two modes: D Dorian and Eb Dorian. Even though this modal approach is something new, there is a lot that is traditional about this tune. The form is a standard AABA pop song form. The head is based on a simple Call and Response pattern but the bass makes the call, which is not typical, and the piano or the piano and horns respond. The A sections are in D Dorian and the B section simply moves everything up a half step to Eb Dorian. The introduction, played by piano and bass, is slow and rubato.

Bill Evans came up with a new way of voicing chords, built on mostly 4ths rather than the traditional 3rds. This was novel at the time and added so much to the novelty and flavor of *So What* that they became known as *So What Voicings*. How they are played for the response during the head is shown below.

Figure 17.4

Each soloist treats the new challenge of modal improvisation differently:

Miles is lyrical, tuneful, and simple and typically, he plays recurring ideas.

Coltrane is more intense. He tends to play fast flurries of notes leading to long notes. He sounds like he is exploring the modes by listening to how each note relates.

Cannonball superimposes bebop-like chord progressions on the modes and plays Bebop-like fast lines.

Evans' solo is simple with some complex chords and single notes. The chords are more like colors than harmonies. During the piano solo the horns play the *So What* figure that was the response in the head but now as the call by placing it on the first beat of the measure instead of the third beat. Evans plays coloristic chords while comping throughout and creating a unique atmosphere.

What to listen for:

1. How the slow intro leads to the head
2. The Call and Response between bass and band
3. The bass walking for solos
4. The characteristics of each solo (see above)
5. How the "So What" response gets turned around into the call during the piano solo
6. How tension is created during the B sections and how it is released with the return to the A section

SO WHAT

Miles Davis—Trumpet
Cannonball Adderley—Alto Sax
John Coltrane—Tenor Sax
Bill Evans—Piano
Paul Chambers—Bass
Jimmy Cobb—Drums

Intro
Piano and bass—out of tempo - rubato

	8	8	8	8
0:35	A	A	B	A
Chorus 1	Head - Call & Response————————————————
	Call - bass————————————————
	Res - piano	pno + horns————————————
1:31
Chorus 2	Miles trumpet solo————————————————
	simple-lyrical-tuneful-cool- develops a motive————
2:28
Chorus 3	Miles Trumpet solo continues————————————
3:25
Chorus 4	Coltrane tenor sax solo————————————————
	more intense than Miles- sequences short motives
	Plays fast flurries of notes leading to long notes
4:20
Chorus 5	Coltrane tenor sax solo continues————————
5:16
Chorus 6	Adderley alto sax solo————————————————
	superimposes bebop-like chord progressions and blues
6:11
Chorus 7	Adderley alto sax solo continues————————
7:06
Chorus 8	Evans piano solo————————————————
	Call & Response - Call - horns, Response - piano
8:03
Chorus 9	Head	Call & Response————————————
	bass walks	Call - bass————————————
	pno-head res	Res - pno + horns————————
8:59
Coda	Call & Response continues - bass and piano - fade

THE OTHER TUNES

There are four other tracks on *Kind of Blue* and another remarkable aspect of this album is that all five cuts were first takes. CD reissues of the album contain one extra take on *Flamenco Sketches*. Wynton Kelly replaces Bill Evans on *Freddie Freeloader*. Evans has already left the band by the time of the recordings and Kelly was Miles' current pianist. Kelly shows some influence from Evans but infuses much more blues and bebop into his playing.

FREDDIE FREELOADER is a variation on a traditional blues progression and the most traditional-sounding cut on the album. Wynton Kelly's playing here clearly differs from Evans' more introspective approach and gives this track a slightly different feeling from the others.

BLUE IN GREEN is a haunting ballad that treats a modal melody with a circular chord progression that never seems to end but rather keeps circling back on itself. The harmonic progression can speed up or slow down on the whim of the soloists. This is another radically new procedure for jazz and another example of leaning toward *freedom* in the 1960s. This notion of freedom is one that makes the improvisers less confined by the structure of the tune, itself, and more free to be in the moment.

All Blues is a modalized blues and is triple meter. Triple meter was virtually nonexistent in jazz until the mid-1950s and became more commonplace by 1959. The I and IV chords of a traditional blues in G are replaced by a G Mixolydian and a G Dorian mode. The tune features a repetitive bluesy bass and saxophone riffs.

Flamenco Sketches is the most radical track on the album. There is no head or planned melody, rather just a series of five modes. The length for each mode is not even predetermined. The tune is completely improvised and even the form is improvised. Each soloist plays on each mode as long as he likes and then cues the band when to change to the next mode. This is music that is much in the moment and, again, *freedom* is lurking as the music becomes less and less preplanned. As radical as this procedure is, the music does not sound radical; it is, rather, slow and pretty and colorized by Bill Evans' lush harmonic ambient underpinnings.

WYNTON KELLY

Pianist Wynton Kelly (1931–1971) played with Miles from 1959 to 1963. He had strong roots in Bebop and Blues and had a light buoyant touch similar to Red Garland. He was also influenced by Bill Evans and incorporated some of Evans' chord voicings into his playing. As with all Miles' rhythm section players, Kelly was a master accompanist and had a great sense of swing.

SO WHAT
Live Video 1959

What this 1959 TV performance of *So What*. It is from a show called *The Robert Herridge Theater*. The group by now has played the tune for a little while and all, especially John Coltrane, are more comfortable with the tune and the new concept.

Miles Davis—Trumpet
John Coltrane—Tenor Saxophone
Wynton Kelly—Piano
Paul Chambers—Bass
Jimmy Cobb—Drums
Other Musicians—Under the direction of Gil Evans

MILES DAVIS AND GIL EVANS

Miles Davis collaborated with arranger/composer Gil Evans to make several recordings beginning as early as 1947 with Birth of the Cool. From the late 1950s into the early 1960s, they also recorded four studio albums and one live album. These were essentially concerti for trumpet and orchestra. Evans was always an experimental arranger who sought to combine instruments in new and interesting ways. Duke Ellington did likewise but Evans, although inspired by Ellington, did not copy him but evolved his own original style and approach. Evans featured Miles on these projects and surrounded him with large ensembles that were not typical jazz big bands. Evans used tuba, French horns, flutes, and even bassoons, along with the creative use of mutes on the brass to envelop Miles with a colorful, sonorous ambience. The studio albums are ***Miles Ahead***, ***Porgy and Bess***, ***Sketches of Spain***, and **Quiet Nights**. *Sketches of Spain* is considered to be a masterpiece of Third Stream Music and the most inspired work of their collaboration. Miles' actual first experience with playing modally was on Evans' arrangement of ***I Loves You Porgy*** from *Porgy and Bess*. Evans continued to collaborate with Miles behind the scenes in several later recording projects without receiving acknowledgment at the time, but more on this in Chapter 21.

THE DUKE 1959

Watch this clip from a TV show called *The Robert Herridge Theater*. The showed featured Miles for an entire half-hour and included three tunes from the *Miles Ahead* album with Gil Evans. Notice the unusual instrumentation that Gil Evans was known for. *The Duke* was written by Dave Brubeck in honor of Duke Ellington. Miles is actually not playing a trumpet but rather a flugelhorn, which plays like a trumpet but has a mellower sound. The flugelhorn became popular during the 1960s and beyond. Gil Evans conducts his arrangement for this performance.

Part 4

By the 1960s all hell broke loose as some jazz musicians began to stretch the limits of harmony and rhythm into what many thought was an incomprehensible conglomeration of clutter and noise. Others, however, found new and meaningful ways to play jazz that still appealed to many jazz fans.

Freedom was a key word both politically and artistically during this time and many equated Jazz, as an African American art form, with the Civil Rights struggles going on at the time. To be free in jazz meant little or no presuppositions and preplanning. There was an attitude that one should be free to express oneself without the constraints of chords, tempos, or even tunes. Free Jazz was the name given to this new music. Freedom, however, came with a price; hardly anyone was buying it.

Other jazz musicians were more traditional in their approach yet still strived to be new. New approaches to improvisation and group interaction were sought and implemented for a new Post-Bop music that still appealed to many during the early sixties. This music was freer than traditional jazz but not as free as Free Jazz. As the sixties progressed the freer music got freer as it approached Free Jazz and for most traditional jazz fans jazz seemed to be dead. Younger people were embracing the new Rock music and finding artistic satisfaction in it. Jazz musicians of all styles were struggling to survive during the sixties as Rock music and culture took over the youth culture.

Miles Davis' answer was; "If you can't beat 'em, join 'em," and join them he did. He created Fusion, which attempted to combine jazz with the contemporary Pop music of the day. For the traditionalists, this was the final death knell, while for others it was the saving grace. Either way, jazz was not the same during the seventies, as jazz musicians seemed to fall like dominos after Miles gave the initial push. Some questioned if Fusion was even jazz and cherished their old fifties albums more than ever.

All seemed lost through the seventies until Keith Jarrett in 1983 came out with an album titled ***Standards Volume 1***. Standards are the old Pop songs that jazz musicians had been playing for years but seemed to have forgotten about. Jarrett, who was involved in Free and Fusion, seemed to have had enough and resurrected the old tunes.

Freedom, Fusion, and Federation

How refreshing it was at the time and when someone of Jarrett's stature went back to the old tunes, others took note. The album and the trio he recorded with went on to great commercial success. People, perhaps, were going through withdrawal after years of Fusion and Free. One by one they all seemed to come back to the fold and the old became the new.

Jazz, ever since, has become largely an historical music; one where all styles coexist. Nothing much new happened after Fusion but jazz survives well into the 21st century and one can only hope for a century as diverse and interesting as the last.

Chapter Eighteen

The Bill Evans Trio

Bill Evans (1919–1980), born in Plainfield, New Jersey, is the *Father of Modern Jazz Piano*. Almost all jazz pianists from 1960 to the present day are influenced by him. He changed the way jazz was played on the piano both technically and stylistically. His unique approach to both harmony and rhythm influenced non-pianists as well as pianists, and many of his original tunes have become mainstays of the contemporary jazz repertoire. Evans had classical training and received a degree in piano performance from Southeastern Louisiana State University. He first came to public attention when played with Miles Davis' band in 1958 and was a equal partner to Miles in the conception of *Kind of Blue*, which is almost universally acclaimed as the most important, influential, and best jazz album of all time. Evans was with Miles' band for only nine months and left in 1958 to pursue his own trio. Miles brought him back, however, in 1959 to record *Kind of Blue*. The trio that he eventually formed with Scott LaFaro on bass and Paul Motian on drums pioneered an original concept of each player's role in a rhythm section and paved the way for much freer jazz in the 1960s. Their first album, ***Portrait in Jazz***, was a critical success. And their last recording from the Village Vanguard in 1961 is among the greatest in jazz history. LaFaro's untimely death in an auto accident devastated Evans and he did not play the piano for six months. Eventually he stated playing again and continued to lead trios for the rest of his life. He remains to this day the most important and influential Post-Bop pianist. Unfortunately, Evans' drug problems, first with heroin, and later with cocaine, led to his early death in 1980.

Figure 18.1: Bill Evans, 1969.

BILL EVANS' PIANO STYLE

Bill Evans revolutionized jazz piano playing in several ways. Although he was classically trained, he did not play with a classical touch as John Lewis did. His phrasing and articulation was not derived from the Classical or jazz worlds and no one ever made the piano sound quite the way he did. Although in a much different way, like Thelonious Monk, he evoked new sounds from the piano not just from the notes he played but also from the way he played them. Evans' chords often became colors more than harmonies and like Impressionist painters blur colors and images, he blurred sounds and tones by using the damper pedal to make musical soundscapes. Evans' classical training is evident in his chord voicings that derive from Chopin, and French Impressionists composers, Debussy and Ravel. Evans even blurs rhythm by displacing or replacing the meter in unpredictable ways. His solos are almost always organic in that ideas grow and transform in subtle ways. Sound, texture, harmony, melody, and rhythm combine to create ideas that rely on each element equally and one cannot separate a particular melodic statement from its precise underlying chord voicing or texture.

BILL EVANS' INNOVATIONS

1. **Use of the damper pedal**
   The damper often is erroneously called the sustain pedal. Dampers lay on top of a piano's strings. When a key is pressed down, a hammer is activated to strike the appropriate strings and the damper on top of those strings is raised at the same time to allow the strings to vibrate. When the key is released the damper returns to the string to stop the vibrations. Pressing down the damper pedal raises all of the dampers on the piano at the same time and keeps them raised until released. This enables the pianist to move his or her hands away from the keys that produced certain notes while the notes are still sounding in order to play other notes. Pedaling is a subtle part of piano technique and was rarely used before Bill Evans other than to connect bass notes to chords while playing with a striding left hand. Evans used the pedal to create blurry effects on purpose and the resulting sounds are decidedly different from the well-defined and clearly articulated lines of the Bebop pianists.

2. **Rootless chord voicings and clusters**
   The root of a chord is the lowest note of that chord in is basic position (root position) and determines the letter name for the chord. The root of a D major seventh chord is D, the root of a C minor ninth chord is C, etc. Rootless voicings leave the root out and by doing so, upper extensions of chords can be played more easily with one hand. By playing roots of chords, the pianist essentially doubles what the bass

would most likely play anyway and by eliminating the root not only is the pianist freer to incorporate other, more colorful notes, but also the bassist is freer to play substitute roots and chords. Evans is not the first pianist to use rootless voicings; Erroll Garner, Ahmad Jamal, and Red Garland notably used them before him, but Evans is the first to use them consistently and the one who systemized their forms and use. For Evans, a voicing becomes a sound or a color that can represent a chord and even one particular voicing can represent several different chords. Evans' voicings are played primarily in the middle register of the piano around middle C. This makes for a light sound and texture that leaves the bass player free to roam around the lower range without clashing with the pianist's left hand.

Below are some seventh chords in root position followed by two typical rootless voicings for those chords.

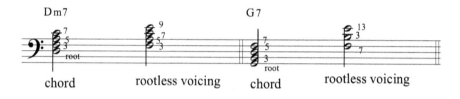

Figure 18.2

Rootless voicings are not chords but are used to represent or imply chords. They can be ambiguous and a single particular voicing can represent several different chords. The voicing shown below can represent or imply other chords and can be used with different roots.

Figure 18.3

Cluster voicings contain notes a half step apart that "rub against" each other. Evans typically uses them as chord fragments that may or may not contain roots. Fragments, like rootless voicing, are often ambiguous and any one particular voicing can represent several different chords.

Figure 18.4

3. **Right-hand–left-hand rhythmic unison**
Bill Evans invented a new way to play **block chords**. The technique is quite simple. The right hand plays single-note lines while the left hand plays a chord voicing with each right-hand note. In actual practice, the left hand plays along with most but not necessarily all of the right-hand notes. This technique ingeniously combines the best of two worlds: the rich texture and colors of block chords, including **locked-hands** techniques, are preserved while the right hand is free to play quick, articulated, and expressive lines.

Figure 18.5

EVANS' IMPROVISATION APPROACH

Motivic Development and Transformation

Evans developed an organic approach to improvisation that grows and develops ideas along the way. New phrases often refer to and/or develop previous ones and the music grows as Evans spins out permutations and variations. He not only uses motivic development, as for example Sonny Rollins often did, but he also engages in motivic transformation that gradually and subtly transforms an initial motive into a new one.

Rhythmic Displacement

Evans used rhythmic displacement in several ways. He sometimes superimposed different meters on the prevailing meter by either keeping the same beat and grouping accents in a different pattern, for example, playing in groups of three beats while the meter is grouped in four beat units, or by superimposing a different beat and metric pattern, for example, playing three beats in the space of two beats of the prevailing meter.

SCOTT LAFARO

Much as Bill Evans revolutionized jazz piano playing, Scott LaFaro (1936–1961) did so with the bass. He is the Father of Modern Jazz Bass and changed the way the bass was played both technically and stylistically. Technically he lowered the string toward the fingerboard, which made the strings easier to press down. He also plucked the strings with alternating fingers rather than by separate movements of the hand for each note. These changes enabled him to play extremely fast, in fact, faster than anyone before him. The changes, however, sacrificed some of the volume of sound he was able to produce. The relatively low volume the trio played and the use of a microphone made this sacrifice inconsequential for the music this group produced. Stylistically, LaFaro brought the bass from the background to the foreground and rid the bass of its time-keeping role. He often plays melodies along with Bill Evans and somehow manages to keep an implied bass line going while he does so. Thus, the bass is the last rhythm section instrument to be liberated from its time-keeping role. For the earliest styles of jazz, all rhythm section instruments kept the pulse. Count Basie freed the piano from doing so by comping instead during the Swing Era. Kenny Clarke freed up the drummer during the Bebop Era by decreasing the emphasis on the pulse and adding other layers of rhythm by dropping bombs, etc. It was LaFaro who now most consistently let go of the walking bass line and added new melodies as well as rhythms to the rhythm section.

This does not mean the music is not organized around a beat or pulse; it most certainly is and one can snap one's fingers to the music as with traditional jazz. It is now, however, the pulse is implied rather than being obviously stated and modern jazz musicians had no desire to play for dancers as earlier jazz musicians often did. LaFaro was an outstanding soloist and was prominently featured in the trio. Bass solos became much more common because of him. LaFaro could also walk a bass line when he wanted to and did so more in the early days of the trio. LaFaro inspired all future bassists with his technical facility and creative innovations.

PAUL MOTIAN

Paul Motian (1931–2011) was a crucial member of the Bill Evans Trio. He contributed to three-way conversation by lightly playing or implying the beat while using the drum set to produce colors as well as rhythms. One of the remarkable aspects of the trio was even though each player was playing an independent part, the music remained uncluttered and comprehensible. Paul Motian was the perfect drummer to accomplish this, and his sensitivity and musicality allowed Evans and LaFaro to *boldly go where no rhythm section has gone before.*

RHYTHM SECTION INTERPLAY

The Bill Evans Trio is historically significant because it pioneered the concept of rhythm section interplay. It blurred the distinction between background and foreground and each member approached the music as equal partners rather than a leader with accompaniment. This process leads the way to the *freer jazz* of the 1960s.

Freer jazz relies less on predetermined parameters and roles than traditional jazz but still adheres to a formal structure. This group also is in the forefront of **Post-Bop** jazz that really began with ***Kind of Blue***. Elements of Bebop and Swing were becoming farther and farther removed from the newer jazz of the sixties and the concept of rhythm section interplay was very much a part of it. We will see the effects and influence of the Bill Evans Trio most notably on the Miles Davis rhythm section of the mid-1960s.

VILLAGE VANGUARD 1961

In June 1961 the Bill Evans Trio recorded for the last time. Scott LaFaro died in a car accident ten days later. The recording was done during live performances on a Sunday at the famous Village Vanguard in New York. Originally, two albums were issued from the recording: *Sunday at the Village Vanguard* and *Waltz for Debby*. Currently the complete recordings are available on *Complete Live at The Village Vanguard 1961*. These recordings capture the trio at its peak and present their innovative approach at its best. These are widely considered to be among the best jazz recordings ever made.

ALICE IN WONDERLAND 1961
SUNDAY AT THE VILLAGE VANGUARD
Bill Evans Trio

Bill Evans transformed this Disney theme into a jazz waltz and a jazz standard. Dave Brubeck recorded it before Evans, but it is most associated with Evans and most often played as he conceived it. It is in triple meter, which was a rarity in the mid-fifties, but by now was fairly commonplace. Most jazz treatments of triple meter are referred to as jazz waltzes and Evans probably more than anyone else performed them. The feel here is very open with the **macrobeat**, the first beat of every measure, as the main pulse. The bass never walks or plays the **microbeat** pulse, every beat. The form is AABA but each section is 16 measures long rather than the typical 8 measures. Evans plays the first two A sections rubato by himself and bass and drums enter on the bridge. The three-way conversation among the trio is clearly heard in the recording, (as well as the conversations from the live audience). LaFaro manages to play bass and an inner counter voice to Evans's piano. Motian complements both with tasty, unobtrusive brushwork. Evans' innovative approach and unique style are audible throughout and all of the characteristics of his playing are heard and it is evident to the listener that we are in Post-Bop territory here, from the sounds of the piano, the chords, and the pedal, to the rhythms, to the absence of an audible pulse. Although this not a modal tune, Evans approaches it modally by thinking of scales rather than chords to construct his melodic lines. This approach will become fairly standard with many Post-Bop Players. The playing on this record is fairly radical for its time but it is so pleasant and pretty that one hardly noticed.

What to listen for:

1. Evans' unique touch and sound on the piano during the rubato beginning
2. The bass and drums entrance on the bridge
3. The 3-way conversation among the trio
4. The absence of an audible pulse throughout
5. Evans organic improvisation through the development and transformation of ideas
6. Evans' blurry playing from pedaling and his almost constant right-hand–left-hand unison
7. LaFaro's virtuosic bass playing, especially during his solo
8. The freshness and newness of this music in relation the previous jazz

ALICE IN WONDERLAND

Bill Evans—Piano
Scott LaFaro—Bass
Paul Motian—Drums

	16	16	16	16
	A	A	B	A
Chorus 1	Piano-Alone -head-----	--------------------------	-------------------------	--------------------
	Rubato----	----------------------	------| bass and drums - in tempo	
1:13				
Chorus 2	Piano solo -----	-------------------------	-------------------------	-----------------
	Bass plays both bass notes and melodic lines--------------------			
2:23				
Chorus 3	Piano solo continues-----	-------------------------	-------------------------	---------------
	Bass continues-----	-------------------------	-------------------------	---------------
3:32				
Chorus 4	Bass solo-----	-------------------------	-------------------------	---------------
	Piano comps lightly-----	-------------------------	-------------------------	---------------
4:41				
Chorus 5	Bass solo-----	-------------------------	-------------------------	---------------
	Piano drops out			
5:48				
Chorus 6	Piano solos again-----	-------------------------	-------------------------	---------------
	Bass- as before-----	-------------------------	-------------------------	---------------
6:55				
Chorus 7	Piano -head-----	-------------------------	-------------------------	---------------

WALTZ FOR DEBBY 1965

Watch this 1965 video from a British TV show with Chuck Israels on bass and Larry Bunker on drums. Israels played with Evans for a few years after Scott LaFaro died. **Waltz for Debby** is one of the many jazz waltzes that Evans composed. The head is played once as a waltz and then in four-four time. The meter remains in four until the end. Israels and Bunker play much like LaFaro and Motian from the original trio.

Chapter Nineteen

Free Jazz—In and Out of Control, Ornette Coleman and Charles Mingus

I n 1959, alto saxophonist Ornette Coleman (b. 1930) and his quartet caused quite a stir at an East Village jazz club in New York called the Five Spot Cafe. Word was out that a very unusual jazz band was creating very unusual music with very unusual sounds. As many music fans went to the Five Spot to see what all the commotion was about, they came away with strong opinions either for or against what they heard. Reputable musicians such as John Lewis of the Modern Jazz Quartet and Classical conductor and composer Leonard Bernstein had high praise for the music, while most, including Roy Eldridge and Miles Davis, had high disdain. What was all the fuss about? There were two aspects of their performance that troubled most jazz listeners: first they did away with preset forms, chords, scales, or keys to improvise on; and second they played many non-tempered notes along with many screeches, squeaks, and squawks emanating from their horns.

Figure 19.1: Ornette Coleman, 2011.

Jazz improvisation was always a "playing on" something, be it a tune, a chord progression, or a scale or mode. While Ornette Coleman's group played written tunes, they did not really improvise on them. The tunes were more of a point of departure from which the players could go wherever they wanted to without being restricted by them. It is important to know that even though they did away with preset forms, chords, scales, and keys on which to improvise, it does not mean that they did not use these parameters. It just means that none of these were predetermined as in earlier jazz performances. In Free Jazz, the players can improvise on chords, scales, etc., if they so choose but they choose so in the moment rather than ahead of time. A tremendous burden then is placed on the accompanying musicians to hear what the soloist is doing and make sense of it tonally and also rhythmically, for that matter. While non-tempered notes, inspired by Blues singing, have always been a part of jazz, this group seemed to carry it to extremes to the point where they no longer sounded like expressive Blues inflections but rather like inept musicians incapable of playing in tune. The screeches, squeaks, and squawks the horn players played for expressive purposes also seemed like the undesirable sounds made by amateur beginners. In fact the group looked like amateurs; Ornette Coleman was playing a white plastic alto saxophone and Don Cherry was playing a pocket trumpet, a rare compacted trumpet that was used in 19th century military units that could fit in your pocket. They appeared to be making noise by playing toys, which added to the derisive attitude of most watchers and listeners. These musicians, however, were serious about what they were doing and had a huge influence on Jazz in the sixties. *Freedom* is a word associated with the Civil Rights movement of the fifties and sixties and many Black musicians who played Free Jazz equated the two. Playing on no preplanned structures was not new in 1959; Lennie Tristano, who was one of the first Cool Jazz musicians, had dabbled in it as early as the late forties.

The following shows a key difference between traditional jazz and Free Jazz approaches to improvisation.

Traditional Approach

```
              A      A      B      A
Chorus 1 head----------------------------------------->
Chorus 2 solo----------------------------------------->
Chorus 3 solo----------------------------------------->
Chorus 4 head----------------------------------------|
```

Free Jazz Approach

```
A      A      B      A                       A      A      B      A
Head---------------------------solos>>>>>>>>>> head----------------------------|
```

Where in the traditional approach the solos are played on the repeating structure of the tune, in most Free Jazz the tune serves as a starting point for improvised solos that are "free" from the tune and simply go according to the whims of the players at that particular time before the tune is typically restated at the end. While to most listeners the improvisations sounded haphazard and random, Ornette often developed ideas and motives in an organic manner not that dissimilar to that of Bill Evans in what is referred to as Motivic Chain Associations. New ideas are born from previous ones and can gradually change to the point where they morph into new ones.

When Ornette Coleman and a few others began playing in this manner in the late fifties, it was referred to as the Avant Garde or "the new thing." It was not until Coleman recorded an album he called *Free Jazz* in 1960 that the movement got its more familiar name. Although Free Jazz never became popular, it did have a major influence on the Freer Jazz of the sixties. We will hear its influence on John Coltrane, Miles Davis, and others.

THE SHAPE OF JAZZ TO COME 1959

Ornette Coleman's first important album, *The Shape of Jazz to Come,* introduced most listeners to Ornette in particular and Free Jazz in general. The Ornette Coleman Quartet featured Don Cherry on cornet, Charlie Hayden on bass, and Billy Higgins on drums. The absence of a piano or guitar avoids stated or implied chords that would encumber the soloists.

LONELY WOMAN

Lonely Woman is probably the most traditional tune from the album and the most palatable to those who find Free Jazz offensive. It has a haunting, slow melody that is treated with the inflections and sound effects that are associated with this music. The form is AABA but the measures for each section are not predetermined. Rhythmically and tempo-wise the tune proceeds on three simultaneous layers: the bass plays out of tempo double stops (two notes at a time), the drums are playing at a very quick tempo, and the horns play a seemingly unrelated rubato slow melody on top. During the head, the horns play in octaves, harmony, or occasionally the sax plays independently. Ornette does the only solo, although Cherry joins him during the B section. The form is adhered to during the solo with an obvious reference to the B section of the head but measures are not counted and are really hard to determine anyway since there seems to be three different and unrelated tempos going on. There is a fade-in and a fade-out with bass and drums that act as an intro and coda.

What to listen for:

1. The fade in with the rubato bass and fast drums
2. The highly inflected in-the-cracks haunting horn melody
3. Ornette's solo against the seemingly unrelated background
4. Cherry's entrance on the B section of the solo
5. The return of the head in similar fashion
6. The brief horn coda
7. The fade out with bass and drums

LONELY WOMAN

Ornette Coleman—Alto Sax
Don Cherry—Cornet
Charlie Hayden—Bass
Billy Higgins—Drums

Intro - Fade in
　　　Bass- double stops
　　　Drums—fast tempo

	A	A	B	A
0:19 Chorus 1	Horns in octave or harmony————————			
1:46 Chorus 2	Sax solo————————————————			
			|cornet—|	
2:54 Chorus 3	Horns in octave or harmony————————			

4:19
Coda　　　　　　　　　　Fade out
　　　　　Horns——————\|Bass- double stops
　　　　　　　　　　　　Drums—fast tempo

FREE JAZZ 1960
The Ornette Coleman Double Quartet

The New Thing, as it was often called, started to be called Free Jazz after Ornette Coleman released an album called *Free Jazz* in 1960. The Ornette Coleman Double Quartet consists of two separate fully functioning quartets with two horns, bass, and drums in each one. Placed in opposite ends of the recording studio, they play uninterrupted for thirty-seven minutes with only a few things preplanned. The two quartets were separated on two stereo channels as follows:

LEFT QUARTET   RIGHT QUARTET

Ornette Coleman—Alto Sax   Freddie Hubbard—Trumpet
Don Cherry—Trumpet   Eric Dolphy—Bass Clarinet
Scott LaFaro—Bass   Charlie Hayden—Bass
Billy Higgins—Drums   Ed Blackwell—Drums

There are some prearranged orders for solos and a few themes but otherwise the music seems random and even chaotic at times. The idea with this kind of endeavor is to be in the moment. Although most people found the album incomprehensible, it did influence many jazz musicians and much of the music of the sixties.

FREE JAZZ
The Ornette Coleman Double Quartet

Listen to an excerpt from Ornette Coleman's *Free Jazz*. This segment, excerpted on the Smithsonian Collection of Classic Jazz, takes place in the middle of the performance.

OTHER FREE JAZZ PLAYERS

Cecil Taylor

Pianist Cecil Taylor (b. 1929), was one of the first notable Free Jazz players. While Ornette Coleman's group preferred no chord instrument so as to avoid traditional chordal associations, Taylor avoids it by percussively playing dense clusters of notes in complex rhythms that create almost constant tension. He was partly influenced by Dave Brubeck in his dense rhythmic chording and also by Thelonious Monk's penchant for stark dissonances. Taylor treats the piano as the percussion instrument that it essentially is and even though he produces definite pitches, the dense clusters of adjacent notes give the effect of approximate pitches or tonal regions distinguishable only by their relative distance from each other. Taylor played solo piano as well as with small groups.

Eric Dolphy

Multi-instrumentalist Eric Dolphy (1928–1964) was a real virtuoso who played flute, alto saxophone, and bass clarinet. His mastery of these instruments enabled him to play wild-like solos that continually jumped to different registers. Although to the casual listener it seemed these notes were random, closer examinations shows true pitch relationships that are only displaced into different octave. These types of relationships were being explored as well by composers in the Avant Garde Classical world of the time. He famously played with Chico Hamilton, Charles Mingus, and John Coltrane.

Albert Ayler

Tenor saxophonist Albert Ayler (1936–1970) perhaps stretched the limits of Free Jazz too far. He essentially screams at the listener most of the time while coaxing sound effects from his horn. His tunes are very basic and simple but his ensuing improvisations tend to go off the deep end as far as most listeners are concerned, even those who otherwise embrace Free Jazz.

CHARLES MINGUS

Bassist and composer Charles Mingus (1922–1979) remains one of the most enigmatic figures in jazz history. He studied trombone then cello while in school but switched to bass when he realized the limited market value for a Black classical cellist at the time. His music is stylistically as hard to pin down as is his personality. His inclusion in this chapter on Free Jazz is quite arbitrary as it would be in any chapter. His music is unique but inclusive of almost all jazz styles before and after him. He was a virtuoso bass player who pioneered a more modern way of playing the instrument, both musically and technically. He often used the bass as a melodic instrument and played extremely fast lines by alternating fingers to pluck the strings. His playing experience was as varied as it could get at the time: he played New Orleans style with Louis Armstrong; Swing with Lionel Hampton; and Bebop with Charlie Parker, Dizzy Gillespie, and Bud Powell. He is often associated with Hard Bop because of the many Gospel/Blues tunes he wrote and performed. He dabbled in Third Stream music and also anticipated Free Jazz, although he generally disapproved of it, he explored in it in a controlled environment.

Figure 19.2: Charles Mingus, 1976.
Copyright © Tom Marcello (CC BY-SA 2.0) at http://commons.wikimedia.org/wiki/File:Charles_Mingus_1976.jpg

In many ways Mingus is the opposite of Ornette Coleman. He was perhaps foremost a composer, who like Jelly Roll Morton and Duke Ellington, liked to control his music. Although his players mostly improvised, Mingus controlled the mood, feeling, and tempo of the music. There are sections where the players might freely improvise but those sections are determined by Mingus within a larger compositional framework. Mingus was also a throwback to 19th century Romanticism; he used music as a form of self-expression and often he expressed his outrage and frustration with racial discrimination. His compositions are often programmatic: ***Pithecanthropus Erectus*** depicts the rise of mankind who evolved from apes to his eventual downfall. ***The Clown*** has a narration that goes with the music that uses an unappreciated circus clown as a metaphor for jazz musicians. ***Haitian Fight Song*** expresses Mingus' thinking about racial prejudice and persecution. He has said he cannot play it right unless he thinks about them as he plays. He also wanted his players to feel what he was feeling and his legendary temper could take over when they did not. He has been known to physically assault band members as well as chastise audiences for lack of attention. Mingus was never one to hide his emotions within and without music.

Mingus wrote for and performed with various sized ensembles throughout his life. Like Morton and Ellington he often told players what to play rather than write out specific parts. Sometimes these instructions were nonspecific: "Play something like this, or express this or that emotion, etc." The music often had complex polyphonic lines going against each other, written or improvised. When he instructed the players to play freely without reference to the tune or chord changes, it was always to express chaos or anger or rage. Mingus' tunes often change tempos in the middle of a performance but even when they did, he, not the soloist, controlled when it would happen. The tempo changes could be not only twice or half the current speed, but also a third faster or slower. Tempo changes in jazz are rare, other than occasional double-time, but Mingus used them as structural compositional devices to expand the scope of a jazz performance. In this regard he was similar to John Lewis of the Modern Jazz Quartet, who likewise sought to broaden the formal dimensions of the standard 12-bar Blues or 32-bar pop song form.

HORA DECUBITUS 1963
MINGUS MINGUS MINGUS MINGUS MINGUS
Charles Mingus

Hora Decubitus is a Latin term used in prescription medicines that is usually abbreviated *hor. decub.* It means *at bedtime.* It is a 12-bar Blues form built around a simple riff-like theme. Despite the title the tune is anything but calming. Mingus sets the tone playing the first chorus by himself with an aggressive bass line using octave jumps. Then Jerome Richardson enters on the baritone saxophone play the main theme of the head. This Blues head is in a a^1 b form; the a^1 phrase begin a fourth higher on the IV chord and ends like the first phrase on the I chord. The theme keeps repeating while new parts are added to it for four more choruses. All the while the polyphonic cacophony that ensues builds to a chaotic Free Jazz–like tension until Booker Ervin's tenor saxophone solo. The background parts that join the solo are Ellingtonian in their structured dissonance against the saxophone. Eric Dolphy solos next on the alto saxophone in his typical asymmetrical style. He jumps registers constantly and seemingly plays free of any melodic coherence or adherence to the chordal structure. Dolphy, however, knows exactly what he is doing and his lines would sound more normal if those wide leaps were transposed to lie within one register (see above section on Dolphy). After Richard Williams' trumpet solo, the head returns three more times; polyphonically at first then in unison (octaves) for the last chorus, which solidly grounds the tune and the tensions encountered along the way. The ending features a drawn-out "Amen" ending, IV-I, where all the players engage in a free improvisational final cadence.

What to listen for:

1. Mingus' aggressive solo bass introduction
2. The equally aggressive head (main theme) first played on the baritone sax
3. The build-up of tension as instruments and melodies are added
4. Ervin's tenor sax solo with and without background parts
5. Dolphy's wild but highly structured alto sax solo
6. Williams' trumpet solo
7. The return of the head during the 18th–20th choruses
8. The grounding of tension during the last unison head chorus
9. The Free-Jazz-like ending

HORA DECUBITUS

Charles Mingus—Bass
Jaki Byard—Piano
Walter Perkins—Drums
Richard Williams—Trumpet
Eddie Preston—Trumpet

Eric Dolphy—Alto Sax
Booker Ervin—Tenor Sax
Jerome Richardson—Baritone Sax
Brit Woodman—Trombone
Don Butterfield—Tuba

Chorus 1: bass solo

Chorus 2: head begins—bar. sax—main theme

Chorus 3: Other saxes join bar. Sax—in unison and harmony

Chorus 4: saxes continues main theme—trombone plays counter line

Chorus 5: alto sax plays new counter line, others continue as before

Chorus 6: trumpet adds a riff as others continue

Chorus 7: tenor sax solo (Booker Ervin)

Choruses 8–9: solo continues with band playing background figures

Chorus 10: solo continues with rhythm section

Choruses 11–12: alto sax solo (Eric Dolphy) after short band intro

Chorus 13: solo continues with band playing background figures

Chorus 14: solo continues with rhythm section

Choruses 15–16: trumpet solo (Richard Williams) after short band intro

Chorus 16: solo continues with band playing background figures

Chorus 17: solo continues with the main theme in the background

Choruses 18–19: head—main theme and counter lines from first head

Chorus 20: all horns play main theme together

Ending: free-like improvisation by all over IV-I "Amen" cadence

Chapter Twenty

John Coltrane

Saxophonist John Coltrane (1926–1967) was perhaps the most influential jazz musician of the 1960s. "Trane," as he was commonly referred to, was not just a master musician; he was a force that dominated the Post-Bop world of jazz.

Figure 20.1: John Coltrane, 1963.

He was born in Hamlet, North Carolina, and moved to Philadelphia when he was a teenager where he studied music at the Ornstein School of Music and later at Granoff Studios and with Dennis Sandole. In 1945 he enlisted in the navy and played in the navy band in Hawaii. Coltrane was virtually unknown until he played in the Classic Miles Davis Quintet of the fifties (see Chapter 16). There he served as the perfect foil to the cool, laid-back Miles Davis. Jazz critic and historian Ira Gitler described Coltrane's playing of a lot of notes as sounding like "**sheets of sound**." Miles actually fired Coltrane in 1957 because of his drug and alcohol problems and suggested that he clean himself up and play with Thelonious Monk's band. Miles knew Monk was looking for a sax player and he thought the experience would straighten Coltrane's head out. Coltrane was always searching for something intangible both musically and spiritually. Miles also told him that he would hire him back when he was off the drugs, which he did in 1958. Trane then became a member of the Miles Davis Sextet, which added Cannonball Adderley on alto saxophone. After playing on the historic *Kind of Blue* album with Miles Davis, Coltrane formed his own quartet in 1960 and continually evolved his music until his death in 1967 from liver disease, due to complications of earlier drug abuse.

Coltrane influence the jazz world in three major ways:

First was his **dedication**. He practiced incessantly and was constantly exploring and finding new ways to play his music. He devoured Nicolas Slonimsky's *Thesaurus of Scales and Melodic Patterns*, which offers a very intellectual, mathematical approach to music. He even practiced on gigs while others were soloing.

Second, he brought a **Eastern influence** into jazz. Although Yusef Lateef's album ***Eastern Sounds*** predates Coltrane's ***My Favorite Things***, Coltrane was the one mostly responsible for adding an Eastern aesthetic to jazz in the sixties.

Third, he brought **spirituality** into the jazz world. While he was purging himself from drugs and alcohol in 1957, he became very religious. His first wife, Naima, was a Moslem who got him interested in Islam, but Coltrane remained devoted to his Christian upbringing and also embraced various Eastern religious and philosophical thinking. Coltrane's spirituality becomes most evident in his albums: ***A Love Supreme, Meditation***, and ***Ascension***.

Coltrane's work can be divided into three style periods:

1. Early: 1955–1960—Chord Change obsession period
2. Middle: 1960–1965—Modal period
3. Late: 1965–1967—Free Jazz period

EARLY PERIOD 1955–1960

During this period Coltrane seemed to be obsessed with chords and chord changes (progressions). He searched for all the possibilities he could find on chord substitutions and progressions. He challenged himself by devising exercises that would not only change chords quickly at very fast tempos but also changed to distantly related keys a rapid rate. Much of the material that jazz musicians played during this time came from "The Great American Songbook" that was composed mostly of the great Pop standards written during the 1920s through 1940s. These songs typically change keys within the usual 32-measure form. The keys, however, are usually closely related; for example, the keys of C major is closely related to the keys of G major and F major since there is only one different note in the scales of these keys. C major has no sharps or flats, whereas G major has one sharp (F-sharp) and F major has one flat (B-flat). Coltrane wrote tunes that changed to distantly related keys; for example the key of E major is distantly related to C major because the E major scale has four sharps as opposed to none. What were originally exercises became full-fledged tunes that Coltrane recorded under his own name while was still playing with Miles Davis' band. These tunes serve to this day as intellectual challenges for jazz improvisers. One needs to have a firm grasp on the theoretical implications of these chord progressions in order to create a convincing improvisation. Coltrane mastered this technique through his incessant practicing.

GIANT STEPS
From GIANT STEPS 1959

The album *Giant Steps* was another landmark album that was recorded in 1959. This was a remarkable year in the history of jazz recording that also included Miles Davis' *Kind of Blue*, Dave Brubeck's *Time Out*, and Ornette Coleman's *The Shape of Jazz to Come*. For all practical purposes, the tune *Giant Steps* put an end to Bebop. Coltrane seemed to stretch the Beboppers' delight in complex chords and chord progressions to its limit and the language that became Bebop all but stopped evolving after *Giant Steps*. It became the ultimate intellectual challenge to jazz musicians because of its rapid and distantly related key changes as well as its very fast tempo. The chord progression continually modulates (changes key) by major thirds every one or two measures going from B major to G major to Eb major. These three keys outline an augmented triad, Eb-G-B, and symmetrically divide the octave into three parts. Coltrane's interest in this kind of symmetry stems from his study of Slonimsky's book and his interest in 20th century Classical composers such as Igor Stravinsky and Bela Bartok, who employed symmetrical techniques in their compositions. When *Giant Steps* first came out, musicians were amazed that Trane could play such a complex tune at such a fast tempo, but after the solo had been transcribed, they could decipher how he managed to do so. Coltrane thought in groups of notes rather than single notes and he practiced note patterns that he was able to plug into any solo. In the example below, each note of the upper staff is translated into a note pattern; a 1-2-3-5 pattern in the first measure and a 1-3-5-7 pattern in the next measure. Coltrane used these patterns and others, mixing them up in different ways in playing through tunes with complex progressions.

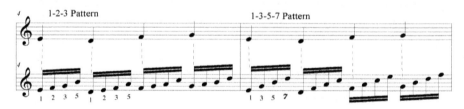

Figure 20.2

Although the chord progression is complex and tempo is extremely fast, the melody, itself, the head to Giant Steps, is very simple consisting mostly of half notes.

GIANT STEPS 1959

John Coltrane—Tenor Sax
Tommy Flannigan—Piano
Paul Chambers—Bass
Art Taylor—Drums

Listen to **Giant Steps**. The head is played twice before Coltrane's improvised solo. Notice the speed with which he plays his solo along with the very fast tempo.

MIDDLE PERIOD 1960–1965

After Coltrane's experience with **Kind of Blue** in 1959, he made a 180-degree turn and abandoned his infatuation with chord changes and embraced modality in its place. In essence, he went from lots of chords to no chords, or at least no predetermined chords. In his Modal Period, Coltrane evolved the whole concept of playing on modes more than Miles Davis and Bill Evans did. While Miles and Evans did no new explorations of modality right after **Kind of Blue**, Coltrane stretched the limits of freer jazz in the early sixties by his free-like modal improvisations. He discovered that once a modal underpinning grounds the tonality, he could play almost anything over it. It is during his Second Period that Coltrane found musicians who shared his musical concept and also an audience who appreciated what his band was playing. Coltrane became an international jazz star and was in demand all over the world. Being a rather shy person, he was never very comfortable with his newfound celebrity. During this time, Trane became interested in music of other cultures, especially Indian, Middle Eastern, and African music. He became friendly with the famous Indian sitar player Ravi Shankar and studied Indian music with him. What is sometimes referred to as Indian Classical music is mostly improvised and is based on certain scales called ragas that are akin to Western modes. Ragas have certain colors or moods associated with them and Indian musicians improvise long, complex melodies and rhythms based on them. Coltrane was now approaching his improvisations in a similar way and his additional interest in certain Indian philosophies brought a new Eastern aesthetic into the jazz world. It is during this time that Coltrane started playing the soprano saxophone. Although not new to jazz, the soprano sax was rarely used before. The great New Orleans musician Sidney Bechet most notably played it and later Johnny Hodges occasionally played it with the Duke Ellington band. But the sound of the soprano sax was new to the ears of most jazz musicians and listeners when Trane first recorded with it. Theories abound as to why he started playing the soprano sax when he did, but an obvious reason seems to be that it has a similar sound to Eastern and Middle Eastern wind instruments. Coltrane was also being influenced by free jazz and by prominent Free Jazz saxophone players Eric Dolphy and John Gilmore. He now incorporated screeches and squawks along with the sheets of sound into his repertoire. With a new band and new sounds, John Coltrane was about to set the jazz world on fire with a radically new kind of music and he did it with a simple and popular song from a Broadway musical called *The Sound of Music.*

JOHN COLTRANE QUARTET

After trying out several players in 1960, Coltrane found the players he was looking for his working quartet: McCoy Tyner on piano, Elvin Jones on bass, and Steve Davis on bass. Tyner and Jones proved to be perfect complements to Coltrane's new modal concept and their unique approaches to their instruments became crucial for Coltrane's new tonal and rhythmic explorations. In 1962 Jimmy Garrison was added on bass and it is the group with Garrison that became known as the Coltrane Classic Quartet.

MCCOY TYNER

McCoy Tyner (b. 1938) grew up in Philadelphia where he became friends with Coltrane and his family. He first came to national attention when he played with Art Farmer's and Benny Golson's Jazztet. Coltrane hired him in 1960 and he stayed for Coltrane's entire middle period. While with Coltrane, Tyner developed a unique approach to comping on the piano, one that made use of full resonant chords played with low register octaves and fifths with the left hand and middle register lush harmonies with the right hand. While soloing, he often played chords built in fourths in the left land and melodies derived from pentatonic scales in the right hand. **Pentatonic scales** are five-note scales that are often used in simpler folk music from around the world. Coltrane's interest in Eastern music also inspired Tyner to explore ways of incorporating these simple scales into their music. Fourths are related to pentatonic scales since one can derive a pentatonic scale by playing five perfect fourths in a row.

Figure 20.3: McCoy Tyner, 1973.

Tyner abstracted various **quartal** chords (chords built in fourths) from the modes he was playing on and by superimposing different pentatonic scales over them, he created a very complex juxtaposition of simple independent parts. He also sometimes played ringing octaves with his right hand in cross-rhythmic patterns. Quartal harmonies are tonally ambiguous and Tyner's use of them makes less for traditional harmonic implications than it does for color and rhythmic interest. What Bill Evans began with *Kind of Blue*, McCoy Tyner evolved into a highly personal style, one that influenced many Post Bop pianists, most notably Chick Corea. The quartet's historic version of *My Favorite Things* is impossible to imagine without his unique playing style.

Excerpt of McCoy Tyner playing Afro Blue in 1961

ELVIN JONES

Elvin Jones (1927–2004) is one of the two most influential Post-Bop drummers. Like McCoy Tyner, Jones' contribution to Coltrane's middle period is enormous. Jones took the polyrhythmic (polymetric) concepts of some of the previous drummers to the extreme. He was able to play a complex overlay of different rhythms and meters that produced an exciting rhythmic impulse to Coltrane's music. It is in the sixties with drummers like Elvin Jones that jazz comes closest to the West African Polymetric drumming that originally inspired Ragtime and Jazz at the turn of the 20th century. Jones often sounds like an entire percussion section and Coltrane's new harmonically static modal music allowed Jones the freedom to focus the music on rhythm. Often he and Coltrane would engage in duets that reached a kind of hypnotic ecstasy. Jones' unique playing style became crucial to Coltrane's vision and the historic recordings he played on seem unimaginable without him.

Excerpt of Elvin Jones playing *My Favorite Things* in 1961

MY FAVORITE THINGS

Coltrane's recording of *My Favorite Things* from the album *My Favorite Things*, released in early 1961, is one of the most radical and revolutionary recordings in all of jazz history. It became a major sensation and made John Coltrane a superstar in the jazz world. With this recording Coltrane brought an Eastern influence, a new approach to modality, and the soprano saxophone into the forefront of the worldwide jazz community. As radical as his treatment of this Broadway show song was, it became a major popular jazz hit, partly because of the song's familiarity. Coltrane took a show tune with no jazz connection at all and transformed it into a masterpiece of Post-Bop Freer jazz by doing what jazz musicians have always done; that is, he used the tune as source material to interpret in a deeply personal way.

The soprano saxophone, although not entirely new to jazz, was new to most listeners and the sound Coltrane made on it has a distinctly Eastern flavor. The tune is in triple meter and although this was not a novelty by 1961, the rhythm section's treatment of it was felt in six rather than in three and was not played like a typical jazz waltz. The entire rhythmic feeling of the music has a swaying back and forth character to it and this along with an almost constant drone (a repeating low E) in the bass added to the Eastern flavor of the music. Rather than improvise on the form of the tune as was done in tradition jazz, the band takes a modal approach but one that is based on the structure of the tune. Richard Rodgers ingeniously wrote the main melody of the song so that it could be harmonized in a minor key and then a major key without changing a note. Tyner and then Coltrane improvise during interludes between statements of the A section of the tune. The return to the head during the A sections signals that a change of mode will occur for the next interlude. The reiterations of the theme also serve as reference points for the listener—that we are indeed listening to *My Favorite Things* from *The Sound of Music*, written by Rodgers and Hammerstein. With this recording we are truly in a Post-Bop world that has little resemblance to Bebop, Swing, or any jazz before it.

What to listen for:

1. The Hypnotic swaying triple meter feel
2. The exotic sound of the Coltrane's soprano sax
3. How this version of *My Favorite Things* differs from the original show song
4. Tyner's full resonant chords throughout
5. The droning bass for most of the performance
6. Tyner's ringing octave in his right hand during his solo
7. The return of the A section during the solos
8. The changes between minor and major during the solos
9. Coltrane's use of sound effects and screeches
10. The polyrhythmic drumming of Jones

MY FAVORITE THINGS

John Coltrane—Soprano Sax
McCoy Tyner—Piano
Steve Davis—Bass
Elvin Jones—Drums

Intro - piano
16

Head   A | inter | A | inter | A¹ | B | inter
        sax——————|————————|——————————|———————————|—————————|————————|——————
        E minor——————————————————————| E maj——————————————|E min———————
        16 |8 | 16 | 24 | 16 |16 |16

2:18
piano   A | inter | A | inter | A¹ | inter | A
solo   Piano———
        E min |————————————————————| E maj——————————————| E min———————————
        16 |32 | 16 | 152 | 16 | 32 |16

7:02
sop sax inter | A | inter | A | inter | A | B |inter|end
solo   sop sax——
         | E min——————————————————————————————| E maj | E min———————————————
         8 | 16 | 136 | 16 | 136 | 16 | 16 | 32

AFRO BLUE

John Coltrane—Soprano Sax
McCoy Tyner—Piano
Steve Davis—Bass
Elvin Jones—Drums

Watch this 1961 video of **Afro Blue**, written by Latin percussionist Mongo Santamaria, from **Jazz Casual**, which was a TV show hosted by jazz writer Ralph Gleason. It is modal and in triple meter, and has much of the flavor of **My Favorite Things**.

A LOVE SUPREME

Many consider **A Love Supreme** to be Coltrane's finest recording. It was recorded in December 1964 and released in February 1965. It is a four-movement suite intended to be heard as a complete work in a prescribed order. Coltrane's spirituality is obvious here as the title refers to the love of God. Coltrane in his liner notes thanks God for rescuing him from his addictions in 1957 and composed a poem addressing his thoughts that was printed on the album cover. The music is highly intense and inspired, not at all for casual listening, yet became very popular. It is probably the culmination of Coltrane's Middle-modal period. The music is even freer than before but still anchored by modes or at least a prevailing tonality. It appealed to the Rock crowd as well as to jazz fans, and its free-like improvisations over a modal underpinning serve as a model for sixties Rock guitar solos. The four movements are

I. Acknowledgement
II. Resolution
III. Pursuance
IV. Psalm

Acknowledgement is based on the opening bass motive (A Love Supreme motive) played after a rubato introduction, and a separate motive Coltrane plays on top of it. Coltrane develops his motive first and then works of the bass motive eventually playing it in all twelve "keys." Toward the end of the movement Coltrane, chats the words "A Love Supreme" to the bass motive in the original key, F minor, and then drops it down a whole step to Eb minor, the key of the next movement, **Resolution**.

Figure 20.4

The rhythm section is in constant flux throughout, providing an undulating current underneath Coltrane's searching, searing solo.

Resolution, which begins with a bass solo by Jimmy Garrison, is a simple 8-measure tune with chord changes but treated modally for the most part. The third movement, *Pursuance*, begins with an Elvin Jones drum solo before proceeding with a minor blues tune. After Coltrane plays the head, Tyner plays a typical energetic, driving solo that features quartal voicings in his left hand and melodic lines based on pentatonic scales in his right hand. The performance is modal for the most part but Coltrane seems to ignore the form for a while during his solo. In the last movement, *Psalm*, Coltrane recites on the saxophone the printed poem that he composed for the album cover, although most were not aware of this at the time. One can easily follow the words as Coltrane intones them on his horn while the rhythm section plays a nonmetric rubato sustained background. There is no real preplanned head or melody as Trane lets his own poem guide him along.

ACKNOWLEDGEMENT 1964

John Coltrane—Soprano Sax
McCoy Tyner—Piano
Jimmy Garrison—Bass
Elvin Jones — Drums

Listen to the first movement of **A Love Supreme**. Notice the fanfare-like opening and distinctive bass motive that succeeds it. Coltrane then works off a different motive before picking up the bass motive and sequencing it, eventually starting it on all twelve pitches. At the end of the movement Coltrane, who actually overdubbed his voice a few times, chants; "A Love Supreme" to the bass motive.

BALLADS

During his modal, Freer jazz period, Coltrane did not entirely abandon playing standards. In the album *Ballads*, released in 1963, Coltrane plays lyrically and simply while almost singing the songs through his horn. He stays close to the songs' melody throughout, eschewing his usual sheets of sound. *John Coltrane and Johnny Hartman*, also released in 1963, teamed Coltrane with balladeer vocalist Johnny Hartman. Hartman's deep, rich baritone voice was a perfect match to Coltrane's deep, penetrating tenor saxophone. The very relaxed Hartman vocals contrasted nicely with Coltrane's more assertive playing. The album is widely considered to be one of the great jazz vocal albums of all time, with definitive versions of some great standards, including *Lush Life*, *You Are Too Beautiful*, *and They Say It's Wonderful*.

LUSH LIFE

Johnny Hartman—Vocal
John Coltrane—Soprano Sax
McCoy Tyner—Piano
Steve Davis—Bass
Elvin Jones—Drums

Listen to *Lush Life* from the album, *John Coltrane and Johnny Hartman*. A 19-year-old Billy Strayhorn wrote this famous song, which is amazing considering the sophistication of the music and lyrics. Strayhorn was Duke Ellington's alter ego who wrote and arranged many tunes for the Ellington band. Hartman's rich baritone comes through on this recording and he and Coltrane shine on this track. Hartman sings the verse and the chorus, after which Coltrane solos on the chorus up until the last 16 measures, where Hartman comes back in.

LATE PERIOD 1965–1967

In the last few years of his life, John Coltrane fully embraced Free Jazz. His music was getting progressively freer throughout the sixties and he continued his searching by expanding his group and playing with less preplanning. He added Rashied Ali as second drummer and the added rhythms perhaps overcomplicated the already complex drumming of Elvin Jones. Coltrane added some additional horn players as well and both Jones and McCoy Tyner, unhappy with Coltrane's new direction, left the band by the end of 1965. The music now took on the character of Ornette Coleman's ***Free Jazz*** album with a playing-in-the-moment approach that seemed to most listeners as formless chaos. Throughout his middle period, Coltrane managed to attract listeners because his free-like improvisations were always grounded on a formal and/or tonal structure. Now, however, that structure was gone for the most part and the music became increasingly difficult to follow with much simultaneous improvising with little or no harmonic, tonal, or rhythmic consistency. Coltrane continued his spiritual quest with albums such as ***Ascension*** and ***Meditation***, but was increasingly losing the vast audience he had acquired during the preceding years. It was really John Coltrane who put Free Jazz on the map. Because of his great stature in the jazz world and his great following, he legitimized Free Jazz in the eyes and ears of many musicians and listeners. One can only imagine where all of this would have taken him had he not succumbed to liver cancer in 1967. John Coltrane has become a jazz icon and is revered and almost worshipped by many fans and musicians to this day.

ASCENSION 1965
(Excerpt)

Listen to this excerpt from Ascension. The music is very dense and chaotic with very little preplanning, similar to Ornette Coleman's ***Free Jazz*** album. The band is a larger 11-piece ensemble, which adds to density of sound with much collective improvisation going on.

Chapter Twenty One

Miles Davis in the Sixties

After *Kind of Blue* in 1959, Miles Davis' band went through several personnel changes. In 1963 he assembled another great quintet with another great rhythm section. Tenor saxophonist **George Coleman** was eventually replaced by **Wayne Shorter** in late 1964 and it is the group with Shorter that became known as Miles Davis' second great quintet. The group consisted of great young players who nudged Miles into a newer, freer direction. Miles continued to play essentially the same material from the fifties that made him famous: some pop standards like *Autumn Leaves* and *Bye, Bye Blackbird*, some jazz standards like *Walkin'* and *'Round Midnight*, and two tunes *from Kind of Blue*: *So What* and *All Blues*. The new rhythm section, however, played in a freer, more aggressive manner than Miles' previous rhythm sections and Miles himself began to change his playing from a cooler, laid-back style to a more assertive one.

His new rhythm section is widely considered to be the third (chronologically) great rhythm section in jazz history. Out of the three great rhythm sections in all of jazz history, it is no coincidence that Miles Davis led two of them. A big part of Miles Davis' talent and some might say genius is his knack for assembling the right musicians at the right time who play extremely well as a group. The rhythm section consisted of **Herbie Hancock** on the piano, **Ron Carter** on the bass, and **Tony Williams** on the drums. These young players brought some of the newer currents in jazz into the group, including Free Jazz, Bossa Nova, and Rock. They extended the Bill Evans Trio's concept of rhythm section interplay to accompanying the horn soloists and were extremely interactive with them. Like the Evans trio, they often blurred the distinction between background and foreground. The band was able to spontaneously and seamlessly change tempos, moods, and feels all within the performance of any single tune.

When **Wayne Shorter** joined the group, the group changed direction to one that became freer in its approach and more abstract in its material and playing. Shorter is a gifted saxophonist and composer whose tunes contained nontraditional melodies and harmonies. The band began to border on Free Jazz without ever going all the way. Each new album showcased new concepts of jazz structures and improvisational approaches on those structures. After having taken Freer Jazz about as far as it could go, in 1969, Miles did a 180-degree turn and created a new genre called Fusion. Fusion was an attempt to woo the Rock crowd and have a more popular appeal. Indeed it worked and for as many who said Miles sold out, there were those who thought he rescued jazz from becoming an esoteric music for a cultural jazz elite.

MILES DAVIS SIXTIES QUINTET
RHYTHM SECTION
HERBIE HANCOCK

Pianist Herbie Hancock (b. 1940) is one of the five major Post-Bop pianists. Born and raised in Chicago, he was classically trained and was considered to be a child prodigy. He first came to public attention when he played with trumpeter Donald Byrd in 1960 and more so when Miles Davis hired him in 1963. Hancock seemed to be influenced most by his two immediate predecessors in Miles' band: Wynton Kelly and Bill Evans. He employed Evans' rootless voicings and clusters in his left hand but played more blues-inflected right-hand melodies. His melodies often contain short sequential note patterns as well as sequences of longer lines. His comping was aggressive and his novel use of rootless voicings in the left hand with filled-in high-register octaves in the right hand gave his chords a clear and ringing sound that cut through the rest of the band. He was equally adept at soloing and accompanying, and influenced other Post-Bop players in both areas. Hancock wrote and recorded several funky Soul Jazz hits before and during his stay with Miles Davis, most notably *Watermelon Man* and *Cantaloupe Island*. His *Maiden Voyage* (see below) is one of the great Post-Bop standards. In the seventies, Hancock led a major Fusion band (see Chapter 22).

Excerpt of Herbie Hancock playing Autumn Leaves in 1964

RON CARTER

Bassist Ron Carter (b. 1937) was born in Ferndale, Michigan, and later moved to Detroit. Classically trained on the cello and bass, he earned bachelor's and master's degrees in music. He played with several notable jazz artists before famously joining the Miles Davis Quintet in 1963. Carter was the rock of the rhythm section and anchored the sometimes flailing tangents initiated by Herbie Hancock and Tony Williams. He was able to play extremely fast tempos and change feels at will. And it was Carter who initiated many of the tempo and feel changes that the rhythm section engaged in. As the quintet's music became more abstract after the addition of Wayne Shorter, Carter masterfully made sense of their freer "time no changes" approach that relied more on one's ears than predetermined chord structures. During and well after his stint with Miles Davis, Ron Carter has been a much-in-demand player who has played on literally thousands of recordings.

Excerpt of Ron Carter playing Autumn Leaves in 1964

TONY WILLIAMS

The remarkable drummer Tony Williams (1945–1997) was the most amazing member of the rhythm section. Born in Chicago, he grew up in Boston and started with Miles Davis at the age of seventeen. A true prodigy and one who was totally original, he transformed drumming in the Post-Bop jazz world of the 1960s. He, along with Elvin Jones, was one of the most influential drummers of the time. He played the drum set in ways no one ever thought of before him. For example, he often would not consistently play the hi-hat on beats 2 and 4 as drummers had been doing since the swing era, or he might play it on every beat, even at fast tempos. He also engaged in complex polyrhythmic overlays that were continually changing. He had an innate sense of the **macrobeat**, the large beat, the first beat of every measure, for example, that he could subdivide in myriad ways into units of twos, threes, fours, etc., or sometimes all at once. Williams was extremely interactive and would often come to the foreground during another solo. As the group evolved into the later sixties, he would often dominate the music. If Ron Carter was the anchor of the group, Tony Williams was the waves that rocked the boat.

Excerpt of Tony Williams playing I Fall In Love Too Easily in 1967

MILES DAVIS QUINTET 1963–1964

While the quintet continued to play older material, they did so with ever-increasing freedom. **George Coleman**, tenor saxophone, was out of the Hard Bop tradition and served as a foil to Miles much as Coltrane had done with the fifties quintet by generally playing many more notes than Miles. At first, the young rhythm section played much more interactively and aggressively behind Coleman than Miles, thinking Miles preferred the more laid-back style accompaniment that the fifties quintet gave him. Miles, however, eventually urged them to play more freely behind him and the band began to explore a freer approach throughout each performance. They began to stretch the limits of form and style by playing standards with an elasticity that made each tune so flexible and pliable that it could be a slow ballad, an up-tempo swing feel, and a Latin tune all in one. This changing of feels and tempos (really double-time, half-time, etc.) was so seamless and natural that it was hard to believe that it was all improvised in performance, which it was. Make no mistake, however, that Miles was not in charge; it was clearly his leadership that made all this possible, tacitly or otherwise. Several outstanding live albums were made during this period, including *Miles in Europe, Four and More,* and *My Funny Valentine.* The last two albums were from one concert at Lincoln Center in New York.

SO WHAT 1964
FOUR AND MORE

Miles Davis—Trumpet
George Coleman—Tenor Sax
Herbie Hancock—Piano
Ron Carter—Bass
Tony Williams—Drums

Listen to this live 1964 version of *So What* and compare it to the original 1959 recording on *Kind of Blue.* Noticeable immediately is the much faster tempo and overall intensity of the 1964 version. Miles is playing much more aggressively as he is inspired and nudged by his young rhythm section. Notice the very interactive drumming of Tony Williams and how he fills the spaces that Miles leaves for him. Herbie Hancock is equally aggressive in his comping with his rootles voicings with right-hand octaves cutting through the band. Hancock's solo is textbook in Post-Bop piano playing with its freer modal approach, linearity, sequences, and rhythmic impulse.

MY FUNNY VALENTINE 1964

Miles Davis—Trumpet
Wayne Shorter—Tenor Sax
Herbie Hancock—Piano
Ron Carter—Bass
Tony Williams—Drums

Watch this video performance of the Rodgers and Hart classic Pop song, **My Funny Valentine** from Milan, Italy. By this time Wayne Shorter (see below) had replaced George Coleman on tenor saxophone. This version represents how the quintet approached the older Pop standards during this period. They change tempos and feels and textures on the spur of the moment. The form of the song is AA^{1}BA^2 –Tag, the tag is an extra 4 measure at the end. After a rubato piano intro, Miles plays a very free and very slow rubato variation of the original melody for the A section and a very slow tempo is established at the A^1 section and continues for the rest of the first chorus. The second chorus starts to double-time the tempo, which means the feeling is now twice the speed but the tune is not proceeding any faster. The rhythm section goes into a Latin feel for the B section of the second chorus and back to the double time for the A^2 section before slowing down again at the tag. When Wayne Shorter comes in, the music seems to stop and becomes very abstract and mysterious. Listen to how the band continues to change feels as it goes on to the end. This band was unique in approaching music in this way and seemed to reach the limits of transforming Pop songs into artistic jazz performances. Without altering the structure of the tune, they solved the dilemma of formal complexity and spontaneous creation.

BOSSA NOVA AND ROCK INFLUENCES

Jazz has always absorbed popular music styles from its very beginning and when Pop styles changed during the fifties and sixties, they effected a change in some of the new jazz of the time. This was true more for the younger players, which included Miles Davis' rhythm section. Bossa Nova and Rock influenced much of the newer jazz of the sixties, either directly or in more subtle ways. What these diverse types of music have in common are an underlying pulse that divides the beat into two equal eighth notes, thus superimposing eight beats under the four-beat pulse (twice as fast) and a bass part that is conceived at half the speed of the beat in two beats per measure. They also have well-defined, active background rhythms.

Bossa Nova was a new style of Latin music from Brazil that combined elements of Samba and Cool Jazz. It began there during the 1950s and was introduced to Americans most notably by tenor saxophonist **Stan Getz** and guitarist **Charlie Byrd** on their 1962 album, *Jazz Samba*. *Desafinado*, written by one of the inventors of Bossa Nova, **Antonio Carlos Jobim**, became a top-forty hit, simultaneously putting Bossa Nova in this country and starting a Bossa Nova craze. Stan Getz was a Cool Jazz musician who went on to great fame from this and many other Bossa Nova recordings. His recording of Jobim's *The Girl from Ipanema* with Brazilian singers **Joao and Astrud Gilberto** became a number-one hit and remains popular to this day.

Bossa Nova differs from the Afro-Cuban Latin music that inspired Dizzy Gillespie in the 1940s. Afro-Cuban music is based a rhythmic concept called the clave. The clave is a strict rhythm pattern that organizes the rhythms around it. It is sometimes played on an instrument called the claves but often is not played at all. Bossa Nova is much freer in its rhythmic conception; its background rhythms are flexible and unpredictable, for the most part, like jazz comping. In Bossa Nova the background rhythms are often more active than the foreground melodic rhythms. There can be long-held notes in the melody that float on top of an undulating accompaniment. This, in some ways, is a reversal of the Bebop norm of very active melodies against slower moving accompaniments. In Swing everything relates to the steady pulse played by the rhythm section, in Bebop the melodies themselves propel the music, and in Bossa Nova the background rhythms carry the music forward as the melodies either float on top on directly plug into them.

The newer style by now referred to as **Rock** evolved from fifties Rock & Roll was in full sway by 1965 and Herbie Hancock and the other young rhythm section players of Miles Davis band having been no strangers to it, incorporated elements of it into their playing with Miles. In Rock, the background rhythms, played mostly by electric bass, electric guitars, and drums, become crucial elements of the tune; the arrangement, for the most part, is not independent from the tune. The performance of *My Funny Valentine* described above is just one of hundreds of ways of playing the tune. The older Pop standards are flexible that way and any arrangement or style can be added to them. The newer Rock Pop songs, however, are typically not nearly as pliable and without, let's say, a particular bass part, a particular song would not make as much sense.

The layering in Rock is different from layering in jazz. In Rock, the rhythm section lays down a groove over which the melodies are played. In traditional jazz it is not so much a groove as the pulse itself on which the melodies and everything else occur. That is the essence of swing; it relates to the beat. **Ahmad Jamal** is an exception in the jazz world because he approached his music by establishing a groove. *Poinciana* in a prime example of this; the bass and drums lay down a groove on which Jamal floats freely by plugging into and out of it. Afro-Cuban music works off a groove as well as Bossa Nova to some extent, but Bossa Nova is more flexible and jazz-like to begin with and thus was more adaptable to jazz. Bossa Nova, which was influenced by jazz in the fifties, will now influence jazz in the sixties, either directly as in the music of Stan Getz and others or indirectly as in *Maiden Voyage*.

THE GIRL FROM IPANEMA 1963
Stan Getz

Stan Getz—Tenor Saxophone
Joao Gilberto—Vocal and Guitar
Astrud Gilberto—Vocal
Antonio Carlos Jobim—Piano and Composer

Listen to this classic Bossa Nova record that became a number-one hit. It is sung in both Portuguese and English with solos by Stan Getz and Antonio Carlos Jobim.

MAIDEN VOYAGE 1965
HERBIE HANCOCK

Like John Coltrane during the 1950s, Herbie Hancock recorded several albums under his own name while with Miles Davis' band. His 1965 album *Maiden Voyage* was an artistic and commercial success. The title tune became a Post-Bop standard and exhibits two new influences in the sixties jazz world: Bossa Nova and Rock. *Maiden Voyage* is neither Bossa Nova nor Rock but elements of both pervade the performance. A complex, undulating 2-measure rhythm pattern played by the piano and bass underpins the entire head of the tune. Although the rhythm is not strictly from Bossa Nova or Rock, its accent on the second beat of the first measure of the pattern clearly relates to them. On top of this background rhythm floats a melody of mostly long-held notes, many lasting three full measures. Again, the slow moving foreground melody over the active background rhythm is reminiscent of Bossa Nova. The tune is also modal and in an AABA 32-measure form. Each section consists of two modes that last for 4 measures each, so there is a slow harmonic rhythm that matches the slow moving melody. Out of the only four chords that are used in the tune, three are suspended chords. A suspended chord is one where the normal third is replaced by a fourth; this literally gives the chord a suspended sound with no sense of direction or resolution. The use of suspended chords in *Maiden Voyage* influenced a lot of the newer jazz during the sixties and seventies. These chords go well with modal playing and the more static aesthetic that goes with it. The chords in *Maiden Voyage* do not lead from one to another, as in traditional Western music, but rather simply shift from one to another. Each chord generates a mode to improvise on. After the head the players are freed from the *Maiden Voyage* (MV) rhythm and play off it or around it, and plug into and out of it during the solos. The music goes through many moods and textures and this is a key difference between this and Bossa Nova or Rock. Drummer Tony Williams does not participate in or establish any groove, but rather fills in spaces and complements the rhythms around him while playing or implying the underlying eighth-note feel that comes from Rock and Bossa Nova.

The band on this recording is essentially the Miles Davis band without Miles Davis. Along with Miles' rhythm section, **Freddie Hubbard** plays trumpet and **George Coleman** plays tenor saxophone. The famous recording is an example of Post-Bop Freer jazz and Modal jazz.

Figure 21.1: Maiden Voyage Rhythm (MV rhythm).

What to listen for:

1. The Maiden Voyage rhythm during the intro
2. The slow moving melody against the MV rhythm during the head
3. The freer way the rhythm section accompanies the solos
4. The changing moods and activity during the solos
5. The rhythm section's reactions to the soloists
6. The overall suspended feeling and the unresolved nature of the music

MAIDEN VOYAGE 1965
HERBIE HANCOCK

Herbie Hancock—Piano
Freddie Hubbard—Trumpet
George Coleman—Tenor Sax
Ron Carter—Bass
Tony Williams—Drums

Intro piano, bass, drums
  8

	A	A	B	A
0:17 Chorus 1	Head - tpt+sax——————————————————————— unison———————————— | sax MV rhy | unison— piano and bass play consistent rhythm pattern (MV rhy)			
1:20 Chorus 2	Sax solo————————————————————————— starts slowly——————————|much faster |slows down rhy sec - freely playing off MV rhy————————			
2:21 Chorus 3	Trumpet solo———————————————————— slowly and melodically———————————————— pno- new rhy | MV rhy | pno sparse | MV rhy			
3:22 Chorus 4	Trumpet solo continues——————————————— faster notes | slower-faster | fast runs | slower Rhythm section reacts—————————| pno-harp-like |tpt- fast at end pno- new rhy sparse bass strums | calmer			
4:23 Chorus 5	Piano solo—————————————————————— Mood changes | high | faster- Bebop-like piano- sparse– |drums sparse———————| dr respond			
5:23 Chorus 6	Piano solo continues——————————————— repeated figure| MV rhy——————fast figures| winds down | drums react | MV rhy			
6:24 Chorus 7	Head - tpt+sax———————————————————— unison————————— sax MV rhy | unison— piano and bass play MV rhy———————			
7:26 Coda	music fades————————————			

Figure 21.2: Herbie Hancock, 1976.
Copyright in the Public Domain.

MILES DAVIS QUINTET 1964–1968

When **Wayne Shorter** joined the group at the end of 1964, the Quintet went in a new direction. Shorter came from a Hard Bop background and was lured away from Art Blakey and the Jazz Messengers. His playing became less hard boppish and more abstract with Miles Davis. His compositions did, as well, and he nudged the group into a new kind of jazz that had little resemblance to earlier styles of jazz. While the band played material similar to what the quintet had been doing for the previous few years in live performance, they embarked on a series of studio albums that kept pushing the envelope with each successive issue. The music became freer and more abstract and went about as far as it could over into Free Jazz without actually going all the way. Gone were the standards that populated most of Miles' earlier albums. Shorter was now writing most of the tunes with others written by Miles and the rest of the band. The forms of these tunes were nontraditional, the harmony was essentially non-functional, and the melodies and rhythms were almost totally removed from swing, or bebop, or any other kind of music. The thematic material often consisted of melodic fragments separated by silence. The rhythm section often supplied a polymetric layering that often blurred any sense of pulse or beat. While still adhering to the tunes for improvisation, the soloists were free to ignore the chords or anything else, including the tune at times. What differentiates their approach from Free Jazz is that the tune was never totally ignored and served as a reference even if the players were thinking about the tune in different terms. Chord voicings were often used in place of chords. A lead sheet might contain a three-note ambiguous voicing (F-B-E), for example, that can imply several different chords. Each player then is free to think of it any way he wishes at any particular time.

The band called their unique approach **TIME, NO CHANGES** because they adhered to the tune, as it would keep returning in time as in traditional jazz, but were not restricted by chords, or even scales or modes. Motivic and thematic reference and development became the primary procedure for the improvisations, and each soloist masterfully exploited the possibilities inherent in the new approach. All of this made for difficult listening, however, and even if they were adhering to some formal structure, the average listener could not follow it, so it might as well have been Free Jazz. From 1965 through 1968, Miles was breaking new ground and challenging his players and his listeners along the way with innovative ways to play jazz, but by doing so, his record sales were dwindling and was losing his audience to the point where he could hardly fill up a club anymore. One of the biggest stars in jazz in 1959 now seemed to have alienated many of his followers with an incomprehensible new music.

WAYNE SHORTER

Saxophonist Wayne Shorter (b. 1933) is one of great players and composers in jazz history. Born in Newark, New Jersey, he first came into prominence when he joined Art Blakey's Jazz Messengers in 1959. He became music director for that band and wrote many original tunes for them. Blakey was not happy when Miles Davis lured Shorter away in 1964. Shorter began to shed his Hard Bop roots with Miles and essentially changed not only his own direction but that of the entire band as well (see above). For several years Miles had been searching for someone like John Coltrane and finally found that someone in Shorter. He could play as fast as Coltrane and was as serious and dedicated as well. Shorter's presence profoundly influenced the Miles Davis Quintet and inspired them to new heights in the freer climate of the sixties. In the seventies he co-led one of the leading Fusion groups, **Weather Report**. He has remained active and continues to play original tunes reminiscent of his earlier work.

Excerpt of Wayne Shorter playing *Agitation* in 1967

Figure 21.3: Wayne Shorter, 1977.
Copyright © Jean-Luc (CC BY-SA 2.0)
at http://commons.wikimedia.org/wiki/
File:Weather_Report_%28Wayne_
Shorter%29.jpg

DIRECTIONS IN MUSIC BY MILES DAVIS EXPERIMENTAL ALBUMS 1965–1968

Here is sampling of the quintet's albums from 1965 to 1968.

E.S.P. 1965

Wayne Shorter's *E.S.P.* is a tune built on melodic fourths with nontraditional chord changes.

Eighty-one, written by Miles Davis and Ron Carter, is a blues form that features suspended chords and a quasi-rock feel.

MILES SMILES 1966

Wayne Shorter's **Footprints** is a minor blues underpinned by a polymetric three-against-two feeling or a two-against-three feeling, depending whom you are listening to. Miles and Wayne Shorter play a quasi-unison head that is intentionally not always in sync: à la Ornette Coleman and Don Cherry.

Freedom Jazz Dance, written by Eddie Harris, is another tune based primarily on melodic fourths. It has no real chord progression and sits primarily on one chord. Ron Carter plays a fragmented bass line based on the theme itself and Tony Williams plays a complex layered background that has hands and feet in constant motion.

THE SORCERER 1967

The Sorcerer, by Wayne Shorter, has a short head based on one idea. TIME, NO CHANGES is clearly evident during the solos that play off the head itself.

Masqualero, also by Shorter, is an abstract tune based on an ABA form. The theme consists of short seemingly unrelated fragments. The rhythm section is freely floating in the background often coming to the foreground. Again the TIME, NO CHANGES approach is in full sway.

NEFERTITI 1967

Wayne Shorter's **Nefertiti** is an unusual tune that keeps circling back on itself, quite literally in this performance that the horns continually play without any improvised solos. It is the rhythm section, mostly Tony Williams and Herbie Hancock that dominates, as their background becomes foreground. The traditional roles of melody and accompaniment are reversed in this performance, as melody remains constant. Miles and Shorter purposefully play the head not quite in sync.

Another Shorter tune, *Pinocchio*, is based on variants of the theme and has a circular unresolved feeling to it. The horns do solo on this one but the head is played four times at the beginning and in between solos.

MILES IN THE SKY 1968

This is the first album that Miles used electric instruments on, and is shows him transitioning from his very abstract freer, Post-Bop music to the more accessible Fusion style that he is credited with inventing. Gil Evans also becomes actively involved in the concepts and writing of the music.

Stuff, written by Miles Davis, has a Rock groove that accompanies a very long playing of the head that is repeated five times and lasts over five minutes. Electric piano and bass is used and although not as strict as in succeeding albums, the bass and drums are relegated primarily to playing a groove.

Paraphernalia, written by Shorter, adds George Benson on electric guitar to the otherwise acoustic band. He plays an almost constant repeated note (octave Ds). The tune has two sections, a kind of static A section in quadruple meter and an B section with chromatic chords in triple meter. For solos, the A sections on the background repeated note are open ended and the B sections are cued by the soloists. This is yet another new approach to improvisation pioneered by this band.

FILLES DE KILIMANJARO 1968

This album represents the quintet in transition. **Chick Corea** and **Dave Holland** replace Herbie Hancock and Ron Carter on half of the album and the electric instruments are used more than on the previous album. Once again Gil Evans becomes actively involved.

Petits Machins (Little Stuff), written by Miles Davis, is a tune of almost constant tension with a lot of pedal tones in the bass. Miles develops a motive based on alternating minor and major thirds that links it to the Blues tradition. The solos are essentially free, following ideas from the head but not in a strict form.

Mademoiselle Mabry, credited to Miles Davis but most likely conceived by Gil Evans, was actually a reworking of Jimi Hendrix's *The Wind Cries Mary*. The procedure here is unique; the rhythm section is essentially restricted to playing fixed notes and rhythms throughout in an 18-measure sequence that constantly repeats. There is really no head; Miles simply starts improvising on the fourth occurrence of the sequence. The drums fill in here and there. Again Miles is experimenting with new formal procedures and reversing tradition roles—in this case the accompaniment is strict, while the horns having nothing preplanned.

FOOTPRINTS 1966

Miles Davis—Trumpet
Wayne Shorter—Tenor Sax
Herbie Hancock—Piano
Ron Carter—Bass
Tony Williams—Drums

Watch this video of the quintet performing Wayne Shorter's **Footprints**, which was originally recorded on the **Miles Smiles** album. Notice the looseness with which the horns play the head in fourths. Tony Williams is very much in the foreground at the beginning of the performance. Notice the changing moods and seemingly changing tempos that this group typically engaged in. Notice how the music really quiets down at the beginning of Wayne Shorter's solo and almost stops as Herbie Hancock plays repetitive cluster sounds, which gives way to his piano solo. Notice how Hancock plays off the theme and goes off on his own, unaccompanied, before the band comes back in for the head. This is in a 12-bar Blues form but because of the *time no changes* approach, it is hard to follow at times.

FUSION

In 1969 Miles Davis abandoned his connection to earlier jazz completely and created a brand new music that became known as Fusion. In theory, Fusion combines elements of jazz with Rock to create a new, third kind of music, much as Third Stream attempted to do with jazz and Classical music in the fifties. The term *Rock* included any of the popular styles that emerged in the sixties, including Rock, Soul, and Funk. Although this was not a total shock, since Miles had hinted at and had been experimenting with Rock grooves even as far back as 1965, the jazz world was surprised when he totally committed to Fusion in 1969. The electric instruments and Rock grooves were here to stay and Miles never looked back. As we have seen, Miles Davis was always searching for something new and after finding it and influencing many others, he would abandon it and start the process over again. He went from Bebop to Cool Jazz to Hard Bop to Modal Jazz to Freer Jazz to Fusion within a twenty-five-year span.

Miles Davis, in many ways, ingeniously solved the problem plaguing jazz musicians during the 1960s; i.e., how could one keep playing freely and still connect with an audience? When the Rock 'n' Roll of the fifties evolved into Rock of the sixties, the music went from being a kind of juvenile dance music for teenagers to a more serious, artistic form of expression that provided an environment for artistic improvisations, much as jazz has always done. Some guitar players like Jimi Hendrix were being compared to John Coltrane and groups like the Beatles were being compared to the great composers and lyricists of the Great American Songbook. James Brown and Sly and the Family Stone were creating Funk, which layered rhythms in new, complex, and interesting ways. Jazz had always been based partly on Pop music and now that Pop had changed, why shouldn't jazz change along with it? But jazz had also been based on a complex harmonic language since the thirties and evolved into a rhythmically subtle and supple music. Many thought that Fusion was a regression in these areas and simply an attempt to attract the Rock audience in order to made more money. Many were saying Miles Davis had sold out! But all he had really done was to continue to play freely but now with a danceable groove beneath it. The tunes typically had little or no harmonic change and were generally solidified by an **ostinato** (repeating) bass part. The improvisations were essentially freely modal and mostly open ended with no adherence to form during solos. What anchored the music now was the groove and just about anything could go on top of it. For as many fans as Miles alienated and lost for embracing Fusion, he gained a lot more and now joined Jimi Hendrix, Sly, and others playing to huge crowds in large arenas.

NEW SOUNDS OF FUSION

Electric guitar—Although not new in jazz, Fusion players made the guitar sound like and played it more like the Rock players, using electronic effects, reverb, echo, wa-wa pedals, etc. Most previous jazz players treated it like an amplified acoustic guitar, eschewing any embellished sound.

Electric bass—This came into common usage in Rock/Pop world in the late fifties. The first popular model was the Fender Bass manufactured by the Fender Guitar Company. Sometime called a bass guitar, the new instrument had a profound effect on Rock and Pop music. Since the bass could now be as loud as any other instrument, it took on a life of its own by producing well-defined, rhythmic bass parts, as opposed to more or less keeping the pulse.

Electric piano—The instrument of choice was the Fender Rhodes Piano. This was essentially a mechanical instrument like an acoustic piano but with metal tines rather than strings producing the tones. The tines were inaudible without amplification. The sound was not like a piano at all but it played like a piano with hammers and dampers, etc. The instrument eventually was simply called a Rhodes and dominated the jazz and Pop worlds of the seventies.

Synthesizers—Invented by Robert Moog in 1968, synthesizers, theoretically, could synthesize any sound imaginable. This could include known sounds of instruments to electronic sounds and noises. These instruments were awkward to use at first, requiring the manipulation of many patch chords and dials to produce a single sound. In the 1970s, the Mini Moog and other similar instruments made their use more practical for live performance.

Percussion—Percussionists became common in Fusion bands, they not only provided new layers of rhythms, but they also produced sounds and colors that augmented the sonic palette of the music by using conga drums, tambourines, finger cymbals, bell trees, shakers, etc.

Trumpet—Even though Miles played his normal trumpet, he added electronic effects through a microphone by using reverb, echo, and even a wa-wa pedal.

IN A SILENT WAY 1969

In a Silent Way was Miles Davis' first album that can be labeled entirely Fusion. The whole concept, sound, and instrumentation were entirely new. Three electric keyboards (two pianos and an organ) and electric guitar created a complex texture of sound and rhythm that filled in a middle ground between the soloists and the restricted drums and bass groove. Herbie Hancock returned for this recording to play electric piano along with Chick Corea. **Joe Zawinul** was added to play organ and **John McLaughlin** was hired to play guitar. The entire album has a consistency of sound and mood, mostly on the soft side, and the players adeptly stay out of each other's way while subtly complementing each other. The album was heavily edited, which is something else foreign to traditional jazz. **Teo Macero**, the record's producer, was also a composer whom Miles entrusted to edit hours of tape. Miles, himself, then edited from there and the music you hear on the record is not at all the way they played it. The repeating parts on the edited tracks give the tunes a sense of form that did not exist during recording. The music is mostly static with little or no harmonic change.

Figure 21.4: Miles Davis, 1986.

BITCHES BREW 1969

The album that really got Fusion going was **Bitches Brew**. Whereas **In a Silent Way** was restrained and almost ambient in its pervasive sounds and mood, *Bitches Brew* was in-your-face music that hit you over the head. The aggressive, almost arrogant attitude of the Rockers was present, especially in Miles' playing. The music was much freer and almost out of control, only to be reined in through careful masterful editing by Teo Macero. It is with this album that Miles finally breaks through to the Rock crowd; they were prepped for it from the long-winded solos of Jimi Hendrix, Eric Clapton, the Grateful Dead, et al. The album was a huge commercial success and was Miles' first gold record. Once again Miles added many players to his working quintet that now included Wayne Shorter on soprano saxophone, Chick Corea on electric piano, Dave Holland on bass, and **Jack DeJohnette** on drums. **Bennie Maupin** used the rarely played bass clarinet as a kind of rhythm section instrument, supplying random-like undertones that gave an exotic flavor to the proceedings. Extra keyboards, drums, bass, and percussion were also added to the ensemble in various ways.

BITCHES BREW

Listen to this excerpt from the beginning of the tune **Bitches Brew**, from the album **Bitches Brew**. The original track is twenty-six minutes long. The intro is played in free rubato with a lot of echo and reverberation. The trumpet and bass play many repeated noted (Cs) while the keyboards and guitar play random-like chords. After two minutes and fifty-two seconds, everything stops; the bass plays an ostinato (repeating line) and is joined by bass clarinet and percussion. Drums, keyboards, and guitar reenter next and eventually Miles improvises on top of a very busy, dense background. His solo is essentially modal with Blues notes and inflections. The density of sound owes partly to the instruments used: there are two electric basses, two drummers, two percussionists, and two keyboardists, in addition to trumpet, soprano saxophone, and bass clarinet.

What to listen for:

1. The rubato intro beginning with basses, keyboards, and guitar
2. The trumpet entrance with echo and reverb
3. The repeated notes of the trumpet and bass
4. The silence followed by the bass ostinato that sets up the groove
5. The drums' rock groove
6. The dense overlay of keyboards and guitar behind the trumpet solo
7. Miles' simple modal, bluesy solo against all the goings-on

BITCHES BREW

Miles Davis—Trumpet
Wayne Shorter—Soprano Sax
Bennie Maupin—Bass Clarinet
Joe Zawinul—Electric Piano
Chick Corea—Electric piano
John McLaughlin—Electric Guitar

Dave Holland —Bass
Harvey Brooks—Elec. Bass
Lenny White—Drums
Jack DeJohnette—Drums
Don Alias—Congas
Juma Santos—Percussion

INTRO- rubato
Bass, keyboards, guitar

0:41   Trumpet enters—with a lot of echo and reverb
         Trumpet and bass play a lot of repeated notes (Cs)
         Keyboards and guitar fill with random-like chords

GROOVE - in tempo
2:52   Everyone stops and bass plays a 2-measure ostinato
         quickly joined by bass clarinet and percussion

3:34   Keyboards and guitar enter playing random-like chords

3:54   Miles enters and improvises solo

Chapter Twenty Two

Fusion in the Seventies

itches Brew was a defining moment in jazz history; it drew a line in the sand, so to speak. Who was willing to cross that line? Who risked being obsolete by not crossing it? Traditional jazz seemed all but dead: *traditional* in this case meaning pre-Post-Bop. After the so-called 1967 Summer of Love when the Beatles released their *Sergeant Pepper's Lonely Hearts Club Band* album, Western culture seemed to change. It was now the Dawning of the Age of Aquarius, peace and love, LSD and marijuana. Rock reigned supreme, the Supremes rocked the Soul world, and jazz seemed to be a relic of the establishment. These were antiestablishment times; what was old was bad and what was new was good, no matter how good it was. Even after Miles Davis crossed the line, many of the players who initially joined him retreated to experimental free-form jazz. His three keyboardists, Herbie Hancock, Chick Corea, and Joe Zawinul, along with saxophonist Wayne Shorter, all formed groups that explored a newer sounding Free Jazz with electric and acoustic instruments. All, however, formed full-fledged Fusion bands by the mid-seventies. Economics was a big factor in crossing the line but also a desire to communicate to a wider audience. The free-form improvisational approach did not attract a large audience, neither the traditional jazz audience nor the rock audience. This kind of music seemed to be caught in the middle. One by one they decided to not only embrace Fusion but also to pursue a much more commercial version of it than Miles Davis did. Though there were cries of selling out, these musicians thought of themselves more in the tradition of a Benny Goodman or Count Basie during the Swing Era who was playing what the people wanted, based on the Pop music of the day.

Although Fusion is often defined as the merger of jazz and Rock, it is more specifically a merger of jazz with Soul and Funk. In the previous chapter the term *Rock* was defined as including Soul and Funk along with what is more specifically Rock music. Rock's rhythms are more rigid than Soul's and more redundant as far as separate parts go; in Rock several instruments might be playing the same rhythm, whereas in Soul music, the rhythm is more layered with different rhythms played by different instruments. Fusion almost always favors this latter approach. Funk uses some very complex rhythms that are layered to fit together as interlocking parts. A key difference between Fusion and all of this other music is a lack of repetition: Fusion, being more jazz-like, tends to layer rhythms but in a looser, more flexible way. They are more improvised as opposed to the usually strictly repeating patterns of the Pop-oriented styles. Also Fusion was mostly an instrumental music that emphasized improvisation. But where Miles Davis' brand of Fusion was very free and unpredictable as far as form and soloing, the newer Fusion of the seventies became more strictly arranged with clear-cut formal divisions.

FUNK
JAMES BROWN AND SLY STONE

Funk is the invention of James Brown (1933–2006). He created a brand-new kind of music during the 1960s that still influences Pop music to this day. Whereas traditional jazz is based on the quarter-note pulse and Rock on the eighth-note pulse, Funk's rhythmic conception is based on the sixteenth note. While in Rock the eighth notes are usually being played, in Funk every sixteenth note is not necessarily heard. Brown has his band play superimposed different interlocking repetitive riffs that are based on the underlying sixteenth-note pulse. Typically there are separate riffs played by the bass, guitar, and horns, as well as an independent rhythm on the drums that form a complex rhythmic overlay. These usually occur in two-measure repeating patterns. The example below shows how the parts might relate for one measure. In this case every sixteenth subdivision is played as a composite rhythm of all the parts. This is not required; it may or may not happen.

16th Note Interlocking Riffs

horns	1		4		7	9		12 13 14	
guitar	1	3	5 6	8	10 11	13	15 16		
bass	1 2	4	6	9	12	15			
16ths	1 2 3 4 5 6 7 8 9 10 11 12 13 14 15 16								
BEAT	1	2	3	4					

Another key feature of Funk is the emphasis on the first beat of the measure. This is very different from the typical Rock and Soul music emphasis on beats 2 and 4. Funk is actually closer to traditional African rhythmic practice than most Jazz or Soul music.

Another original concept of James Brown was the way he formed his music in static harmonic blocks of rhythmic activity. In order to comprehend the complex overlay of complex rhythms, the harmony becomes static. Having harmonic and rhythmic complexity at the same time would sound too chaotic for most listeners. This is true for any kind of music. The famous Russian composer **Igor Stravinsky** composed in a similar way, using very complex simultaneous rhythms on static harmonic backgrounds. Like Stravinsky, Brown holds on to a single chord, or sometimes two alternating chords, for a relatively long time before shifting to a new chord with new riffs. Usually he alternated between two harmonic blocks. The blocks are open-ended and go on until he cues a change. On top of the entire goings-on, Brown talks, shouts, screams, and sometimes actually sings.

Sly and the Family Stone was a successful Pop group of the late sixties and early seventies that summed up nearly all of the Pop trends of the sixties. Their leader, Sylvester Stewart, aka Sly Stone, combined elements of Funk, Soul, Acid Rock, Folk, Rock, and Jazz Rock into new music that was enormously popular. This group was really a family that consisted of males and females as well as Blacks and Whites. Sly wanted to bring everyone and everyone's music together. It is really Sly's version of Funk that had the major impact on seventies groups like **Earth, Wind, and Fire**, and the Fusion bands. His influence on Miles Davis and Herbie Hancock, who even wrote a tune called *Sly*, is most obvious. Sly's music sometimes had no harmonic change at all, which gave it a ritualistic feeling. James Brown, himself, was also influenced by this. Unfortunately, drugs got the better of Sly and the great promise of his early career never fully panned out.

FOUR FUSION BANDS OF THE SEVENTIES

MAHAVISHNU ORCHESTRA

John McLaughlin (b. 1942) is a British guitarist who formed the Mahavishnu Orchestra in 1971. Drummer Tony Williams introduced him to Miles Davis in 1968 and Miles used him on his first two Fusion albums, ***In a Silent Way*** and ***Bitches Brew***. He then played in Tony Williams' short-lived Fusion group named **Lifetime Emergency Trio**. After studying Indian music and philosophy, he formed the

Mahavishnu Orchestra, which combined elements of Acid Rock and Indian music. McLaughlin was very influenced by Acid Rock guitarist Jimi Hendrix, and the band played at extremely loud volumes with distorted sounds. The band featured **Jan Hammer** on keyboards and synthesizers, **Billy Cobham** on drums, Jerry Goodman on violin, and **Rick Laird** on electric bass.

Figure 22.2: John McLaughlin, early 1970s.

BIRDS OF FIRE 1971

Listen to this recording of *Birds of Fire*. The opening gong sound immediately relates it to Indian music. The meter is in an 18-beat pattern, which is also akin to the music of India. The music is very intense with wild frenzied solos and aggressive drumming by Billy Cobham. Notice the synthesizer sounds, which were quite new at the time.

HERBIE HANCOCK
AND
HEADHUNTERS

Herbie Hancock, one of the major Post-Bop pianists and composers, became a star in the jazz world, not only through his exposure with Miles Davis' band but also from his own successful albums. His funky Blues tune **Watermelon Man**, written in 1962, became a hit in the jazz world, first with his recording and again with a Latin version by **Mongo Santamaria**. His **Maiden Voyage** remains a staple of the Post-Bop repertoire (see Chapter 21). After leaving Miles Davis in 1968, Hancock formed a sextet that dabbled in Free Jazz while exploring the possibilities of electronic keyboards and synthesizers. Public reception was not very enthusiastic for his new music, however, and in 1973 he formed a new band, Headhunters, which was much more commercially oriented. He credits his experience with Nichiren Shoshu Buddhism for changing his focus to a more accessible music. He had been attracted to the music of **James Brown** and **Sly and the Family Stone** and now incorporated some of their style and techniques. Hancock's brand of fusion is very Funk oriented. His 1973 album **Headhunters** became a huge hit and sold over a million copies. At that time it eclipsed Dave Brubeck's **Time Out** album as the largest selling jazz album in history; it was later eclipsed by Miles Davis' **Kind of Blue**. Some questioned whether the album should be classified as jazz but Hancock never minded his critics and continued to play Fusion with occasion returns to his Post-Bop roots.

Figure 22.2: Herbie Hancock, 2006.

CHAMELEON 1973
HEADHUNTERS

Herbie Hancock—Keyboards
Bennie Maupin—Tenor sax
Paul Jackson—Electric Bass
Harvey Mason—Drums
Bill Summers—Percussion

Listen to the hit tune **Chameleon** from the *Headhunters* album.

The Funk and Soul roots of this music are evidenced from the 2-measure opening bass riff that repeats for most of the track. It is based on two chords that alternate throughout the first section of the tune. The repeated Bbm7-Eb7 is derived from a Dorian mode and was commonly used by Rock band at the time; Santana's **Evil Ways** is an example. Various overdubbed keyboards play riff-like figures based on the sixteenth-note subdivision of the beat over the bass line. The saxophone then enters and repeats a four-measure figure that is eventually broken up with another line that ends the head after almost four minutes. Hancock's synthesizer solo follows. Notice how he takes advantage of the nontraditional sounds that that a synthesizer can make along with a lot of playing in the cracks that he cannot do on a piano.

After the end of this edited version, the band switches to a more spacious groove on which Hancock solos on the Fender Rhodes piano. After Hancock's solo the original groove returns.

CHICK COREA
AND
RETURN TO FOREVER

Pianist Armando "Chick" Corea (b. 1941) is one of the major Post-Bop pianists and composers. He replaced Herbie Hancock in Miles Davis' band in 1968. In 1970 he and bassist Dave Holland left the band and formed a group call **Circle**, which essentially played Free Jazz. In 1971, like Herbie Hancock, he abandoned Free Jazz in an attempt to reach a wider audience. His new group did not exactly play Fusion at first but rather embraced Latin and particularly Brazilian music in an attempt to have a groove-based music. Along with bassist **Stanley Clarke** and sax and flute player **Joe Farrell**, two Brazilians, drummer/percussionist **Airto Moreira** and singer **Flora Purim**, were in the band. The Brazilian influence was apparent on their recordings, which featured a lot of samba-based music. Corea used primarily the Fender Rhodes electric piano during this time and that, along with the groove-based music, appealed to the Fusion audience. This version of *Return to Forever* issued two albums: **Return to Forever** and **Light as a Feather**. **Spain**, from *Light As A Feather* enjoys great popularity to this day.

Figure 22.3: Chick Corea.
Copyright in the Public Domain.

In 1973, inspired by the Mahavishnu Orchestra, Corea formed a new group that fully went over to a more Rock-oriented Fusion. Stanley Clarke, now playing electric and acoustic bass, remained from the previous band and drummer **Lenny White** and guitarist **Bill Connors** were added the band. This group continued to play some Latin-influenced music but played more of a Rock-sounding Fusion with loud distorted electric sounds. Their first album, ***Hymn of the Seventh Galaxy***, recorded in 1973, was very popular. In 1974, **Al Di Meola** replaced Bill Connors on guitar.

Stanley Clarke advanced the art of electric bass playing and famously invented the thumb-slapping technique that became popular in Pop music. This group continued its commercial success and although it disbanded in 1977, they have reunited several times in recent years to go on tours. Corea is a major jazz composer and much of his music is more compositional in nature than improvisational. His Fusion music tends to be more structured than the freer, more spontaneous music of Miles Davis and even more than Herbie Hancock's music.

HYMN OF THE SEVENTH GALAXY 1973

Chick Corea—Electric Piano and Organ
Bill Connors—Electric Guitar
Stanley Clarke—Electric Bass
Lenny White—Drums and Percussion

Listen to the title tune from the *Hymn of the Seventh Galaxy* album. It has allusions to heavy metal music with its high-energy loud distorted electric sounds. This is a good example of Corea's compositional approach to his music. After some synthesized sounds, the head begins in octaves with guitar, organ, and bass. The tune is based on three short ideas for the most part that are varied in several ways. The guitar solo that follows is not based on the form of the head. After the short guitar solo, the head returns but not in the exact way as in the beginning. Corea does not solo on this tune but his compositional manipulation of a few ideas rivals Thelonious Monk's writing and his larger sense of form recalls John Lewis' attempts.

Figure 22.4: Return to Forever, 1976. Lenny White, Stanley Clarke, Chick Corea, Al Di Meola.

WEATHER REPORT

After playing on *Bitches Brew*, keyboardist **Joe Zawinul** and saxophonist **Wayne Shorter** formed Weather Report in 1970. At first, the group mixed acoustic and electronic instruments with a Free Jazz approach. Like Herbie Hancock and Chick Corea, however, they began to move in a more commercial direction with music that became more and more arranged. They ultimately became the most popular and longest lasting of the Fusion bands. Zawinul was a master synthesizer player and programmer who synthesized many unique sounds and textures. He surrounded himself with multiple keyboards and switched instruments, sometimes playing two at once, seamlessly. After several personnel changes, virtuoso electric bassist **Jaco Pastorius** joined the group in 1975 and attracted even more listeners to the band. Pastorius explored new sounds and ways of playing the electric bass and was known for playing harmonics, which produce high notes outside of the bass's normal range. Pastorius, along with Stanley Clarke, discovered new techniques and explored new possibilities on the relatively new instrument more than anyone else during this time.

Joe Zawinul (1932–2007) first came to widespread attention playing with Cannonball Adderley's band during the sixties. By that time Cannonball was mostly playing Soul Jazz, which had elements of popular Soul and Gospel music of the time. Zawinul pioneered the Fender Rhodes electric piano and was the first prominent pianist to play one. He first played it on *Mercy, Mercy, Mercy*, a tune he wrote, which became a huge crossover hit. He later wrote and played on *In a Silent Way* for Miles Davis and performed on *Bitches Brew*.

Figure 22.5: Joe Zawinul, 2007.

Copyright © Joe Zawinul (CC BY-SA 3.0) at http://commons.wikimedia.org/wiki/File:Joe_zawinul_2007-03-28_live_in_freiburg.jpg

As the group progressed, Zawinul became more important to the overall sound, style, and conception of the band. The music became more compositional and arranged, sometimes with little real improvisation. Wayne Shorter, who is among the elite saxophonists of all time, seemed to be relegated to a few toots here and there. Zawinul got more and more synthesizer-savvy as time went on and dominated the sound and sounds of the music. The album *Heavy Weather* became a hit and the tune *Birdland*, from the album, remains their most popular tune. The group also mixed in elements of what is now called **World Music** by incorporating various ethnic sounds, melodies, and rhythms.

BIRDLAND 1978

Joe Zawinul—Keyboards, Synthesizers
Wayne Shorter—Soprano and Tenor Sax
Jaco Pastorius—Electric Bass
Peter Erskine—Drums

Watch this live performance of *Birdland*. Notice all of the keyboards surrounding Joe Zawinul. Listen to the low opening synthesizer riff and the melody that Jaco plays with harmonics on the bass. Notice how he also bends the strings. Shorter then comes in with a new melody along with synthesizer. They then play a bluesy riff against a rising bass line that culminates in a new melody played by Shorter, now on tenor sax. After about one minute and fifty seconds, the main theme comes in that acts as a chorus. It is a very catchy tune, played by Shorter and Zawinul and sung by Jaco, which is easy to remember and has all the makings of a Pop song hook section. After a section of repeating descending chords, various sections of the tune repeat with a long chorus section at the end. Like Chick Corea's *Hymn of the Seventh Galaxy*, this music is more composition than improvisation. The problem of form facing some jazz musicians in the fifties seems to be partly solved by these Fusion groups but at the expense of improvisation. So was it really solved? Let us now look at the eighties to see where all this went.

Chapter Twenty Three

Keith Jarrett

Pianist Keith Jarrett was born in 1945 in Allentown, Pennsylvania. He is as eccentric as he is eclectic, as distinctive as discerning, and as captious as off the cuff. He, along with Bill Evans, Herbie Hancock, McCoy Tyner, and Chick Corea, is one of the five major Post-Bop pianists. He was a real child prodigy who began playing public performances when he was five years old. After briefly playing with Art Blakey and the Jazz Messengers, he gained notoriety playing with the Charles Lloyd Quartet during the second half of the sixties. After Lloyd's band broke up he played with Miles Davis' Fusion band from 1970 to 1971. After leaving Miles' band he led several groups during the seventies, including a trio with bassist Charlie Hayden and drummer Paul Motian, which was augmented to a quartet with the addition of saxophonist Dewey Redman. This group was known as Jarrett's "American Quartet." He also led a "European Quartet" that featured saxophonist Jan Garbarek. During the seventies, while performing with these groups, he also began to perform and record as a solo pianist. It is mainly through his solo playing that he reached a wide non-jazz audience as well as a jazz audience. In 1983 Jarrett shocked the jazz world when he recorded an album of standard pop songs with a trio. The tradition of playing standards all but ceased during the seventies and what seemed at the time to be a risky step backwards, turned out to be a huge critical and commercial success that, in the ears of many, rescued jazz from the solipsistic excesses of Free Jazz and the simplistic juvenilia of Fusion.

Jarrett, from the beginning, has been a flamboyant performer who totally immerses himself into the music he performs. He often stands up or squats as he plays while singing along or grunting and groaning to the music. While these antics annoy some, Jarrett makes no apologies, as his total immersion is the only way he channels his creative urges that may even, as he has implied, travel through him rather than from him. Jarrett is also a competent Classical pianist who has recorded and performed works of Bach, Mozart, and several other contemporary composers, and it is interesting to watch Jarrett perform written music in a very staid manner as opposed to the way he performs improvised music.

Jarrett is a composer of jazz and Classical works and plays various other instruments, including soprano saxophone, organ, clavichord, and a variety of percussion instruments.

Figure 23.1: Keith Jarrett, 2003.

CHARLES LLOYD QUARTET

Keith Jarrett made his mark on the jazz world when he played with the Charles Lloyd Quartet from 1965 to 1969. Charles Lloyd (b. 1938) played tenor saxophone and flute, and led one of the most popular jazz groups of the sixties. The band included Jack DeJohnette on drums and Cecil McBee on bass who was replaced in 1967 by Ron McClure. Although the band was strictly acoustic, it appealed to a segment of the Rock audience. Lloyd masterfully blended elements of Free Jazz with Rock or Latin grooves, along with Eastern musical influences. Jarrett who was only 20 years old and DeJohnette, who was 23, shared Lloyd's eclectic tastes and brought their youthful openness and enthusiasm to the music of the band.

Some of the music that the group played might be considered as a sort of proto-fusion but it was purely acoustic. The music could even sound folkish at times and even though the improvisations often could be quite free, there seemed to be an inclusiveness in it that was largely missing from other more belligerent Free Jazz. The quartet often played venues associated more with Rock than jazz, including the Monterey Pop Festival and the Fillmore Auditorium in San Francisco; it was not unusual to see Dead Heads and hippies among the jazz fans at a Charles Lloyd Quartet performance.

The 1966 album *Forest Flower: Live at Monterey* is one of the few million-selling albums in jazz history. Lloyd's original two-movement tunes, *Forest Flower: Sunrise* and *Forest Flower: Sunset* became hits in the jazz world. *Forest Flower: Sunrise* is a complex tune with an unusual form and unusual harmonies. There are also changes of feel built into the tune, going from Latin to swing to almost Rock. The tensions created by these fluctuations are grounded by *Forest Flower: Sunset*, which vamps on a repetitive two-chord calypso-like groove. Jarrett's solos on both parts are outstanding and technically brilliant. Here he exhibits his knack for taking the music *outside* (free-like, random-like) but bringing it back *inside*.

Jarrett's formative years with Lloyd were crucial for his later development as a player. The quartet's eclectic approach, Pop sensibilities, and universal appeal continue to be Jarrett's modus operandi to this day.

LOVE SHIP 1968
THE CHARLES LLOYD QUARTET

Charles Lloyd—Tenor Sax
Keith Jarrett—Piano
Ron McClure—Bass
Jack DeJohnette—Drums

Watch this except from the 1968 television show *Jazz Net*. The young Keith Jarrett clearly shows Bill Evans' influence with impressionistic rootles voicings, rhythmic displacement, and organic improvisation. Notice the rhythmic suppleness and interplay of this rhythm section that was inspired by the Bill Evans Trio.

MILES DAVIS FUSION BAND

After the Charles Lloyd Quartet broke up in 1969, Miles Davis asked Keith Jarrett to join his new Fusion band as a second keyboard player; Chick Corea was already with the band. When Corea left the band in 1970, Jarrett was the sole keyboardist who played the Fender Rhodes electric piano, the RMI electric piano, and an electric organ: sometimes two keyboards simultaneously. Unlike most of his generation, Jarrett eschewed electric instruments but acquiesced in this case for a chance to play with Miles Davis. His rhythm section mate from Charles Lloyd's group Jack DeJohnette was the drummer in this Miles Davis band and their reunion added new energy to this group. Many consider this to the best of Miles' Fusion groups.

EXCERPT FROM A BERLIN CONCERT 1971

Watch this except from a performance with Miles Davis in 1971. Jarrett is accompanied only by a percussionist while he plays the Fender Rhodes and an electric organ simultaneously. This is a free-form improvisation that will become common for Jarrett on acoustic piano soon after (see below). Here he clearly takes advantage of the electric keyboards' eliciting unique sounds by combining the instruments. Jarrett and the percussionist work off each other and he treats the keyboards more as percussion instruments at times. As usual, he is totally immersed in the music and physically contorts his body as he makes countless facial expressions.

SOLO CONCERTS

In 1971 Jarrett recorded a solo piano album, *Facing You*, for ECM records. ECM was a new German label run by Manfred Eicher who encouraged Jarrett along with Chick Corea and Paul Bley to record solo piano albums. Unlike the other two pianists, Jarrett embarked on solo piano career and continued to record and perform as a soloist. Other than several isolated solo piano recordings by Thelonious Monk, Bill Evans, and a few others, the art of solo jazz piano, a staple of jazz from its beginning, seemed to die along with Art Tatum in 1956. In some ways, Jarrett revived this tradition but his approach was radically new. His were true improvisational performances in that he started with no preconceived material, *a tabula rasa*, as it were: no tunes, no keys or modes, no chord changes; this smacks of Free Jazz but Free Jazz performances typically have a point of departure usually in the form of a tune, to get things started. Free Jazz also typically sounds dissonant and chaotic for the most part. Jarrett's solo performances are truly free and almost anything goes; this can include music that sounds joyously consonant as well as dissonantly chaotic. It is difficult to categorize much of what he plays; it could be jazz, Classical, Gospel, Blues, Folk, Rock, etc.; sometimes it is all of those and more. Jarrett, then, becomes a pure improviser with nothing upon which to improvise. Traditionally, Jazz improvisation involves a layering on of something; usually a tune or a scale or a chord progression. But in a way, Jarrett, by starting from nothing, is improvising on the whole history of music—whatever came before his actualization at the moment. Indeed, this is risky business and Jarrett truly looks and sounds as if the music is being channeled through him as he plays. The whole history of music idea is not that farfetched, as Jarrett has already experienced much of it from the European classics to non-western music and most music in between. These solo concerts often take on a ritualistic atmosphere as the high priest weaves his magic in front of a seduced audience.

After the success of his first solo album, *Facing You*, which had predetermined tunes, his subsequent albums, *Solo Concerts* (1973) and *The Köln Concert* (1975) with no predetermined material became even more popular, appealing to a wide audience. *The Köln Concert* is the most popular of all; it still sells well and is one of largest selling albums by a jazz artist in history, having sold more than 3.5 million copies. Something magical happened that night in Cologne, Germany. Jarrett almost did not perform that night because of the flawed piano but as great pianists often do, he not only made the best of it, but he also adapted his playing to the idiosyncratic mechanics of the instrument as if the piano was playing him. He also played off the acoustic environment of the Cologne opera house. It was truly a remarkable, inspired performance. Jarrett make the piano sing, weep, and dance; his complete technical mastery of the piano is evident, not only on the fleet rapid-note passages, but in the static slow sections with long-held notes that reverberate through the concert hall, buoyed by his not-always-*sotto voce* singing along.

During the seventies Jarrett usually simply walked on stage, sat down at the piano, and started playing uninterrupted for about forty minutes to an hour; after an intermission he would do the same for the second half of the concert. In later years, he has played shorter segments with defined endings, lasting anywhere from three to twelve minutes or so. His later playing is more esoteric and abstract, for the most part, and less visceral and groove oriented. Overall, Jarrett does not overwhelm us with his dazzling technique as Art Tatum and Oscar Peterson would, but rather impresses us with his complete mastery of the piano and the sheer musicality of his playing—from the longest held single note to the rapid-note lines to the complex interlocking multiple parts. It is more about the music than about him and more about the music than about what's hip or current. Like other great artists, Jarrett transcends style and genre and communicates directly to the human spirit. For example, like opera singer Luciano Pavarotti and cellist Yo-Yo Ma, the music comes through no matter what musical predispositions a listener might have.

THE KÖLN CONCERT 1975
Part 1 (excerpt)

0:00 Jarrett begins by mimicking the signal chimes at the Cologne Opera House that alert the audience to be seated for the start of a performance—a clear indication that this performance was not preplanned. He uses this as a point of departure from which enters a quasi gospel feel

2:16 A static harmonic section based on a rhythmic vamp

2:52 Vamp leads into a still rubato section where he mostly alternates an A minor with a G major chord using long notes in the left hand and rapid cascading figures in the right hand

6:22 Jarrett stomps his foot to the beat—Still alternating the 2 chords

6:44 foot stops as music calms down—back to rubato - Still alternating the 2 chords

7:14 definite tempo established—LH plays quasi ostinato (repeating part) vamp while the same chords alternate every 2 measures.

8:38 vamp stops and music becomes still again—rubato—alternates same A minor and G major chords with cascading RH runs and figures

9:44 in tempo again—repetitive groove - alternating same two chords—crescendos

10:18 groove continues –begins to work in some passing chords

10:52 continues but suddenly softer

11:20 continues adding more passing chords and rapid RH lines

11:57 continues—crescendos—LH gets an octave lower in range

12:45 continues—softer—LH back to previous range—gentler –more lyrical melody emerges—chord progression begin to change from the alternating A minor to G major chord to a more chromatic and unpredictable one

14:00 tempo slow down (ritardando)

14:14 rubato- motion becomes disjunct—2-note stepwise motive emerges

15:09 music pauses - excerpt ends here but Jarrett continued

THE STANDARDS TRIO

In 1983 Jarrett recoded an album called ***Standards Volume 1*** with bassist Gary Peacock and drummer Jack DeJohnette. Standards are songs from the Great American Songbook, those that have stood the test of time. Most jazz singers sing standards and pop songs in general have served as material for jazz musicians since the beginning. However, by 1983, standards seemed to be gone from most jazz musicians' repertoires and essentially moribund. Much as in the Rock world from the sixties on, jazz bands were expected to write their own material. Jarrett, himself, had been doing that with his own groups up until this time. His American and European Quartets played mostly his own compositions, which were mixtures of traditional jazz, Rock, Gospel, and an acoustic kind of Fusion. ***Standards Volume 1*** seemed to come from out of the blue; it literally shocked the jazz world. The concept was so old that it was new. Don't mistake this, however, for some kind of nostalgic, retro homage to bygone days; the music *was* new and fresh with a modern bent on its performance. Jarrett, Peacock, and DeJohnette had been on the forefront of contemporary jazz since the sixties and had extensive experience in Freer Jazz, Free Jazz, and Fusion. Now playing standards in 1983, they brought those experiences to bear upon this time-honored material. This was not their father's ***My Funny Valentine***. The trio adapted the freer interplay conception of the Bill Evans Trio and Miles Davis' sixties rhythm section to create a newer, original approach to familiar tunes.

A hallmark of the trio's playing is their rhythmic suppleness. Although the beat is always steady, it seems to fluctuate amid the polymetric superimpositions of each player. They often think more in terms of the macrobeat, which could be the first beat of every measure or even of every two or four measures. Each player might subdivide that macrobeat into different groupings, twos, threes, fours, etc. Jarrett, also, is able to lift his melodies away from the pulse into different time dimensions; essentially playing rubato while the real beat never moves: Sonny Rollins does something similar in his playing. Like Miles' sixties rhythm section, they change the feels and smoothly transition from virtually doubling or halving the tempo. They sometimes lock into grooves or vamps that can linger a while at the ends of tunes. The players' admiration for the Ahmad Jamal Trio is apparent in their affinity for a groove and their spreading the responsibility equally for the music they make.

Before the first standards session the trio agreed that they only would play songs they all liked and knew the words to. No one sings (Jarrett's humming aside) but they thought it was important to know and feel the essence of a song through its lyrics. Indeed, one can *hear* Jarrett *singing* many of these melodies as he plays them. Knowing the words to a song can help an instrumentalist phrase the melody, much as it did for Billie Holiday and Frank Sinatra. Some musicians, however, feel that knowing the lyrics has no bearing on how they play a particular song. Interestingly, Bill Evans, one of Jarrett's influences and one with whom both Peacock and DeJohnette played, said he paid no attention to the words of a song.

What began as a single recording session has blossomed into a partnership that has lasted over thirty years. The group has been a huge artistic and commercial success, and very influential. It seemed like the jazz world was starved for standards again and one by one most musicians came back to the fold—Miles Davis is a notable exception. Jarrett's trio proved that the material is not nearly as important as what you do with it. By resurrecting the standard song, Jarrett resurrected jazz itself. Fusion and Free had run their course and now was time for a federation of styles. In a sense, Jarrett created what might be called *Post-Hip*. Now, nothing was hip so everything was hip; the old was new and the new was old; *new to be new* was replaced with *knew to be known* again. Everybody knows the standards and they function like Platonic forms that earthly endeavors strive to attain. Listeners are eager to hear Jarrett's version of **My Funny Valentine** along with Miles Davis,' Chet Baker's, Frank Sinatra's, Ahmad Jamal's, etc. They are different, yet they are all **My Funny Valentine**. So in reality there are *My Funny Valentines* that are perhaps shadows of an ideal **My Funny Valentine**, just as *my funny valentine* is different from *your funny valentine*.

This trio has set new standard for playing standards and rightfully belongs among the great piano trios of jazz history and among the greatest groups in jazz, past and present.

JACK DEJOHNETTE

Figure 23.2: Jack DeJohnette, 2006.
Copyright © Ric Brooks (CC BY-SA 2.0)
at http://commons.wikimedia.org/wiki/
File:Jack_DeJohnette.jpg

Drummer Jack DeJohnette (b. 1942) is one of the greatest in jazz history. He combines Tony Williams' inventiveness, Elvin Jones' rhythm complexity, and Max Roach's melodic sensibilities into a highly original organic approach to playing the drums; one that is above all musical. His association with Keith Jarrett goes back to the Charles Lloyd Quartet during the sixties and Miles Davis' Fusion band of the early seventies. He has also played with Bill Evans and Free Jazz bands, and like Jarrett, brings all of his varied experience to the trio. He can lay down any kind of groove and above all swing when called for. He also plays the piano and this as well as his experience with World Music has made him simpatico with Jarrett for almost fifty years.

GARY PEACOCK

Figure 23.3: Gary Peacock, 2003.

Bassist Gary Peacock (b. 1935), like DeJohnette, comes from a varied jazz background, having played with such stylistically varied musicians as Art Pepper, Bill Evans, Albert Ayler, and Miles Davis. Scott LaFaro's influence is evident in all of his work as he can capably play an equally interactive role with drums and piano. But like Jarrett and DeJohnette, Peacock can swing when called for and lay down infectious grooves.

STELLA BY STARLIGHT 1985

Keith Jarrett—Piano
Gary Peacock—Bass
Jack DeJohnette—Drums

Watch this video performance of *Stella by Starlight*, one of the Great American Songbook standards written in 1944 by Victor Young with lyrics added by Ned Washington. It has served as a vehicle for jazz musicians ever since. The early performance by the "Standards Trio" demonstrates the intuitive interplay and inventiveness of the group. All do admirable solos and Jarrett leads the way with his piano as well as his inadvertent singing and choreography.

Chapter Twenty Four

Jazz from the Eighties

U nfortunately there is not much to say about jazz since 1980 other than that from the previous chapter on Keith Jarrett. Or perhaps it is better said as: "depends on whom you ask." Once Jarrett and company returned to playing standards, jazz seemed to come full circle, which meant it stopped evolving. What follows here is just an opinion but most would agree the jury is still out on the significance of the jazz of the last thirty-plus years.

SMOOTH JAZZ

Fusion devolved into *Smooth Jazz*, which is a sort of *muzak* version of Fusion. Muzak is the original "elevator" or "dentist office" music: bland, unobtrusive background music that was originally designed to increase industrial production from bored workers. Muzak was a company name that now generically means piped-in music to businesses or music played while a business puts your phone call on hold. Musicians use the term pejoratively and many jazz musicians refer to Smooth Jazz as "Fuzak." Even Miles Davis, who never abandoned Fusion, played a quasi-Smooth Jazz music during the eighties that included hits of the day by Michael Jackson and Cindy Lauper. In the Pop world, the Yamaha DX-7 became the preferred keyboard that replaced the Rhodes (née Fender Rhodes) during the decade. It was a digital synthesizer as opposed to the mechanical Rhodes and older analog synths. Its sound was lush and amorphous and added a wash of sound that enveloped the music. The digital revolution began in the eighties and personal computer technology spilled over into the music world as MIDI (Musical Instrument Digital Interface). MIDI is a way that digital keyboards can "talk" to each other and be controlled by a computer. Many "live" performances of Pop music included pre-existing computerized sequenced tracks. The old days of Joe Zawinul rearranging patch chords on his monstrous analog synthesizers were gone and much of the human element along with it.

Saxophonist Grover Washington Jr., with singer Bill Withers, had a huge hit with *Just the Two of Us* in 1981. The popular success of this record inspired other saxophonists to smooth out their jazz as well. The soprano saxophone became a popular instrument within this genre and the unique sound that John Coltrane brought to Jazz in the turbulent 1960s became the banal sound of the smooth eighties. Although most jazz musicians give little credence to Smooth Jazz, if nothing else, it has become a familiar sound after "can I put you on hold" and ubiquitous on the Weather Channel.

NEOCLASSICISTS

After the electric seventies, a number of young players beginning their careers in the early eighties shunned Fusion and electronics, and attempted to revisit various pre-Fusion styles. Young trumpeter Wynton Marsalis was the unofficial leader of this group that became known as the Neoclassicists. Marsalis played with Art Blakey and the Jazz Messengers when he was just 18 and began to lead his own bands when he was 21. Marsalis revisited Hard Bop and music based on Miles Davis' sixties quintet at first and then embraced the entire history of jazz, including early jazz from his native New Orleans. Marsalis is currently director of Jazz Studies at the prestigious Juilliard School for the Arts and founder and director of Jazz at Lincoln Center. He is also an accomplished classical player who has had equal success in the Classical music world. He has been an articulate spokesman for jazz in general and its historical significance in American culture. With all these accomplishments, Marsalis remains a somewhat controversial figure. Many say his playing lacks a certain authenticity in that it is derivative rather than original. His technical virtuosity possibly works against him in this regard, as it all seems too easy for him. Some criticize what is perceived as his selective view of jazz history. Whatever one's opinion, Marsalis has been the most visible player and spokesperson for jazz since the early 1980s.

The problem with the neoclassicists is just that; it is a looking back, a reproduction rather than anything original. It makes jazz a historical moribund music rather than an evolving vital music as it had always been.

This nostalgia for *the good old days* is well intentioned and instructional, but adds little to the legacy of jazz. Recordings make re-creations moot; why would one want to hear someone try to sound like Louis Armstrong when he or she can hear Louis Armstrong, himself, on records? Attempting to sound like Louis Armstrong can be instructive to a trumpet player learning to play, but offers little to the astute jazz listener who has heard it before and with apologies to George Santayana, *those who learn their history too well might be condemned by repeating it.*

One should not confuse the playing of old material (standards, etc.) with the playing of older styles. The Keith Jarrett Trio, for example, plays old standards but not in an old way. They do not attempt to play *Autumn Leaves*, for example, the way the Bill Evans, Erroll Garner, or Ahmad Jamal trios played it. Likewise the playing of new material does not make the music new if the performance is derivative from the past. But then, is there anything new in jazz?

CD REISSUES: THE OLD BECOMES NEW

When *high fidelity* recording and playback became available during the fifties, recording artists of all genres rerecorded much of their popular material to take advantage of the better sound that high fidelity had to offer. The arrival of stereo in the late fifties offered similar opportunities. By and large, however, unless records were perennially popular, after the initial pressings were released, they were no longer available on the market. The advent of digital compact discs, however, led to a different scenario. Instead of re-recording older material, record companies transferred existing tapes to the digital CD format. Thus, hundreds of old recordings were issued as new CDs. Wynton Marsalis was now competing with the younger Miles Davis and Clifford Brown and jazz fans were either rediscovering or discovering the great masters of the past. The increased time capacity of CDs over records made the issuing of previously unreleased tracks possible. Never-heard alternate takes of issued cuts as well as never-released tunes were now part of the present.

The reissue craze actually began on vinyl during the seventies when Dial and Savoy records released complete sets of everything Charlie Parker recorded for them, most of which consisted of alternate takes. Several other labels followed suit and alternate takes became common on reissued LPs. All of this exploded as CDs replaced LPs during the eighties and jazz aficionados, enticed by the added tracks, eagerly replaced their LP collection with CD proxies. Reissues began to outsell new albums as *jazz as history* seemed more appealing to most listeners than contemporary jazz.

The *"i"* revolution of the early 21st century that included tunes, pods, pads, and phones, increased the availability of music of all sorts on all sorts of devices. Now, one can sit at home and conjure up Louis Armstrong, Benny Goodman, or Art Tatum from his or her thumb or fingers. Ironically, the album concept pioneered by Frank Sinatra in the 1950s that the Beatles introduced into the Rock world in the 1960s began to lose significance during the new century, as listeners were able to purchase individual songs as opposed to complete albums. Currently, digitally remastered and remixed recordings are replacing original CD issues, as listeners buy yet newer tinkered-with versions of their old favorites. As the old get newer, the new get older, and the with apologies to T. S. Eliot, it seems that *jazz present and jazz future are both perhaps contained in jazz past.*

JAZZ EDUCATION

Jazz education was virtually oxymoronic until the 1960s. The prevailing mindset was that jazz can be learned but not taught; one learned jazz by listening and playing, by serving an apprenticeship, as it were. For the early jazz players, of course, it was just that, but as early as the late 1920s, musically educated jazz musicians emerged. These players were not educated in jazz but in traditional Western music. As jazz became more written during the Pre-Swing Era, players were required to read music as well as improvise, and arrangers such as Don Redman and Fletcher Henderson were musically schooled at the college level. Teddy Wilson was a college music professor before joining Benny Goodman. While music education became more normative for jazz musicians, jazz education remained elusive. Most colleges and universities did not take jazz seriously and although some student-run jazz bands were tolerated, the idea of receiving credit for playing or learning about jazz seemed absurd to most "legitimate" musicians and teachers.

During the forties, Lennie Tristano devised theories about jazz and Bebop in particular that he was able to teach to others (see Chapter 14). His theoretical approach led to Cool Jazz and also to criticism for what was perceived as overly intellectualizing jazz. Despite the criticism, jazz education became a possibility in the minds of some musicians and educators during the fifties and several schools offered accredited courses in jazz. In 1947 the University of North Texas pioneered a Jazz Studies degree and in 1957, the Lenox School of Jazz was started in Eastern Massachusetts. It was a summer program directed by John Lewis of the Modern Jazz Quartet, and was essentially the beginning of modern jazz education. Saxophonist and educator Jerry Coker began doing jazz clinics at colleges during the sixties and wrote books and articles that took much of the mystery out of jazz by reducing its workings to some basic principles based on generic patterns of notes and chords.

During the sixties the Berklee School of Music put jazz education on the map when it instituted a Jazz Studies degree. It became the most well-known institution to not only offer a jazz degree but to specialize in jazz education as well: Keith Jarrett and Al Di Meola are among those who attended Berklee. By 1980 jazz studies degrees were relatively common and by 1990 practically every major music program offered one.

The proliferation of jazz as an academic discipline has created a new generation of schooled jazz musicians who come the table with an unprecedented knowledge of the theories and workings of jazz. With this, however, comes a sameness, a *lingua franca,* as it were, that is shared by almost everyone. The academizing of jazz has brought with it a jazz academe that serves itself more than a jazz fan base. Students get degrees in jazz studies that qualify them for and enable them to get college-level teaching jobs that perpetuate the jazz scholastic elite by turning out more like themselves. This is not the academe's fault; modern economics is such that it gets increasingly harder to make a living playing music to such a small fan base. The good news is that jazz is now universally recognized as an expressive, legitimate art form; the bad news is it often can become a pedagogical pedantic pursuit of a professional position. Of course this not true for everyone and many first-rate jazz musicians have come through academic programs.

There are probably more good jazz musicians today than any time before but where are the great ones, the innovators? Where is the next Satchmo, Bird, or Trane?

ECONOMICS

Since 1980, economics are such that full-time jazz clubs are becoming increasingly rare. Outside of New York, they hardly exist at all. This is detrimental not only to jazz fans but to the musicians, themselves, not just financially but also artistically. The fact that it is virtually impossible to keep a jazz band working on a regular basis has led to the virtual disappearance of jazz bands. Time was that Miles Davis' bands of the fifties or sixties would work clubs across the country six days a week. Other than the Keith Jarrett Trio, nothing even close to his sixties quintet has been achieved as far as an integrated, intuitively communicative enclave ever since. The reason these bands and others, such as Bill Evans' trios, John Coltrane's quartet, and Duke Ellington's band, were so tight is they played as a unit on a regular basis for extended periods of time. Unfortunately, even for the most prominent of jazz musicians, this is no longer possible. For aspiring players, this lost opportunity further relegates them to school practice rooms to try out their wares as opposed to the baptism by fire of public performances. One wonders how talented younger players, such as saxophonist Chris Potter would flourish in a sixties Miles Davis band–like environment, although he is quite impressive as is. The lack of full-time clubs that has led to the lack of full-time bands has led to lackluster liaisons, for lack of a better word, among contemporary jazz musicians, comparatively speaking.

JAZZ AND POP

Although jazz began in 1900, it really blossomed during the 1920s and not coincidently along with recording, radio, and the Great American Songbook (see Chapter 10). Just as Ragtime influenced the writing of Ragtime songs at the turn of the 20th century, jazz affected the writing of Pop songs during the twenties. Jazz musicians played these songs and non-jazz-related Pop songs as well, effectively turning them into jazz through performance. The sophisticated chords and chord progressions used in the Pop songs from the *Golden Age of American Popular Song* (1920s–1940s) became part of the basic jazz harmonic vocabulary and remains so to this day. All was well when the symbiotic union between jazz and Pop thrived during this age. Even as Bebop began to sever this union, Pop standards and Pop song forms served as a point of departure for modern jazz into the sixties.

As much of Pop music changed after the advent of Rock 'n' Roll in the mid-fifties, jazz musicians either went toward an anti-Pop mindset or tried to adapt to the newer music. The anti-Pop movement has been the focus of sixties jazz in this book, but there were some attempts to play current Pop hits during the sixties. Wes Montgomery, for example, recorded some of them, including **California Dreaming**, and **Going out of My Head**, with elaborate big band arrangements by Don Sebesky. Although these records sold well, they were neither meant to be nor were taken as serious artistic music. But if, as was stated earlier in this book, anything can be turned into jazz, and jazz was an approach to rather than a style of music, can these songs and others like them serve as vehicles for serious jazz interpretations? In general, no, because the melodies, harmonies, rhythms, and forms are too rigid and stifling for a musician to create a continuous improvised solo. The songs from the Great American Songbook usually have a sense of moving forward in time even though sections and forms repeat. The chord progressions of the old standards traverse areas of stability and instability that literally can take the improviser on a jazz journey and there seems to be countless ways of negotiating those harmonic terrains. Harmonic tension and release is built into the songs themselves and the uncrowded melodies leave enough spaces for filling in and interpretive leeway. Most Pop songs from the Rock Era are harmonically static and have busy melodies that leave little space to fill. The verse-chorus forms of most contemporary Pop songs seem to interrupt the forward flow at the arrival of the chorus. These forms are as antithetical to jazz as Classical music forms that are too lengthy and/or complex.

The backgrounds of the newer songs are most often very specific and crucial to what the song is, which leaves little room for rhythmic interpretation. Changing the chords, melodies, and harmonies to most of these songs would make little sense of the song and distort its inner unity. The Pop music of the Rock Era consists not so much of songs as of records of those songs. The record defines the song once and for all, leaving little left to interpret and change. Change is the very nature of jazz and that is why there are thousands of records of **Body and Soul**, and relatively few of the Eurhythmics' **Sweet Dreams Are Made of This**.

Oddly enough some Disco music of the seventies had some elements in common with jazz. In fact some of the old Pop standards were actually turned into Disco songs. Vincent Montana, Jr. and his Salsoul Orchestra combined Salsa and Soul music with jazz to create a new dance music that became enormously popular. His recording of **Tangerine**, a song written in the 1920s and a jazz standard, became a huge Disco hit. Although the background rhythms were well defined, Montana and others realized that they could play jazz-like solos over them because the harmony and chords lent themselves to such exploits.

As eighties Pop drifted toward computers and digital and sampled sounds, jazz drifted farther away—other than Smooth Jazz, which is not really jazz. As Pop song hooks became more repetitious than ever and humans were increasingly replaced by machines, the separation of Pop from jazz seemed to be complete and therein lies much of the problem. When John Coltrane recorded **My Favorite Things**, as radical and far removed from the original song as it was, it was a contemporary Pop song that was in the air at the time. On any given night one might have turned on the television and heard Julie Andrews, or Perry Como, or Dinah Shore, or Ella Fitzgerald singing it. ***Autumn Leaves*** was a hit song and hit record for several artists before Miles Davis or Bill Evans ever recorded a jazz version of it. The average listener could hear and appreciate what a jazz musician could do with familiar material and while this song and others like it are still familiar to many, they are most likely not to younger listeners. Even most young jazz musicians think these songs are jazz songs when originally they were not. In other words, there is a disconnect between jazz and Pop today that never before existed to this extent.

Some jazz players have attempted to reconcile the newer Pop with jazz by creating new *standards* from newer Pop songs. Pianists Herbie Hancock and Brad Mehldau have recorded songs by the Beatles and others. While the attempts are admirable, the music sounds too contrived at times and the concept has not caught on with most jazz players.

Even during the seventies' fascination with Fusion, standards were kept alive by singers. Frank Sinatra and Ella Fitzgerald were still going strong as were other notable singers, including Sarah Vaughn, Carmen McCrae, Ernestine Anderson, Shirley Horn, and Tony Bennett. In more recent years several younger singers emerged and enjoy commercial success singing standard songs. Although nothing much new has come from this new generation, they have attracted a younger audience to the older music. Harry Connick, Jr., Diana Krall, and Michael Bublé have managed to preserve some standard songs while slipping in some more contemporary material.

One of the most original of the younger singers is Kurt Elling. He has taken scat singing and vocalese to new level. Vocalese is the singing of words to previously recorded improved solos. This process began in the 1940s with singers Eddie Jefferson and King Pleasure and was later ingeniously employed by the vocal group of Lambert, Hendrix, and Ross. This group applied the technique to entire instrumental recordings by Count Basie, Duke Ellington, Horace Silver, and others. Elling applies vocalise to more modern jazz tunes and recordings, especially those by Wayne Shorter. He also sings standards with a fresh and original approach.

Another Pop music innovation of the eighties was the proliferation of music videos shown on MTV. It was then almost necessary for Pop music to be seen as well as heard and records had a much less chance of succeeding in sales without an accompanying video. This worked extremely well for Michael Jackson and Madonna but would have been downright silly for jazz musicians to do the same. Pop music is well scripted and easily lip synced so the video montages and collages can be edited and assembled in a variety of ways, which make the sudden scene changes associated with these videos work as visual versions of songs. Jarrett's gyrations aside, jazz is more of a nonvisual medium than Pop and the unscripted improvisations from the musicians are practically impossible to visually sync with lips or fingers. A case in point is a famous film of jazz musicians produced in 1950 by jazz impresario Norman Grantz. To optimize the video and audio quality of the film, he had the musicians record the music in a sound studio and then asked them to pretend they were playing their parts for the filming. The players, of course, could not remember exactly what they played and their inept attempt at syncing is quite obvious to any viewer of the film as well as the musicians themselves; Charlie Parker famously laughs as he watches Coleman Hawkins fumbling as he tries to sync his part. All this is to say that jazz misses out on a major new marketing medium from the eighties.

WHITHER JAZZ?

Jazz began as a kind of folk music around 1900 but transformed into an art music during the 1920s that evolved quickly until the 1970s; it then plateaued during the 1980s where it sits today. It the absence of any viable new styles, all styles coexist. On any given night in any given town one is apt to hear a jazz performance that will feature an eclectic mix of standards, Swing, Bebop, Post-Bop, Latin, and Funk. Today's schooled jazz musicians are equally at home in all styles of jazz and are expected to be fluent in most of them. They are, in effect, much like contemporary Classical musicians who can play music from the 18th to 21st centuries with equal proficiency. If this makes contemporary jazz musicians sound more like the preservers of a hallowed tradition, so be it. The tradition is indeed sacred by now and even if your iPod, filled with great jazz recordings, is more of a museum than a device *au courant*, its contents will transcend its OS and serve as a digital diary of the jazz journey you took through the 20th century.

Bibliography

Carr, Ian. *Miles Davis: The Definitive Biography*. New York: Thunder's Mouth Press, 1998. Print.

Carr, Ian. *Keith Jarrett: The Man and His Music*. New York: Da Capo Press, 1992. Print.

Chambers, Jack. *Milestones: The Music and Times of Miles Davis*. New York: Da Capo Press, 1998. Print.

Collier, James L. *The Making of Jazz: A Comprehensive History*. New York: Dell Publishing Company Inc., 1978. Print.

Crouch, Stanley. *Kansas City Lightning: The Rise and Times of Charlie Parker*. New York: HarperCollins, 2013. Print.

Davis, Miles, and Quincy Troupe. *Miles: The Autobiography*. New York: Simon and Schuster, 1989. Print.

DeVeaux, Scott. *The Birth of Bebop: A Social and Musical History*. Berkeley and Los Angeles: University of California Press, 1997. Print.

DeVeaux, Scott, and Gary Giddins. *Jazz*. New York: W. W. Norton and Company, Inc., 2009. Print.

Elsdon, Peter. *Keith Jarrett's The Koln Concert*. New York: Oxford University Press, 2013. Print.

Friedwald, Will. *A Biographical Guide to the Great Jazz and Pop Singers*. New York: Pantheon Books, 2010. Print.

Friedwald, Will. *Jazz Singing: America's Great Voices from Bessie Smith to Bebop and Beyond*. New York: Da Capo Press, 1996. Print.

Friedwald, Will. *Sinatra: The Song Is You*. New York: Da Capo Press, 1997. Print.

Gelly, Dave, *Being Prez: The Life & Music of Lester Young*. New York: Oxford University Press, 2997. Print.

Giddins, Gary. *Visions of Jazz: The First Century*. New York: Oxford University Press, Inc., 1998. Print.

Gioia, Ted. *The History of Jazz*. New York: Oxford University Press, 1997. Print.

Gridley, Mark C. *Jazz Styles: History and Analysis*. 7th ed. New Jersey: Bud Therien, 2000. Print.

Gioia, Ted. *West Coast Jazz: Modern Jazz in California, 1945–1960*. New York: Oxford University Press, 1992. Print.

Hall, Fred M. *It's About Time: The Dave Brubeck Story*. Fayetteville: University of Arkansas Press, 1996. Print.

Hamm, Charles, *Yesterdays: Popular Song in America*. New York: W.W. Norton. 1979. Print.

Hodier, André. *Jazz: Its Evolution and Essence.* Trans. Davis Noakes. New York: Grove Press, 1956. Print.

Jost, Ekkehard. *Free Jazz.* New York: Da Capo Press, Inc., 1994. Print.

Kahn, Ashley. *Kind of Blue: The Making of the Miles Davis Masterpiece.* Boston: Da Capo Press, 2000. Print.

Kahn, Ashley. *A Love Supreme: The Story of John Coltrane's Signature Album.* New York: Penguin Books, 2003. Print.

Kaplan, James. *Frank: The Voice.* New York: Doubleday, 2010. Print.

Koch, Lawrence O. *Yardbird Suite: A Compendium of the Music and Life of Charlie Parker.* Bowling Green: Bowling Green State University Popular Press, 1988. Print.

Lawn, Richard J. *Experiencing Jazz.* 2nd ed. New York: Routledge, 2013. Print.

Lees, Gene. *Singers & the Song.* New York: Oxford University Press, Inc., 1987. Print.

Litweiler, John. *The Freedom Principle: Jazz After 1958.* New York: Da Capo Press, Inc., 1984. Print.

Lyons, Len. *The 101 Best Jazz Albums.* New York: William Morrow and Company, Inc., 1980. Print.

Lyons, Len. *The Great Jazz Pianists Speaking of Their Lives and Music.* New York: Quill, 1983. Print.

Martin, Henry, and Keith Waters. *Jazz: The First 100 Years.* 2nd ed. Belmont, CA: Thomson Schirmer, 2006. Print.

Mathieson, Kenny. *Cookin': Hard Bop and Soul Jazz 1954–65.* United Kingdom: Canongate Books, 2002. Print.

Nisenson, Eric. *Blue: The Murder of Jazz.* New York: Da Capo Press, 2000. Print.

Nisenson, Eric. *'Round About Midnight: A Portrait of Miles Davis.* New York: Da Capo Press, 1998. Print.

Pettinger, Peter. *Bill Evans: How My Heart Sings.* New Haven: Yale University Press, 1998. Print.

Porter, Lewis, and Michael Ullman with Edward Hazel. *Jazz: From Its Origins to the Present.* New Jersey: Prentice-Hall, Inc., 1993. Print.

Rockwell, John. *Sinatra: An American Classic.* New York: Rolling Stone Press, 1984. Print.

Schuller, Gunther. *Early Jazz: Its Roots and Musical Development.* New York: Oxford University Press, 1968. Print.

Schuller, Gunther. *The Swing Era.* New York: Oxford University Press, 1989. Print.

Shadwick, Keith. *Bill Evans: Everything Happens to Me—A Musical Biography.* San Francisco: Backbeat Books, 2002. Print.

Shapiro, Nate, and Nat Hentoff, eds. *Hear Me Talkin' to Ya: The Story of Jazz as Told by the Men Who Made It.* New York: Rinehart, 1955. Reprint, New York: Dover, 1966.

Shipton, Alyn. *A New History of Jazz.* New York: Bayou Press Ltd., 2001. Print.

Szwed, John. *So What: The Life of Miles Davis.* New York: Simon and Schuster, 2002. Print.

Tackley, Catherine. *Benny Goodman's Famous 1938 Carnegie Hall Concert.* New York: Oxford University Press, 2012. Print.

Tanner, Paul O. W., and David W. Megill. *Jazz*. 12th ed. New York: The McGraw Hill Companies, 2013. Print.

Teachout, Terry. *Duke: The Life of Duke Ellington*. New York: Gotham Books, 2013. Print.

Tirro, Frank. *Jazz: A History*. 2nd ed. New York: W. W. Norton & Company, Inc., 1993, 1997. Print.

Valerio, John. *Bebop Jazz Piano*. Milwaukee, WI: Hal Leonard Corporation, 2003. Print.

Valerio, John. *Post-Bop Jazz Piano*. Milwaukee, WI: Hal Leonard Corporation, 2005. Print.

Valerio, John. *Stride & Swing Piano*. Milwaukee, WI: Hal Leonard Corporation, 2003. Print.

Waters, Keith. *The Studio Recordings of the Miles Davis Quintet, 1965–68*. New York: Oxford University Press, Inc., 2011. Print.

Wilder, Alec. *American Popular Song: The Great Innovators, 1900–1950*. New York: Oxford University Press, 1990. Print.

Williams, Martin. *Jazz Masters in Transition, 1957–1969*. New York: Macmillan, 1970. Print.

Williams, Martin. *Jazz Masters of New Orleans*. New York: Da Capo Press, 1978. Print.

CPSIA information can be obtained
at www.ICGtesting.com
Printed in the USA
BVOW07s1931170118
505580BV00003B/23/P